American War Stories

War Culture

Edited by Daniel Leonard Bernardi

Books in this series address the myriad ways in which warfare informs diverse cultural practices, as well as the way cultural practices—from cinema to social media—inform the practice of warfare. They illuminate the insights and limitations of critical theories that describe, explain, and politicize the phenomena of war culture. Traversing both national and intellectual borders, authors from a wide range of fields and disciplines collectively examine the articulation of war, its everyday practices, and its impact on individuals and societies throughout modern history.

Jon Simons and John Louis Lucaites, eds., *In/visible War: The Culture of War in Twenty-First-Century America*

Roger Stahl, *Through the Crosshairs: The Weapon's Eye in Public War Culture*

Mary Douglas Vavrus, *Postfeminist War: Women and the Media-Military-Industrial Complex*

Simon Wendt, ed., *Warring over Valor: How Race and Gender Shaped American Military Heroism in the Twentieth and Twenty-First Centuries*

American War Stories

BRENDA M. BOYLE

Rutgers University Press

New Brunswick, Camden, and Newark, New Jersey, and London

Library of Congress Cataloging-in-Publication Data
Names: Boyle, Brenda M., 1957- author.
Title: American war stories / Brenda M. Boyle.
Description: 1 Edition. | New Brunswick : Rutgers University Press, 2020. |
Series: War culture | Includes bibliographical references and index.
Identifiers: LCCN 2020005632 (print) | LCCN 2020005633 (ebook) |
ISBN 9781978807587 (paperback) | ISBN 9781978807594 (hardcover) |
ISBN 9781978807600 (epub) | ISBN 9781978807617 (mobi) | ISBN 9781978807624 (pdf)
Subjects: LCSH: War and society—United States. | United States—History,
Military—21st century. | Militarism—United States. | War stories, American.
Classification: LCC HM554 .B698 2020 (print) | LCC HM554 (ebook) |
DDC 303.6/6—dc23
LC record available at https://lccn.loc.gov/2020005632
LC ebook record available at https://lccn.loc.gov/2020005633

A British Cataloging-in-Publication record for this book is
available from the British Library.

∞ The paper used in this publication meets the requirements of the
American National Standard for Information Sciences—Permanence
of Paper for Printed Library Materials, ANSI Z39.48-1992.

www.rutgersuniversitypress.org

Manufactured in the United States of America

For Carter

Contents

American War Stories

Introduction

American War Stories since World War II

War's complete permeation of social experiences means that it is no longer
possible to isolate a battlefield image from everything else.... In this view,
war is no longer a part of culture—it is the culture.
—Jan Mieszkowski, *Watching War*

The new American militarism draws much of its sustaining force from
myth—stories created to paper over incongruities and contradictions that
pervade the American way of life.... [These myths] create an apparently
seamless historical narrative of American soldiers as liberators, with
Operation Iraqi Freedom in March 2003 becoming a sequel to Operation
Overlord in June 1944.
—Andrew J. Bacevich, *The New American Militarism*

War stories are always looking back and looking ahead. They are
telling the story of a war that has already occurred at the same time they
are preparing for a war yet to come. Stories are often told by interested
parties, parties who have particular points of view about specific wars or
wars in general or both. Stories are told to individuals and to nations, and
they play a significant role in determining whether individuals and nations
are willing to go to war. The stories are important because they tell
audiences not simply about wars but about moralities, about men and
women, and about one's place in the social order.
—Susan Jeffords, "Telling the War Story"

James Loewen's analysis of eighteen American high school history textbooks, *Lies My Teacher Told Me*, first published in 1995 and updated in 2018, concludes that the textbooks tell a noteworthy story about the United States as a nation-state, one where progress is inevitable, heroes are infallible and destined for heroism, and the causes of instability like armed conflict abroad or economic collapse at home are mysterious and unknowable. American history and education writ large, Loewen concludes, is ultimately not only seen by students as irrelevant, but it is also a lesson in conformity and utter trust in authority. This story and its alienating results can have dire consequences for a democracy, reliant as it is on a knowledgeable and discerning citizenry: "Students are simply not learning even those details of American history that educated citizens *should* know. Still less do they learn what *caused* the major developments in our past. Therefore, they cannot apply lessons from the past to current issues. Unfortunately, students are left with no resources to understand, accept, or rebut historical referents used in arguments by candidates for office, sociology professors, or newspaper journalists" (342).

One might conclude from Loewen's study that American high school graduates of at least the last several decades have been exposed to a limited storyline about the trajectory of the nation, especially, in light of the epigraphs above, in regard to the role wars have played and continue to play in that trajectory. When asked what they have learned about the American war in Vietnam, for instance, my undergraduate students of the last thirty years consistently report having learned seven lessons from the stories they have been told: (1) only Americans were involved in the Vietnam War; (2) all Americans who served in Vietnam were men; (3) all men who served during the war were in combat; (4) all men fought in the jungle; (5) all men were traumatized by their dehumanizing experience; (6) all men were mistreated on their return from Vietnam; and (7) the 58,000 fatalities were the most tragic of any war in which the United States has been involved. Despite innumerable texts offering substantiated evidence that disproves or at least complicates understandings of that war, my students' attitudes are settled on these few and insupportable lessons. Such mystification of the American war in Vietnam, comments Loewen as recently as 2018, "has left students unable to understand much public discourse since then" (257).

Moreover, lest it be imagined that their curtailed thoughts are a case of young people dismissing as ancient and irrelevant history the lives of their elders, although students of the last two decades have spent the entirety of their lives in an era of "forever wars," their understandings of the post-9/11 wars in Afghanistan and Iraq are similarly circumscribed yet certain. They report being told about or experiencing the events of 9/11 as moments of American horror followed by national unity but have little understanding of the ensuing 2001 and 2003 American invasions, the wars' fundamental differences in causation and conduct, or the ongoingness of those armed conflicts. This surface-level "my country, right or wrong" stance is reflected in Loewen's conclusion: none of the eighteen American history textbooks challenge the official reasons given for the wars (275). "Textbooks find it hard to question our foreign policy because from beginning to end they typically assume the America as 'international good guy' model," and so wars are consistently and simplistically titled in the textbooks, "Fighting for Freedom and Democracy" (267). Still, my students have learned somehow to say, "Thank you for your service," to all in military uniform or military veterans, even though they are unlikely to have served in the military or to have family members who have served and so do not know what that service entails. They accept that all service members are "heroes" without knowing what heroism is or necessitates. They are deeply unfamiliar with any interpretations of 9/11 and the conflicts that are part of the Global War on Terrorism that might challenge or sublimate the "national unity" story they were told.

Subsequently, my students are unacquainted with arguments like Tom Engelhardt's in *The End of Victory Culture* (2007), which claims that the nation-founding American war story is one of an innocent underdog triumphing over devious ambushers, a story first impaired by the USA's dropping of atomic weapons on two

Japanese cities in 1945 and then decimated by the American war in Vietnam. Though the Bush administration saw in 9/11 the opportunity to revive the story of righteous underdog triumphalism, Engelhardt asserts that it was fated to be a short-lived revival given the unprovoked invasion and occupation of Iraq in 2003. My students are also unfamiliar with Susan Faludi's detailing in *The Terror Dream* (2007), like Engelhardt, how another of the nation-founding myths, this one of "invincibility," was used in storytelling post-9/11 to reimpose traditional gender roles, thus producing at great cost the "national unity" my students report. Such a reimposition would aver that only when women in particular were controlled and returned to their rightful, subordinate position and men to their rightful, dominant one would the United States be in a position to wreak revenge. Nor do my students make the connection between entertainment and militarism that Roger Stahl draws in *Militainment, Inc.* (2010), and how the integration of "military" and "entertainment" determines what behavior it takes to perform "American citizen." Stahl recognizes that this trend began during the Persian Gulf War of 1991 and so was to an extent normalized by the time of 9/11's events, though it "gathered a critical mass in 2003" with the invasion of Iraq (5). Just as to Stahl "militainment" has normalized thinking of war as consumable and thereby palatable, so too did the Global War on Terrorism normalize various intrusive domestic policies and practices, including, according to Rosa Brooks's *How Everything Became War and the Military Became Everything* (2016), civil liberties through domestic policing strategies, courtroom secrecy, immigration, and privacy and surveillance, and war-making practices such as the use of drones, an increase in covert activities, and the widespread use of private military contractors (320–322). For most of my students, if they are aware of them, these policies and practices have become background only, indeed, normal "American," and not challenges to liberal democracy.

Finally, like the rest of us, my students cannot have been expected to know much about another outcome of 9/11: "enhanced interrogation techniques," commonly understood as torture, and justified by the federal government. Generally censored, there nonetheless are some stories of torture or abuse available to us that indicate what has been done in our names, stories that are not the ones of a rosy "national unity." In 2004, for instance, we might have seen the widely distributed images and stories told of torture and prisoner abuse at Iraq's Abu Ghraib prison. But the acts depicted ultimately were dismissed as bad behavior by a band of rogue U.S. Army military police, not behavior sanctioned by the U.S. government. Kathryn Bigelow's 2012 Hollywood film, *Zero Dark Thirty*, depicts fictional CIA torture tactics employed to locate Osama bin Laden, but because their authenticity was neither confirmed nor denied by the actual CIA, doubts of their actuality abound. Furthermore, in November 2015, President Barack Obama signed into law a reinforced U.S. prohibition against torture. Nonetheless, a late-2016 Pew Center report found that despite its being illegal under U.S. and international law, nearly half of Americans surveyed thought torture was warranted in some circumstances, suggesting that this, too, had become normalized following 9/11 (Tyson). Reception of a late-2019 report that includes gruesome and detailed sketches of torture made by one of the people tortured by U.S. personnel at the U.S. Guantanamo Bay Naval Base has not yet registered in the public's attitude toward torture. Published by the Seton Hall University School of Law Center for Policy and Research, "How America Tortures" includes narrative description and the first visual depictions of American torture techniques (Denbeaux). Clearly, these are disturbing elements of the armed violence conducted by the United States following 9/11, coloring "national unity" as more nefarious than my students have learned to expect.

Not only are the lessons my students have learned about some of the most consequential American wars since World War II few in number, because the historical record alone does not support the lessons my interlocutors cite, I am fascinated by how they—how all of us—learn these lessons and what lessons they/we may have learned without recognizing them as such. To what stories have my students been exposed that have led to these non-nuanced, black-and-white deductions about the American wars since 1945? What stories have been withheld? What has the study of history told my students, and how might history be deployed in the way Loewen outlines: as a way to assert authority and institute obedience? How is the invocation of "history" used to prop up popular, wishful retellings? To what extent are my students' and other Americans' understandings of post–World War II American wars—in Asia, the Middle East, and other regions before and since—shaped by popular texts and those deemed canonical? How are literary canons constructed, and why, if they assemble "good" literature (a judgment presumably transcending time and taste), do they morph with time's passage? What is, in effect, a "war story," and what cultural work does it achieve? Most importantly, can Americans be prepared for our responsibilities as citizens in a democracy if we do not understand the complexities of the wars undergirding if not founding American culture?

Conventionally, a twentieth- or twenty-first-century American war story is an oral, written, or filmic text that concerns the first-hand, memorable experience of a combat veteran or war correspondent. The experience may be represented as fiction or nonfiction, but the fact of a teller's personal relationship with war is paramount to the story's credibility and purported authenticity. The story may be told hyperbolically or be poorly or ghost written, but it is nonetheless authorized by the teller's experience of war. Apparently, combatants' interpretation of their experience is inarguable; that they participated in combat alone warrants and authenticates the story of that participation. Thus, in this conventional rendition, a war story's value is more in the fact of experience than in the veracity or quality of its telling.

Consequently, and in response to the myths of mistreatment during the Vietnam War, a post-9/11 era's resurgent American veneration of the "troops," readers or spectators are positioned passively and affectively by these tales to receive war stories as the ultimate truths of war to which they almost exclusively may respond emotionally. This positioning applies especially to the vast majority of American citizens, those who since World War II have not had military experience and subsequently do not have the authority on war granted to current service members and veterans. Their emotional response is not to say that readers and spectators are not influenced by war stories. While pleasurable and emotionally evocative they may be, like morality plays the stories also deliver lessons, if about nothing more than that the stories of combatants are the most relevant and reliable source for understanding American war.

More importantly for this current study, however, is that although these experience-authorized texts are understood to be among the culture's principal stories concerning American war, it is possible for them to be compartmentalized as about war and therefore separate from everyday American life. This separation is especially possible since the 1973 end of the draft and subsequent reduction in the number of Americans who have been in the U.S. military and, since World War II, the invisibility of the financial costs of war to the populace.

Once these stories are shelved away and American war making is itself compartmentalized, many Americans may think their lives are relatively untouched by war. The attitudes taught by these shelved, patent war stories persist, however—attitudes that Catherine Lutz characterizes as the "mental armor" (54) that enables at the very least tacit support of American militarism.[1] These attitudes, which are calculated to protect their holders, include four parts: first, war is human nature and therefore inevitable; second, violence is economical and efficient; third, the immensity of the U.S. military profits both the nation and also individuals; and fourth, militaristic imperialism is at once defensive of American national interests and, altruistically, those of other nations (56–57). Moreover, as the armoring attitudes persist, they also obscure the means by which other war stories, those not necessarily told by veterans or not overtly about war making, surface in the culture.

All of these war stories, the told-and-shelved and the obscured, are central to maintaining what the outgoing President Dwight D. Eisenhower warned of in his 1961 farewell address: the growing influence since World War II of the "military-industrial complex":

This conjunction of an immense military establishment and a large arms industry is new in the American experience. The total influence—economic, political, even spiritual—is felt in every city, every State house, every office of the Federal government. We recognize the imperative need for this development. Yet we must not fail to comprehend its grave implications. Our toil, resources and livelihood are all involved; so is the very structure of our society.

In the councils of government, we must guard against the acquisition of unwarranted influence, whether sought or unsought, by the military-industrial complex. The potential for the disastrous rise of misplaced power exists and will persist.

We must never let the weight of this combination endanger our liberties or democratic processes. We should take nothing for granted. *Only an alert and knowledgeable citizenry can compel the proper meshing of the huge industrial and military machinery of defense with our peaceful methods and goals, so that security and liberty may prosper together.* (Eisenhower; emphasis added)

Like Eisenhower, the authors discussed above—Loewen, Engelhardt, Faludi, Stahl, Brooks, Denbeaux, and Lutz—all express concern for the health of an informed democratic citizenry. It is not too audacious to think that members of the military-industrial complex understandably would be most vested in the perpetual conduct of war, and the primary obstacle to such conduct is what Eisenhower terms an "alert and knowledgeable citizenry." The citizenry's attitudes cited by Lutz, however, would seem to permit if not condone the further empowerment of the complex rather than the "proper meshing" Eisenhower cites.[2] According to a 2018 U.S. Army–commissioned RAND analysis entitled *National Will to Fight*, Lutz's attitudes must be taught; the American populace must deliberately be persuaded to back engaging in armed conflict. Based on a historical study of the twentieth century and a focus on two particular cases (the Korean War and Russia/Soviet Union over the century), the report determines that to encourage the national will to fight, "the effective use of engagement and indoctrination and messaging can greatly influence [the] will to fight" and is "most effective *before* a conflict begins" (McNerney et al. 114–115). "In democratic countries," the report concludes, "internal use of information to influence is less threatening and coercive than full-out indoctrination but still can contribute importantly to [the] national will to fight" (116). Clearly, according to this study, the populace must deliberately be moved to accede to (and fund) war, but the moving must not appear to threaten or coerce. Instead, it must appear to persuade, to cajole, to urge the populace to be willing and ready—nay, eager—to send its armed forces into battle. Because the forces so often are regarded as distinct from everyday American life and conventional war stories easily can be compartmentalized, this coaxing cannot happen with the conventional war stories alone. Some other stories must be told, and some must be withheld. But because the United States is a liberal democracy, the stories always must seem benignly encouraging as opposed to overtly propagandizing.

Lutz's "mental armor" attitudes appear foundational to this American disposition to send troops to war, and some of the stories that lay and buttress that foundation are the subject of this study. It posits that residents of the United States, since World War II but now especially in an age of forever wars and pervasive social media, are told stories constantly. Those more easily identifiable as stories about war—and subsequently shelved—are fiction (e.g., novels, poetry, plays, and short story collections) and nonfiction (e.g., journalistic pieces, memoirs of combat veterans, military histories, and documentary films). Barring the rare military history buff, these are the texts to which my students declare they have hardly ever been exposed.[3] Less easily detectable as persuasive storytelling modes, the ones to which Americans now are more likely to be exposed and persuaded to be willing to fight, are texts such as recruiting advertisements, military activities at sporting events, monuments and memorials across the American landscape, invocations to "support the troops" and to thank them for their service, video games, and fictional films dismissed as "just entertainment."[4] These less detectable stories are especially effective as persuasive tools when they interweave tales about war with core American values such as exceptionalism, collectivism, individualism, egalitarianism, and patriotism, so much so that it is often difficult to discern that the story is about war. Invoking these values has didactic effects, teaching the populace how to respond to the U.S. armed forces and also tethering the populace to the forces and their activities. Although both the easily iden-tifiable and less detectable sorts typically focus on the individual, privilege firsthand experience of war, and appeal emotionally, especially to these core American values, the stories do not have to feature in-country combat or be told by a veteran to be counted as lesson-delivering stories of, about, or for war.

Michel Foucault's concept of discipline can help to explain just how these lessons are delivered. As Foucault points out, disper-sion and proliferation of narratives have a greater influence than their centralization; thus, quietly dispensing stories of war through a wide array of texts and genres increases the potential for normal-izing militarism in civilian democratic society. This quiet disper-sion and not overt propaganda is the RAND study's "indoctrination and messaging" key to engendering a "national will to fight." In *Discipline and Punish*, Foucault traces the eighteenth-century devel-opment of panopticism, or "generalized surveillance," and its part in what has become "disciplinary society" (209). There are two vital strategies of Foucauldian panopticism that lead to efficiently per-suasive and networked control within social institutions. First, constituents must perceive, consciously or unconsciously, that their every move is surveilled.[5] Second and consequently, feeling observed, constituents internalize the perceived norms without having to be actively policed (170–177).[6] Foucault concludes about this disruption of the traditional exercise of centralized power:

> On the whole, therefore, one can speak of the formation of a disciplinary society in this movement that stretches from the enclosed disciplines, a sort of social "quarantine," to an indef-initely generalizable mechanism of "panopticism." Not because

the disciplinary modality of power has replaced all the others; but because it has infiltrated the others, sometimes undermining them, but serving as an intermediary between them, linking them together, extending them and above all making it possible to bring the effects of power to the most minute and distant elements. It assures an infinitesimal distribution of the power relations. (216)

Such "infiltration" characterizes the difference between easily identifiable and less detectable war stories, so that the stories abound and, as Rosa Brooks contends, "everything became war and the military became everything." Foucault continues in *The History of Sexuality: An Introduction,* to detail how this network of stories evolves organically, discursively, unobtrusively, and not as the outcome of (apparent) propagandistic compulsion. He counters the dominant notion that the Victorians were sexually repressed, arguing instead that on the contrary, the nineteenth century engendered a multiplicity of ways to talk about sex and thereby coordinated the behavior. Though previously the church had controlled any discussion or practice of sex, the expanding scientific fields of medicine and psychology offered more modes through which to discuss and apply the topic, the effect of which was control exceeding that offered by repression or censorship.

Rather than the uniform concern to hide sex, rather than a general prudishness of language, what distinguishes these last three centuries is the variety, the wide dispersion of devices that were invented for speaking about it, for having it spoken about, for inducing it to speak of itself, for listening, recording, transcribing, and redistributing what is said about it: around sex, a whole network of varying, specific, and coercive transpositions into discourse. Rather than a massive censorship, beginning with the verbal improprieties imposed by the Age of Reason, what was involved was a regulated and polymorphous incitement to discourse. (34)

This "polymorphous incitement to discourse" is the very outcome of the war stories investigated in this study and the seeds of Lutz's attitudes. That is, the more war stories invoke national values as they multiply across and are embedded in the nation's variable discourses, the more encouraged the populace is unquestioningly to support the military's activities.[7]

Finally, in *Maneuvers,* Cynthia Enloe offers a fine-grained case study of how the discourse of militarism is embedded and thereby made to seem normal, so that war is not so unusual or even is a natural, inevitable outcome. Echoing the distinction already drawn in this introduction between American military and civilian life as a result of shelving "war stories," as long as militarism is thought of only as armed conflict, or "government-directed overt violence," militarism appears benign (3). Instead, Enloe contends, the rooting of militarism in everyday American culture, especially in the lives of women, ensures the national will to fight.[8] She writes, "The more militarization transforms an individual or a society, the more that individual or society comes to imagine military needs and militaristic presumptions to be not only valuable but also normal. Militarization, that is, involves cultural as well as institutional, ideological, and economic transformations" (3). Because of the proliferative embeddedness of this militarizing discourse, Enloe explains that a wide range of reading skills are needed to detect the discourse's elements and effects in the culture: "To chart the spread of militarization, then, requires a host of skills: the ability to read budgets and interpret bureaucratic euphemisms, of course, but also the ability to understand the dynamics of memory, marriage, hero-worship, cinematic imagery, and the economies of commercialized sex" (3). This study takes seriously Enloe's exhortation to read differently and aims to practice that different-reading in each chapter.

This schema of discursive proliferation emerging from the ideas of Lutz, Foucault, and Enloe can help to understand the discourse of American war and the centrifugal role that stories play in that discourse. Regarding war and military culture as separate and distinct from American civilian culture is akin to Foucault's claim

that the church alone controlled talk of sex. The burgeoning of outlets for that talk and its subsequent normalization and regulation
by self-policing constituents is analogous to the propagation of stories about war and armed conflict. Americans tell and hear war
stories purposefully that, in this case, both create and reinforce
American values. The more that is said, the more stories that are
told, the more militarism is embedded so that it is seen as normal,
nay, natural, the more strengthened are the assumptions Lutz outlines, the more embedded are the processes detailed by Enloe,
and the more potential there is for the United States to be willing
to fight. This phenomenon can explain the lessons my students
have learned, lessons that ease their acceptance of and often
unquestioning support for their nation at war.

The chapters that follow examine several—not nearly all—of
the types of war stories endemic in American culture since the end
of World War II.[9] The story examined in each chapter may be a
story told or withheld or even heavily revised, but each analysis also
explores how the invocation of a core American value by the story
solidifies the stories' persuasive impact. The stories have been chosen to illustrate two important elements of the book's argument:
first, a diverse array of media (e.g., historical record, war monuments, memoirs and their Hollywood blockbuster film renditions,
recruiting strategies, video games, and athletic events) are involved
in the storytelling; and second, the stories can be seen to invoke
American values. These values, which are neither consistently com-
plementary to one another nor comprehensive of all American
values, include exceptionalism ("State of Crisis"), collectivism
("Staging War"), individualism ("Lone Wolf Family Man"), egalitarianism ("Military Judgment"), and patriotism ("Soldier's
Creed"). By invoking these values, the stories yoke an inadequately
discerning populace to American war and therefore incur a national
will to fight. Furthermore, the chapters of the book are organized
thematically rather than chronologically, so that the discussion
of each medium and American value leads to the next. This weav-
ing together demonstrates the thematic connections while the
variety of media illustrate the dispersion of the stories, Foucault's

"polymorphous incitement to discourse." Thus, the stories examined are only some, not all, that contribute to the current discourse about American war and are more *suggestive* of the various media and the core values that are invoked than *constitutive* of a comprehensive taxonomy, chronology, or applicability to particular conflicts.

Chapter 1, "State of Crisis: Stories of American Exceptionalism, the French, and Masculinities in Vietnam," embraces Enloe's reading differently and examines in uncommon ways the story told in American culture about the U.S. involvement in Vietnam. The chapter contends that not only are Americans often unaware of the post–World War II French war to recolonize Vietnam preceding the American conflict, but they also have not been taught that the United States was actively involved in France's pursuit during this period. The chapter practices this different reading by focusing on the fraught relationship between the French and Americans in Vietnam immediately after World War II's conclusion, with particular attention to State Department documents in the U.S. National Archives. Although post–World War II French or U.S. military forces are not involved in the diplomatic scuffles studied in the 1946 and 1947 archival materials, the military forces are implicated in how the French and Americans compete to influence the Vietnamese people. The scuffles denote French investment in molding the non–Viet Minh Vietnamese to the French mode of warring masculinity and signpost a fundamental disagreement between the French and American allies. More importantly, the scuffles portend the challenges to be faced by the United States after the French withdraw and as the United States becomes militarily involved in Vietnam. This chapter explores the very subtle rhetorical ways by which U.S. exceptionalist thinking asserts its dominance, even over an ostensible ally. These rhetorical exercises have actual impact and can be seen at work in current-day warring narratives.

Chapter 2, "Staging War: Stories of Collectivity at, by, and through the Vietnam Veterans Memorial," moves the book's analysis into the United States and into the current cultural scene. The chapter argues that the Vietnam Veterans Memorial emblematizes the persistent and ongoing revision of the American Vietnam War story. Since the memorial's beginnings in the late 1970s, its conceptualizers' aim first was "to recognize and honor" individual veterans, which evolved into "to heal and reconcile" the nation, a collectivist entity. That the memorial was not completed, especially in regard to the planned "Education Center at the Wall," challenges sustaining that narrative of reconciliation. Instead, the memorial illustrates the tension between the core values of collectivism and individualism through the continued American irresolution about the war in Vietnam and in subsequent American conflicts. Forty years after its inception, the commemorative site still is regarded as incomplete, as in progress. This chapter traces the memorial's development and, ironically, its uses as a rhetorical staging area for the country's armed conflicts since the Vietnam War.

The tension between the American values of collectivism and individualism raised in "Staging War" are taken up in Chapter 3, "Lone Wolf Family Man: Stories of Individualism and Collectivism in *American Sniper*(s) and *Lone Survivor*(s)." It offers an example of how two American genres—personal memoir and narrative Hollywood film—try to resolve this tension. Using Enloe's different-reading of popular texts, the chapter compares the memoir and film renditions of masculinities in two narratives from the recent United States wars, *Lone Survivor* (Afghanistan) and *American Sniper* (Iraq). In examining how the four texts construct masculinities in relation to collectivism and individualism, the chapter concludes that although the courage and honor of collectivist military might is extolled in American culture, these blockbuster films tell us that collectivism is and should be subordinate to the heroics of the individual.

Chapter 4, "Military Judgment in a Neoliberal Age: Egalitarianism and the All-Volunteer Force" queries both the story that the U.S. military is perhaps the most egalitarian institution in the United States and also the story's apparent basis, the integration cases of African American men, women, and people who identify as gay and lesbian. The cases are examined in the context of the all-volunteer force and its neoliberal origins, a context that problematizes service members' transition from citizen-soldiers to consumer-soldiers. The effects of this transition are widespread and include the most recent group of soldiers—people who identify as transgender. The chapter concludes that the integration cases illustrate how what is termed "military judgment" has now become the arbiter of what is democratic.

Following the conclusion of chapter 4 that the military is regarded as the ultimate determiner of what is democratic, the fifth chapter, "The Soldier's Creed: Stories of Warrior Patriotism in Visual Culture," examines in the most recent decade of the all-volunteer-force era the constitution and heralding of "warrior patriotism," what is represented in many recent war stories as the model for performing allegiance to the United States. The chapter examines this rhetorical constitution in visual culture through the stories told by way of military displays at athletic events, recruiting rhetorics that align sports teamwork (especially football) and patriotism, and militaristic video games that purport to offer autonomy and freedom of choice even as they impose uniformity and conformity. The chapter concludes that these stories imply that acceding to authority is the essence of warrior patriotism and, consequently, the paramount way for Americans to display love for country.

To conclude this study of American war stories, the coda, "Prices Paid for the War Stories We Tell," argues that the ubiquity and content of the stories outlined in the preceding chapters exacts a series of costs, most of which are related to how the stories undergird the "mental armor" values cited by Lutz and thereby embed militarism as American culture. This coda takes literally the "prices paid," however, as it returns to Eisenhower's caution about the military-industrial complex in briefly surveying the current-day financial burden to U.S. taxpayers of funding the armed forces. The burdens seem borne willfully and willingly, though, suggesting that Americans have been conditioned by war stories like those studied here to finance without question and to permit weapons and activities without challenge, thereby suffering, without knowing it, the moral injury said to afflict combatants alone.

My American students over the last three decades undoubtedly have been exposed to these war stories throughout their lives, stories that go a long way in explaining their limited or exceptionally shaded understanding of the American wars since the end of World War II. The limits can be explained by the narrowness of "war story" and the inability to recognize Mieszkowski's point in the first epigraph to this introduction: war is culture. Expanding the meaning of "war story" in the United States to account for the stories' dispersion and subsequent constitution of American culture is critical, then, to developing Eisenhower's 1961 "alert and knowledgeable citizenry" and Rosa Brooks's 2016 "engaged and informed citizenry" (362). Though the vast majority of Americans have no firsthand experience with the military or with war and so may imagine their lives are untouched by war and the forces that wage it, the ubiquity and content of these stories teach lessons about American war making. These lessons not only inform what Americans think and feel about their nation's military mission and its members, but they also teach American citizens their role in sending other Americans to war. The health of our democracy depends on Americans paying critical heed to the stories they are told and the lessons they are taught.

1

State of Crisis

Stories of American Exceptionalism, the French,
and Masculinities in Vietnam

Why is "1959" on the Wall? I thought the war started in 1965.

The Americans took over from the French.
—Overheard at the Vietnam Veterans Memorial, fall 2017

The question and answer above illustrate a well-worn war story among Americans: the American war in Vietnam began with the commitment of Marine combat units at Da Nang in March 1965. Not only is the period between 1965 and "the French" elided in this story, but so is the American war's origins.[1] Because it did not begin with a declaration of war, its origin is more a process, a series of starts rather than a fixed point in time.[2] Yet as Mary L. Dudziak points out in *Wartime*, distinguishing between the times of war and peace is essential, not only in regard to what service medals can be won and what kind of civil rights can be exercised, but also as war and peace times pertain to law.[3] Did the American war begin during World War II, with the Office of Strategic Services (OSS) arming the Viet Minh to counter the Japanese occupying Vietnam? Did it begin immediately after World War II, with the United

States' ambivalence about intervening in France's war to recolonize Vietnam? Did it begin with the assignment of American military advisors, first in 1950 by President Truman and then in 1961 by President Kennedy? Did it begin after 1950 and the advent of the Cold War, with the United States funding 80 percent of France's war against the Viet Minh? Did it begin with the bombing of North Vietnam in 1964? Or did it begin in the 1920s as a rescue story, with Hollywood films depicting Vietnamese people as primitive children who needed salvation? The story that the American war began in 1965 prevails, quietening other stories and obscuring the preceding decades of involvement by the United States in Vietnam, as it offers a definitive point in time that absolves—or erases—all potential sins committed previously.[4] This erasure relies on the first of the five American core values discussed in this book: exceptionalism. It maintains that the United States is virtuously and uniquely motivated among nations in all of its foreign commitments and hence is immune to the forces of history.[5] Consequently, the United States could, with its matchlessly good intents, achieve in Vietnam what no other external nation—China, France, Japan, Cambodia—was able to accomplish. "The Americans took over from the French" denotes the unique competence of the Americans and the predictable incompetence of the French.

In "Making Sense of the French War," Mark Philip Bradley argues that stories told about the French and American wars in Indochina are more complex than the typical story of the Cold War's inevitable appearance in Vietnam, of the French duty to combat communism in Vietnam and, flummoxed by the task, being relieved of the burden by the more virtuous and competent United States.[6] Instead, Bradley asserts, to tell the stories of this war era in Vietnam, history should extend its scope beyond the relations between French or Americans with Vietnamese to examine the convoluted web of geopolitical relations among Western allies, and it also should use "novel interpretive frameworks" to decipher those relations (19).[7] This chapter takes both suggestions seriously, the extension and the novelty, exploring as it does diplomatic relations between the French and the Americans in

Vietnam, through 1946 and into 1947, what memoirist Duong Van Mai Elliott calls "the watershed years" (Elliott xiii) and what, in his book's subtitle, historian Stein Tønnesson terms the French war's beginnings. This chapter also is guided by Christopher Goscha's regret about the abundant scholarship on the few years in the late-1950s and early 1960s leading to the 1965 American commitment of combat units in Vietnam, and the comparative dearth on the time leading to the French war (Goscha xi). Specifically, it examines American consular efforts to establish a United States Information Services (USIS) reading room in Saigon during 1946 and 1947, a period of mounting tensions between France and the Democratic Republic of Vietnam (DRV) but more importantly for this chapter, between the two Western allies. According to American archival documents, the reading room—including its physical space, its contents, its staff, and its operating principles—threatened the recolonizing French, as the uncensored availability of books and other reading materials to "Annamites" and Europeans both were perceived by French authorities as censuring them. With analyses of archival documents, both mine and other authors', this chapter uncovers disputes between the French and Americans founded in contending versions of masculinities, versions that might have impacted French or American influence on Vietnamese people but also might have led the United States to deploy itself as an exception to history and into thinking its exceptionalism could accomplish what the French were unable to do. This gendered and geopolitical "state of crisis" is one of many stories obscured by the story of how "the [exceptional] Americans took over from the [unexceptional] French."

Some Obscured Stories

THE UNITED STATES DID NOT CONDEMN COLONIALISM

One obscured account is the United States' ambivalence about supporting France's recolonization of Vietnam after World War II, despite American principles favoring national sovereignty. Through action and inaction, following World War II the United States was implicated in Vietnam's quest for independence and complicit in France's repudiation of that quest. Although the United States supported the self-determination of all nations outlined in the Atlantic Charter of 1941, and sustained Viet Minh resistance to Japanese occupation during World War II, after World War II it did not explicitly advocate Vietnam's independence. This inaction might have been to assure France of U.S. support as it tried to recover economically and politically from World War II, or it might have been that the United States needed France's cooperation to build a bulwark in Western Europe—the North Atlantic Treaty Organization (NATO)—against the Soviet Union. Most importantly in this story, the United States did not disapprove of colonialism per se; it only disapproved of how France had conducted its version in Vietnam for nearly a century.[8] Belief in American exceptionalism led many American officials to think the United States could perform colonialism well, having demonstrated so in the Philippines.

AMERICAN HUBRIS LED TO THE AMERICAN WAR

Such American hubris may have led the United States, first, to militarily and financially support the French war in Vietnam, and second, to enter into direct conflict a decade after the French withdrew. Two scholars draw this connection and tell this story of American overconfidence. In "Chronicle of a War Foretold: The United States and Vietnam, 1945–1954," Andrew J. Rotter outlines eight attitudes during the French war that were replicated in the 1965–1973 American war. These include cultural ignorance and racial condescension toward the Vietnamese (284); certainty that Vietnam was a proxy for the communist Soviet Union, and China after 1949 (287); certainty that Asians were interchangeable, so war against Vietnamese would be identical to war against Koreans (295); belief that Vietnamese nationalism was malleable and easily could be overlaid with American liberal capitalism (298); and concern that American credibility was at stake (302). U.S. foreign policy decision-makers, Rotter concludes, "failed to heed the warnings" of the French war when they opted to take the U.S. to war in Vietnam (306). Mark Philip Bradley tells a similar story when he traces American discourses about French Indochina and the Vietnamese in "Slouching toward Bethlehem: Culture, Diplomacy, and the Origins of the Cold War in Vietnam." Bradley enumerates three discursive eras—the interwar period, World War II, and the Cold War—to investigate the "language and rhetoric by which policy makers framed their choices," frames learned by Americans from the French (13). In close readings of these temporal discourses, he identifies orientalist tropes in all three: "Annamites" are lazy, primitive liars who only can imitate, not initiate, and as a consequence are susceptible to the influences of bad others, even in terms of nationalism. The Americans, Bradley explains, were certain that all but Americans were bad influences, so it was the obligation of the United States to rescue the Vietnamese, whether by supporting the French war or by direct conflict.

THE UNITED STATES AND FRANCE DISPARAGED VIETNAMESE MASCULINITIES

Other mostly unheard stories intimate the French and American wars were largely motivated or facilitated by gendered views of the Vietnamese. As suggested both by Rotter and Bradley, French and Americans cast the Vietnamese as childlike and the Westerners as rescuing patriarchs who could teach the Vietnamese how to live properly. Frank Proschan outlines how the colonial French found the male and female Vietnamese bodies gender-illegible, producing "colonizing discourses" that warranted the French mastery of people who had not followed (presumably universal) gender presentations. These gender prejudices, Proschan contends, are the "intellectual ground on which the colonial enterprise itself was founded and pursued" (458). Scott Laderman notes in his essay about pre-American-war Hollywood films set in Vietnam that these films cast the childlike, impressionable Vietnamese as exploited by communists and as needing proper "tutelage and instruction," a depiction "leaving [exceptional] Americans with a solemn obligation to aid in their rescue" (578, 607). Furthermore, both orientalizing French and Americans saw Vietnamese men as unmanly, thereby simultaneously sowing doubt about the abilities of Vietnamese men to be warriors and statesmen, while also normalizing their own Western manliness (Bradley, *Imagining* 48–49). During the American war, President Johnson was notorious for casting the Viet Cong (VC) and the North Vietnamese Army (NVA) as not manly and the war as a contest for male virility. Rotter cites Johnson's fear of losing the Vietnam War to "an enemy whom Johnson scorned as sneaky, treacherous, and otherwise effeminate" (302). Jonathan Nashel cites LBJ's going one step further when he crows in his 1971 memoir, "I didn't just screw Ho Chi Minh, I cut his pecker off" (141).[9]

THE AMERICANS THOUGHT THEY WERE MORE PROPER PATRIARCHS

Clearly, both French and Americans were motivated to war by orientalist predilections toward Vietnamese people. However, though both regarded colonialism through a gendered lens, thereby deeming their role in Vietnam as patriarchal, neither trusted the other to perform that fatherly role appropriately. As for the Americans, during World War II President Roosevelt "judged the French to be 'poor colonizers' who had 'badly mismanaged' Indochina and exploited its people" (Cain 3). As for the French, near the end of their war they sought to negotiate a settlement with the Viet Minh that would "free them from the Chinese without putting them into the hands of the Americans" (Dalloz 169), who had both a "mania for cleanliness" (144) and, according to the Chinese, a puritan strain (Patti 34). This faith in colonialism but refusal of each ally to trust in the other's version heightened the tension with the Vietnamese and between the two Western allies. What follows is an exploration of the two latter groups vying for dominance, a competition that reveals not only their different geopolitical attitudes but also, and more importantly for this chapter, their variant versions of masculinity.

Gender as a Factor in Foreign Relations

In "Gender Relations, Foreign Relations: The United States and South Asia, 1947–1964," Andrew Rotter suggests that though gender is not commonly explored in the history of U.S. foreign relations, it ought to be. Gender is, he says, "a transnational process," and so "nations and the people who constitute them become gendered [by other nations], and this affects the policies that other nations pursue toward them" (521). Gender does not always call attention to itself in such interactions, however, so researchers— in an echo of Cynthia Enloe's call for reading differently—need to "look for odd things in the documents: stray remarks about personal style or gesture, comments about a people's alleged 'emotionalism,' or 'effeminacy,' and even references to the kinds of parties American hosts put on for their . . . guests." Rotter continues: "What would seem a collection of marginalia to most diplomatic historians becomes a treasure trove of information demanding thick description to someone interested in culture" (522). Deploying a gender lens as one of Mark Philip Bradley's "novel interpretive frameworks" enables the detection and parsing of obscured stories about Western engagement in Vietnam, especially those stories revealing, according to Rotter, how "gender inspired imperialism, allowed it to grow, and justified its frequently torturous evolution" (526). While the colonial context in Vietnam already is gendered through orientalizing discourses that clarify colonialism's masculinist quality, positioning the colonizer as dominant and the colonized as dominated, the particular context in Vietnam requires a more nuanced approach, as at least two Western countries— France and the United States—fought to master the Vietnamese, and in that competition, to determine who would dominate and who would be subordinated. The rest of this chapter tells the story of the two Western masters competing to dominate. Elements of the story include a theoretical undergirding, or "schematic," the American and French histories of masculinities, and diplomatic relations between the two allies once in Vietnam.

R. W. Connell and J. Messerschmidt's gender schematic for homosocial groups within patriarchy offers a "novel interpretive framework" for comprehending the "odd things" occurring between American and French diplomats in Vietnam. Unlike other gender theories that distinguish between women and men or focus on women alone, Connell and Messerschmidt's provides a method to differentiate among men. Starting with the premise that gender is a cultural construct and so is responsive to and reflective of local culture, Connell and Messerschmidt posit that though there is no transcendental signifier, no single masculinity crossing time and culture, nor is masculinity a performance limited to male bodies, masculinity's enactments in any given culture can be broken into a hierarchy of four modes: hegemonic, subordinate, marginal, and complicit. The *hegemonic* mode is dominant though culture-specific; because a hegemonic masculinity is deemed dominant in one culture or subculture does not guarantee it will be deemed dominant in another. Second to hegemonic masculinity is *subordinate*, the mode of masculinity that is actively subordinated by the hegemon. Although less dominant, the subordinate mode mimics and approximates the hegemonic. Given another culture, it might be seen to occupy one of the other three modes. Third in the hierarchy of masculine modes is *marginalized*. It performs a masculinity that does not approximate the hegemonic mode and so is marginalized both by people in the hegemonic and subordinated modes. Connell and Messerschmidt's fourth mode, *complicit*, refers to people who do not perform or value dominance but reap benefits from the hierarchy nonetheless. All of these positions are in relation to one another, shifting across cultures and history. Whomever is in the hegemonic position determines, momentarily anyway, who is in the other categories.

A crucial component of this hierarchical model is that none of these positions are stable or fixed, responsive as they are to culture. Because of this insecurity, the positions require constant maintenance. In Connell and Messerschmidt's interpretive framework, consequently, rather than crisis being an unusual or isolated condition for masculinity, masculinity is by definition a state of crisis. The compulsion to identify one inexorable form of masculinity within patriarchy, a single script that transcends time and culture, is at the heart of this crisis, as people—mostly men—vie to cement their dominance and thereby gain the perquisite to subordinate and marginalize. In effect, those who occupy the hegemonic position, however temporarily, not only have the power to subordinate and marginalize, but they also have the power to determine, at least provisionally, what is "masculine." In this story of Vietnam, the French and Americans, already having tacitly agreed via orientalizing to marginalize the Vietnamese, compete in the state of crisis to assume the definer's hegemonically masculine position. The evidence suggests that the Americans relied on their exceptionalism to compare their masculinity to that of the French.

After World War II in Vietnam, masculinity was especially volatile, as men of many nationalities, including Americans and French, vied to be the hegemonic definer of "masculinity." At stake was dominance in the locale and therefore tutelage of the Vietnamese in what was appropriately masculine (and thereby appropriately ideological). The Americans and French carried to Vietnam their unique states of crisis from their individual cultures, and the differences between their home-country masculinities were exposed in their competition. These differences are traceable throughout their histories, though this chapter necessarily can cite only a limited number of twentieth-century influences on the Americans and French in Vietnam.

The most immediate influence on both parties would have been their performances in World War II. Simply put, the Americans arrived in Vietnam as the war's victor, the hegemonic form of masculinity in world war, temporarily establishing American martial and industrial masculinities as the world's dominant modes (Jarvis). France, meanwhile, as at least subordinated and perhaps marginalized by American hegemony, was recovering from its shameful defeat by Germany in 1940 and occupation until 1944, and of the French Vichy government's collaboration with Japan in

Vietnam from 1941 until the final months of the war.[10] This already fraught situation between the two ostensible allies after the war undoubtedly was compounded by the national experiences of the masculine state of crisis each brought to their involvement in Vietnam.

For instance, despite victory, postwar American relations across the world were impacted by worries about the precariousness of masculinity, according to Andrew Rotter: "Concerned, perhaps, that their own masculinity was at risk—a concern of American men at least as far back as the Revolution . . . policy makers developed patriarchal designs on the weaker members of the family of nations" ("Gender Relations" 528). Americans brought to Vietnam worries about masculine impermanence emerging from the United States' immediate past, too, especially those about its imperialism around the turn of the century. Late in the nineteenth century, explains Kristin Hoganson in *Fighting for American Manhood*, fear of insecure gender roles domestically swayed foreign policy decisions to engage in the Spanish-American and Philippine-American wars, illustrating how angst about growing women's power at the century's end "helped push the nation into war by fostering a desire for martial challenges" (14). "War," Hoganson concludes, "was the best way to foster fraternalism and a regard for high ideals among men and to highlight distinctions between men and women" (201). Early in the twentieth century, explains Warwick Anderson in "The Trespass Speaks: White Masculinity and Colonial Breakdown," a close relationship was evident between masculinities and colonial white American men's experiences in the tropics. Echoing Hoganson in citing the "masculinity crisis" at the end of the nineteenth century, Anderson examines rhetoric used by physicians until the 1920s to describe white men's difficulties as colonial administrators in tropical climates. Explanations for why men "go to pieces" ranged from racial, to character, to sexual, to socioeconomic class (1343). As long as these "mechanistic," or temporary failure-of-will diagnoses were the rationale, "tropical neurasthenia" was regarded as a valid diagnosis. By the 1920s, however, when the rationale for breakdown was diagnosed as not mechanistic but instead "psychodynamic" or pathological, therefore endangering the colonial enterprise's basis, it no longer was employed (1368). It was imperative, Anderson concludes, to maintain the "exemplary colonial identity as at once manly, white, and civilized" (1367). A final example of ongoing American anxiety about the impermanence of masculinity, or its state of crisis, comes from the Cold War, the period during which the French and American wars in Vietnam were fought. In *Manhood and American Political Culture in the Cold War*, K. A. Cuordileone describes this period as an "age of anxiety," one that "in the name of combating an implacable, expansionist Communist enemy, put a new premium on hard masculine toughness and rendered anything less than that soft, timid, feminine, and as such a real or potential threat to the security of the nation" (viii). This "rearguard action" not only displayed "contempt for things effete," but it also promoted "an ideology that insisted on the sanctity of the nuclear family, strict gender-role norms, and sexual restraint," an ideology extant in foreign policy, literature, and 1950s American culture generally (xxi, xiv). This apprehension can be seen to culminate in LBJ's indelicate claim to a privilege of hegemonic masculinity, cited earlier: "I didn't just screw Ho Chi Minh, I cut his pecker off" (Nashel 141).

The French also brought to Vietnam their national experiences of the masculine state of crisis, including their mortifying performance in World War II and their many decades of colonial mastery across the world and in Indochina. These experiences were in the shadow of an already-existing stereotype of urbane, overrefined French, or exemplifying the very effeteness for which the anti-intellectual Cold War Americans had such contempt.[11] According to Christopher Forth and Bertrand Taithe, the French have since the advent of the modern world in the seventeenth century combated that stereotype with martial masculinities, especially during the French Revolution and Napoleonic eras. World War II slowed that struggle: "The 1940 defeat and occupation at the hands of [brawny and unyielding] Germany humiliated French men in the very activities that anchored male identity: work, warfare, and the protection of women and children" (introduction to *French Masculinities* 9). French colonies, however, had always been regarded as compensatory, as places where a French male could be a "complete man": "Colonial masculinity and its actions—conquest, pacification, the building of new countries, settlement, promotion of traditional virtues—was seen as compensation for a deficit of manliness in France. . . . The intellectual, the Bohemian, and the dandy, though common in Paris, were relatively rare species in the colonies" (Aldrich 125–129). While men who became colonials— soldiers, explorers, missionaries, native troopers, and administrators (126–127)—might not have occupied the hegemonic position in France, according to Connell and Messerschmidt's schematic, the colonial option offered to them hegemony and its perquisite to subordinate and marginalize, especially the gender-illegible Vietnamese (Proschan). This compensatory power would have been especially desirable after France's obeisance to the Germans and the diffusion of masculinities among the Vichy government, Paris collaborators, and London-based nationalists. "We know from popular and scholarly representations of this period," comments Miranda Pollard, "that no one image or language of masculinity became hegemonic, either for Vichy or for the resistance, for rural *résistants* or city *collabos*, for women or for men, French or foreign in France" (153).[12] Furthermore, the yearning to invigorate a martial masculine hierarchy in French Indochina after World War II, with French soldiers and diplomats in the hegemonic spots and Vietnamese in the subordinated and marginalized, is evident in the French attempt to build an army for the fledgling State of Vietnam. Despite the appeal to masculinities of French General de Lattre, the officer commissioned in 1950 to construct this military force, with "Stand up like men," the force failed because the appeal was premised on a monolithic French understanding of what it meant to be "like men." François Guillemot explains, "In the context of an independent Vietnam, instructing a new army on the distant model of the colonial army of old gave rise to all kinds of obstacles. A twofold gulf manifested between the Vietnamese of different classes and between the French and the Vietnamese"

(207). This bid to reconstruct a colonial, martial masculine hierarchy after World War II, to define what "like men" should be, appears in a 1963 novel, Pierre Schoendoerffer's *La 317ᵉ Section*. Still lauded as representing the best of France's military, the expeditionary/colonial forces, the novel depicts the French war in Indochina and clarifies the military's still-enduring values of audacity and élan. In his 2017 review of the text, Michael Shurkin quotes a retired French Army colonel: "The French military ethos attaches more importance to courage and *beau geste* than to victory. The greater the difficulties, the greater the courage to face them. At the end, we prefer 'magnificent losers' to 'ugly victors'" (Shurkin). This noble-gesture ethos evokes the risk-taking underlying what Stein Tønnesson repeatedly refers to as France's "test of strength" in Vietnam in the December 1946 days leading to the outbreak of war (163, 64, 66).

Vietnam in 1946

TENSIONS BETWEEN THE FRENCH AND THE AMERICANS

Tensions between the American and French diplomats in Vietnam were patent during the months leading up to the December 1946 outbreak of war between the French and the Viet Minh. The tensions preexisted this period, emerging from France's questionable World War II performances and President Roosevelt's disdain for French colonial practices in Indochina, outlined above, and from the postwar Potsdam settlement that humiliatingly excluded France from supervising the Japanese removal from Indochina.[13] Nationalist Chinese forces were assigned to supervise in the north and British forces in the south; what would happen to Vietnamese sovereignty after the Japanese departure was not determined, although France, with British assistance, quietly positioned itself to reoccupy Indochina.[14] The United States was at best ambivalent and at worst "indecisive" concerning French reassertion of colonial rights to Indochina: the United States did not oppose French recolonization, but it also, at least initially, resisted facilitating France's efforts.[15] "The French," says Frank Cain, "expected supportive treatment from the Americans for their return to the north, similar to what the British rendered to them in southern Vietnam. So, in finding the US to be neutral between the French and the DRV, the French became more antagonistic towards the United States for its lack of support" (21).

TENSIONS BETWEEN THE FRENCH AND THE DEMOCRATIC REPUBLIC OF VIETNAM

French antagonism toward its Western ally doubtless intensified as the French were humiliated by the DRV challenge to their dominance, or hegemonic masculinity. Repeatedly, as Stein Tønnesson details in *Vietnam, 1946*, clashes arose from French assertions of colonialist hegemonic masculinity and Vietnamese resistance to being subordinated or marginalized in their own nation. First, the March 6 Agreement was arrived at only by the "trap" laid by the supervising Chinese in the north (39); neither the French nor the DRV were satisfied with this agreement (70–78), and each only considered it "a stepping-stone to further advancing their position" (83). Second, when talks in France (at Fontainebleau) to resolve their differences faltered, Ho Chi Minh sought a separate peace with the French minister of overseas France, Marius Moutet. This September "Modus Vivendi" also was ineffective at calming French imperialist motivations so that, by early November, the Saigon-based French administrators "were convinced that the only way to safeguard French prestige and power would be to take drastic action and *teach the Vietnamese a lesson*" (101; emphasis added). The "lesson" was taught in the north with the shelling of Haiphong, the strafing of fleeing refugees, and the attack on Langson, which resulted in the deaths of thousands of Vietnamese people (133–138). Later, the high commissioner of French Indochina, Thierry d'Argenlieu, reported it was Vietnamese "imperialist pretensions"— or audacious competition for the hegemonic position—that led to this conflict (143). The third instance of clashing between French and Vietnamese ambitions precipitated the December outbreak of war. Tønnesson titles this instance "the French trap," or the "tests of strength" used by French Saigon-based administrators to provoke the Vietnamese into aggression while keeping the French Paris-based government uninformed of these moves (163–166). "When the powerful see the basis for their power eroding," says Tønnesson, echoing both the trope of élan in *La 317ᵉ Section* and Connell and Messerschmidt's wrestling for dominance in a masculine hierarchy, "they sometimes embark on risky, even reckless, action" (105). Unfortunately, both the French and the Vietnamese "stumbled and fell into war," a conflict that endured until 1954 (174). Though Tønnesson remarks that both the Vietnamese and the French have "something to hide" about this falling (201), he firmly blames the "triumvirate" of French Saigon-based administrators for baiting the Viet Minh into a contest for hegemony (110, 242). "Saigon's vacillation between open belligerence, provocations, waiting games, subtle pressures, and the laying of traps in the four weeks from the Haiphong massacre to the fateful night of December 19, 1946 reflected, not only their expectations concerning the behavior of the Vietnamese government in Hanoi, but even more their need to thwart any harmful intrusion from their own government in Paris" (185).

TENSIONS BETWEEN THE FRENCH AND THE AMERICANS, REDUX

Tønnesson's Saigon triumvirate, which saw the Americans as a challenge to French dominance, also worked to thwart American interventions in the French provoking the DRV into war (156). Although American diplomats in Vietnam appear infrequently and so seem irrelevant to Tønnesson's account, the few represented are significant to the purposes of this chapter. Publicly, "the importance of France for the postwar settlement in Europe immunized it from great power interference in Indochina" (238), but privately, exceptionalist-thinking American diplomats in Vietnam were highly critical of French operations. U.S. Consul General Reed, stationed in Saigon, doubted France's motivations for urging the withdrawal of Chinese forces in the north, certain the French planned a coup for afterward (111). Reed also disbelieved French assertions that Vietnamese in the south would elect to remain separate from those in the north (73). After the French attacks on Haiphong and Langson, which U.S. Vice-Consul O'Sullivan in Hanoi termed a "terrorist measure," O'Sullivan also reported that the French had become "even more belligerent" than previously (133–134). To him, French belligerence signaled its baiting the Vietnamese into war (147): the situation in mid-December was a "powder keg" (197). Nonetheless, the official line from Washington was not to offend France. Although Abbott Low Moffat, head of the Southeast Asia Division in the Department of State, visited Vietnam early in December 1946 and found the lower levels of French leadership mediocre if not deplorable (182), he was instructed by his boss, John Carter Vincent, for the sake of Western European solidarity not to give any indication publicly of U.S. interference in or disapproval of French foreign policy. "Any publicity would be unfortunate," Tønnesson quotes Vincent telegramming (184). This attitude suggests the United States was willing to accept the subordinate masculine position in French Indochina in exchange for the hegemonic position in Europe. Because subordination within Connell and Messerschmidt's hierarchy is not a choice but a position imposed by the hegemon, however, the option to accept subordination or not indicates dominance.

Therefore, just as the U.S. diplomats' critiques were shared only among themselves, judgment of the French by the Americans would have been oblique, inadvertent, or covert, concerned as the State Department was not to offend its Western European ally while also certain of American exceptionalist superiority. Consequently, the competition to dominate—to claim the hegemonically masculine position in Vietnam and the perquisite to subordinate and marginalize—might be seen in the "odd things" Andrew Rotter cites, particularly in efforts to control the story told about the United States and thereby to tutor the Vietnamese. The combination of needing to dominate but to do it inconspicuously can explain the import of the USIS reading room to this contest, as innocuous and benign a collection of books and periodicals might appear. Mark Philip Bradley points out how the room was a point of contention between the Americans and the French in 1946: "Although the aims of this cultural diplomacy were modest, they provoked vociferous criticism from the French, who despite formal U.S. support for their return to Vietnam, were suspicious of what they viewed as continuing American efforts to subvert French authority" (*Imagining* 143).

THE POWER OF BOOKS AND THE USIS READING ROOM

Given the precarity of masculinity and the French desire to reclaim for their country the masculine desserts of colonialism, it is possible the reading room represented a greater or different challenge than Bradley acknowledges. Bradley's "French authority" could be construed as inhabiting an intact hegemonically masculine position with its attendant perquisite to subordinate and marginalize, a position the French thought was contested by ostensibly neutral American reading room "information." In this period of time, printed materials were seen, especially among Americans, as inherently valuable sources of truth: from the Second World War until the 1960s, "faith in books was surprisingly strong" (Laugeson 128).[16] In the United States during World War II, books were regarded as a safeguard against book-burning fascists; "books were to be 'weapons in the war of ideas,' as the Council for Books in Wartime put it" (129). This mantra likely continued into the period immediately following the war's conclusion, informing the institution of USIS reading rooms around the world and in Vietnam, and continuing into the Cold War with the establishment of the United States Information Agency (Anderton).

The postwar mission of USIS reading rooms around the world was to provide information about a previously little-known though now-dominant country. In an October 23, 1946, letter from U.S. Consul Reed to State Department officials Moffat and Wallner, Reed writes that "the sole and explicit function of USIS is to give the peoples of other countries a truthful picture of the aims, policies, and institutions of the United States and to promote mutual understanding between Americans and other peoples as an essential foundation for durable peace." The American public was in favor of providing such information. But it also worried the information would be propagandistic. In a December 1945 *Harper's Magazine* article, editor Frederick Lewis Allen contends the United States was not understood abroad because its story previously had been told in a "slanted" way by the United Kingdom, France, and Germany (553). In telling its own story of exceptionalism, it had to be careful not to produce its own "slant," however: "National censorships and national news services increase a worldwide tendency to substitute for the search for truth a choice between rival national propagandas" (556). In the winter 1946 edition of *Public Opinion Quarterly*, newspaperman and World War II American information officer Dick Fitzpatrick implies that government-sponsored reading rooms, unlike the psychological warfare and propagandistic aims of wartime radio broadcasting, are a corrective to poor or "slanted" information: "America's international information program is the best method of insuring accurate knowledge of America" (582). Fitzpatrick goes further, asserting that Europeans are unaware of the role the United States played in winning World War II: "I think it vitally essential to have all the people of Europe realize the enormous part played in winning the war by the largest democracy in the world. That may have an effect on their political thinking, as well as creating respect for the strength of this country" (586). "Books would be vehicles for providing basic information on America, its people, and its policies," explains Amanda Laugeson in "Books for the World." "They would work to disseminate scientific and technical information that would help build up friendships abroad; and they could help persuade people abroad (who might think otherwise) that America had a distinctive and valuable cultural tradition" (129).

In their analysis of this faith in books, however, Greg Barnhisel and Catherine Turner in their introduction to *Pressing the Fight* propose ideological motives for print-stocked reading rooms: "Print provided a critical medium for defining state power, creating narratives about the nation, and controlling the meaning of history" (4). Duong Van Mai Elliott recalls, for instance, as a frequent visitor to the Saigon reading room in the early 1950s that it was a place "whose mission was to impress underdeveloped countries with American success" (265). In her 1973 study of USIS libraries/reading rooms, Jody Sussman spotlights the problem of the libraries' dual and potentially contending roles of disseminator of information and of propaganda: "While the library has an informational mission to perform, realistically it must also fulfill its political function [of] waging its 'war of words'" (16). This ideological role became extraordinarily apparent during the Cold War in two notable instances. First, Senator Joseph McCarthy's 1953 congressional hearings attacked the USIS libraries worldwide, asserting that in their holdings were communist-authored texts. Reportedly, books were removed from the shelves and some were burned. For more than six months in 1953, anticommunist authorship of a book mattered more than anything else (Sussman 3).[17] Second, in 1965 the U.S. Advisory Commission on Information reported to Congress that nearly seventy attacks on libraries had occurred around the world. The report concluded that, though lamentable, these attacks indicated both the significance and effectiveness of the libraries at telling a story of American exceptionalism (Collett 545).

The power of reading materials in regard to Vietnam and stories obscured is evidenced by the case of Archimedes Patti, an Office of Strategic Services officer who during World War II was assigned to China, worked closely with the Viet Minh combatting the Japanese occupiers of French Indochina, and urged in mid-1945 that the United States produce "propaganda material illustrating the American way of living" (Bradley, *Imagining* 241, note 84). In his 1980 memoir, *Why Vietnam*, Patti bares his disdain for the French and their recolonizing mission in Vietnam and expresses his conviction that the United States would have been best allied with the Viet Minh. He also explains that following the French defeat in 1954, he had a scathing manuscript ready for publication but was censored, ordered as he was in that McCarthyite era not to publish: "Sensitive to adverse criticism of American foreign policy by members of the military establishment, the Department of the Army decreed that any public disclosure of information or opinion by me on the question of American involvement in Viet Nam would be regarded with official displeasure and I would be subject to disciplinary action" (xviii). Clearly, only stories that contributed to the American exceptionalist tale could be told.

"ODD THINGS" IN THE U.S. NATIONAL ARCHIVES

One might argue that censorship of conflict between the two ostensible allies, France and the United States, enabled the American narrative cited at the beginning of this chapter, that the Americans reluctantly but dutifully "took over" from the French, as though they were following the orders of their hegemon.[18] Considering the influence of printed materials and their subsequent censorship also indicates the French were correct to deduce that the Saigon-based U.S. reading room, though seemingly benign, was a hazard to their dominance in Vietnam, to the compensation in French culture that colonial service was supposed to provide to their masculinities, and so their efforts to prevent the room's establishment were warranted. In his account of the conflict over the mission and establishment of the USIS reading room during 1946, as cited before, Mark Philip Bradley characterizes the French response to the reading room as suspicion of "continuing American efforts to subvert French authority" (*Imagining* 143). Bradley's characterization undoubtedly complicates the one-dimensional "took over from the French" story told at places like the Vietnam Veterans Memorial. However, the American archival record indicates, through Andrew Rotter's "odd things," that this American subversion was particularly to the French enactment of masculinity, at once the basis for orientalizing colonialism but also already compromised by France's ignominious performance during World War II. Thus, words and situations alluding to masculine gender performances that appear in the diplomatic telegrams, missives, and reports in the United States archive signal a French-American contest for masculine hegemony.

The USIS in Saigon was authorized by the secretary of state in March 1946, the same month the March 6 Agreement was reached between the Democratic Republic of Vietnam and France (Robinson, July 1, 1946). American Foreign Service personnel arrived that month to staff the Saigon outlet and to fulfill its mission of disseminating information about the United States. The reading room, open to all local and European community members and with a circulating library, was part of the USIS operation. Many of the troubles of USIS generally and the reading room particularly were due to American insistence that its reading room remain independent of French control, while the other Western ally and colonial power, Great Britain, shared a reading room administered by the French. Independence would have been central to the mission of the United States telling its own, exceptionalist story and negating the "slanted" ones, but independence was perceived by the French as "seditious" (Reed, May 31, 1946). In this heated context, three "odd things" related to USIS, especially the reading room, emerge from the United States archival record when one puts on one's gender glasses: infrequent but deeply suggestive language related to male virility; disruptions by USIS staff to the French sense of superiority and dominance; and difficulties in establishing and staffing the reading room.

"ODD THINGS": INFREQUENT BUT SUGGESTIVE LANGUAGE RELATED TO MALE VIRILITY

In reading the 1940s postwar archive of U.S. diplomatic documents in Saigon, one is struck by the restrained rhetoric. Telegrams, per force, are grammatically abbreviated with few articles, let alone modifiers. They convey thoughts in the tersest, most succinct way and often require deciphering of deliberately incomplete sentences. Letters, though conventionally grammatical, more explanatory, and candid, display a similar restraint, perhaps by virtue of the traditions of formal diplomacy. Invariably, even when letters deliver bad news, they begin, "I have the honor . . ." Reports are similar to letters in their grammatical conventionality, explanatory fullness, and frankness, but because the audience for reports is wider than that for letters, the report language is notably controlled and resistant to modifiers that may disclose the writer's emotions.

Because of this typically restrained language in all three genres, less-restrained or evocative words are a stark contrast and so are laden with the subtextual significance Andrew Rotter flags as "a treasure trove."

In the perpetual state of crisis characterizing R. W. Connell and J. Messerschmidt's contest for masculine hegemony, language invoking male virility is conspicuous. Six words especially stand out in the Saigon-based American diplomatic records during the French war: "rivalry," "stiffening," "emasculation," "impotence," "power," and "penetration." Five appear in telegrams or letters from Consul General Reed to State Department officials during the war's 1946–1947 beginnings; the sixth appears in a report from the Office of Policy and Plans in the State Department near the war's end. While the words often are Reed's characterization of French activities and sensibilities, they also suggest the U.S. consul general's sensitivity to the competition in which the United States is engaged with the French.

"Rivalry" is used by Reed in a letter dated October 23, 1946, and addressed to Moffat and Wallner, State Department officials whose purview included Southeast Asia. Titled "Basis for Proposed Conversation with M. [illegible] on French Hostility towards USIS in Indochina," the letter enumerates the ways by which French Indochina officials have impeded the establishment of USIS in Saigon. In his first point, "difficulty in obtaining quarters for USIS," Reed explains that the French resent the potential "rivalry" USIS represents: "French officials informed [USIS Director] Robinson in May that conditions in Cochinchina were too disturbed to permit establishment of a foreign information service in the center of the city where it might appear to be in rivalry with the French information service." This point clarifies two issues, at least according to the Americans: first, the French want to control the narrative of their recolonization of Vietnam; second, the French understand they are in competition to tell that story. Reed regularly discusses the second issue in his missives.

In a telegram dated November 25, 1946—shortly after the French attacks in Haiphong and Langson in the north—addressed to the secretary of state, Reed uses "stiffening" and "emasculate," indicating that the competition perceived by the French is not only about telling the story, but in doing so is also about vying for masculine hegemony. In the partial language of telegrams, Reed writes, "French attitude in negotiations with Vietnam appears to be stiffening," an attitude unlikely to shift. On his return from France, the French Indochina high commissioner "will have orders [to] maintain French point of view." Alone, "stiffening" of the French position is not weighted. Paired with "Vietnam will endeavor [to] limit or emasculate French interests" later in the telegram, however, it evokes the competition for masculine hegemony, with France's "stiffening" a response to or obviation of Vietnamese challenges to its dominance.

After the mid-December outbreak of war between France and the DRV in Hanoi, Reed wrote a December 27, 1946, letter to the secretary of state entitled "Outlook for United States Information Service Program in French Indochina." In it he is not sanguine about the prospects for USIS, citing the rivalry perceived by the French and comparing American and French storytelling objectives. "The fundamental aim of the United States Information Services policy and program is to make information regarding the United States and 'the American way' available to all persons," Reed explains, "whereas the French are manifestly desirous of restricting the dissemination of any information which may lead to an invidious comparison with French achievements, or lack thereof, and which may further aspirations for democratic freedoms and independence among the native people of Indochina." Reed characterizes French obstacles to USIS success as "emasculation," as though this rivalry lies primarily in the realm of male virility, and he cautions that a new challenger, "Communism," may crowd the masculine arena if the French avert their eyes. USIS is "restricted . . . by reason of French blindness to the advantages of the program and their unawareness that the emasculation of that program may well be an invitation for Communist propaganda."

At nearly a year since USIS was chartered and two months since the French-DRV war outbreak, in his February 6, 1947, letter to the secretary of state entitled "Newspaper Attacks on This Consulate General and the United States Information Service; Anti-Americanism," Reed repeats his pessimism about improving French-American relations, describing an alarming anti-American trend in Saigon subsequent to a "French sense of impotence." Exemplifying the anti-Americanism is an article in the local French-language newspaper accusing USIS of promoting racism and German propaganda. Not only is the article's author a known collaborationist in occupied France, Reed contends, but the newspapers also are the French authorities' storytelling voice pieces. This tainting of the United States' reputation through the press, by accusing the United States of "a sham anti-colonialism" concealing "a virulent economic imperialism," is, according to Reed, done out of masculine insecurity: "Coloring the overall picture of anti-American feeling is an undoubted French sense of impotence, in face of her many economic and political difficulties, and the French knowledge that only a miracle can enable France to maintain any substantial part of her previous economic grasp and political power in this erstwhile hotbed of autocratic colonialism." Characterizing the French despair as "impotence" once again demonstrates how Reed conceives of the stakes in Vietnam as about male virility, and in vying to be hegemonically masculine, the French are desperate to control not only their own story but also those that may reflect on or slant the French narrative. This anti-exceptionalist move echoes what Tønnesson writes about the French decision to "teach the Vietnamese a lesson" when they challenged the French in Haiphong (101). "Such situations have historically been among the most dangerous. When the powerful see the basis for their power eroding, they sometimes embark on risky, even reckless, action" (105).

"Power" peppers the archival records of this period, but two instances in particular stand out in regard to hegemonic masculinity. First, in his June 14, 1947, letter to the secretary of state, "Situation in Indochina at Date of High Commissioner's Departure for France," Reed writes that the "autocratic" high commissioner of French Indochina and follower of de Gaulle, Thierry d'Argenlieu, has been replaced. D'Argenlieu's autocracy means that French authorities are "chiefly preoccupied in maintaining the interests, power, and prestige of France in Indochina," their means often tyrannical and, in this competitive context, recognizable as a grasping for hegemonic masculinity via absolute control. Reed laments that "the present situation is far worse than when I arrived in February 1946" and expresses guarded hopes for improved conditions with the new high commissioner, Émile Bollaert. The second notable instance reported by Reed infers power and unfortunately denies hoped-for improvement; in a September 6, 1947, letter to the secretary of state, he explains that a Vietnamese employee in the American consulate was assaulted by the French military police. After the employee was beaten, he was told that "the French, not the Americans, were running Indochina." Subsequent interoffice notes between stateside State Department officials discuss whether this treatment is an isolated case. The answer is no, that it is widespread in Indochina but not in other French Union countries.[19] Clearly, the competition for masculine hegemony in Vietnam is a unique situation, suggesting it is the presence of viable challengers to the hegemonic position, communism and the Americans, that intensifies the storytelling contest.

Finally, the December 1953 report from the State Department's Office of Policy and Plans again deploys more language— "penetration"—invoking male virility. In "Analysis of Information Centers Programs in the Associated States of Indochina," the authors echo the refrain heard from 1946: USIS still needs strengthening, especially because the majority of its book collection continues to be in English when it should be in French and Vietnamese. Three factors influencing the failure of the library to reach its Vietnamese audience include low rates of English-language literacy, difficulties with communication, and the narrow interests of the population. The fourth factor inhibiting USIS's success continues to be with French authorities: their "sensitivity to American ideological and cultural penetration." Once again, the relationship between the French and the Americans is characterized using language suggestive of male virility and the storytelling competition between two Western powers to assert their masculine hegemony—and resist overt subordination, since they appear to have agreed to marginalize the Vietnamese—in Vietnam (State Department).[20]

Alone, these words can seem inconsequential. Taken together in this postwar context of the masculine state of crisis and looking for the "odd things" Andrew Rotter cites, these words are telling. Peculiar as they are, these words also underscore two other "odd things" in the archival record.

"ODD THINGS": DISRUPTIONS BY USIS STAFF TO THE FRENCH SENSE OF SUPERIORITY AND DOMINANCE

The preceding discussion of words clarifies—from the American viewpoint—France's shaky claim to masculine hegemony in Vietnam. As Reed's December 27, 1946, letter suggests, one of the other claimants would have been communism, except USIS kept it at bay. Reed's conclusion that the French were "blind" to this advantage or the prospect of communism infiltrating southern Vietnam is curious, given that Reed also reports throughout the year French convictions that, first, USIS is a "cover" for American "espionage," second, that the espionage is economic, as the consulate employees work chiefly for American business enterprises, and third, USIS Director Robinson and especially Assistant Director Saulnier are sympathetic to the supposedly communist Viet Minh. Reed repeats this last point in his December 27, 1946, letter in listing the "personal factors" obstructing USIS's success. Robinson, Reed explains, had been part of OSS in China before being assigned to USIS-Saigon, a position the French suspect is counter to their story. Furthermore, Robinson's ongoing criticism of French policies and willingness to identify non-French sources to visiting correspondents threatened, the French thought, their utter control over the story of their colonialist masculine venture. As a member of the war-time French resistance, Saulnier also represented a threat to autocratic French masculine hegemony in Indochina, since his resistance activities might have been gauged after the war's end as hegemonically masculine, thereby at least subordinating if not marginalizing the French Indochina autocrats who had not been resisters. In his December 3, 1946, letter to the secretary of state, Reed explains that the French had accused Saulnier of being a Marxist, an accusation "colored by his open opposition to certain French officials and their policy in FIC [French Indochina]." By the time of Reed's August 20, 1946, telegram to the secretary of state, Saulnier had resigned and become a correspondent for the Associated Press, and by Reed's June 20, 1947, telegram to the secretary of state, Robinson had been reassigned to Manila. Thus, opposition to French masculine hegemony was offered by the backgrounds and ongoing activities of both Robinson and Saulnier; once they were gone, one might suppose French suspicions of USIS would have been mitigated. According to the American archival record, however, mitigation did not occur. As late as the December 1953 report previously cited, the French still objected to the "American ideological and cultural penetration" that the USIS reading room enabled (State Department).

"ODD THINGS": DIFFICULTIES IN ESTABLISHING AND STAFFING THE READING ROOM

That it was not "personal factors" the French ultimately objected to suggests it was USIS, in particular the reading room itself, challenging the French status as masculine hegemon in Vietnam, a predicament compounded by the Viet Minh challenge and the poor performance of official French masculinity during World War II. From its 1946 beginnings, USIS-Saigon struggled to acquire appropriate office space, staff, and equipment, conditions that persisted into the 1950s. Though some of these difficulties, especially office space, could be explained by the postwar turmoil of departing Japanese and the influx of internally displaced people as a result of war, USIS personnel reported that most were obstructions deliberately created by the controllers of property, the French authorities. According to the archival record, USIS-Saigon was the only USIS in the world—except for one in Yugoslavia—obstructed as it was by local authorities, suggesting an anomalous set of circumstances in Vietnam.[21] Though independent construction of the exceptionalist American story was the USIS mission, it was

American resolve to keep its information services in Vietnam independent of French control and censorship, representing a refusal to acquiesce to French hegemonic masculinity, that stoked French ire. Though the autocratic French were unable to impose their will through physical violence on the Americans as they did on the Vietnamese, they were able to initiate a series of passive-aggressive obstacles that made Reed, in his December 27, 1946, letter, question whether USIS-Saigon ought to continue. Obstacles founded by the French and recounted in American archival materials over the course of 1946–1947 include the following: impeding USIS's finding suitable office space; accusing USIS American and European staff of sedition and treachery; accusing USIS of racism and collaboration with Axis powers; inhibiting a free local and international press with censorship, threats, arrests, and repression; threatening and physically harming numerous Vietnamese USIS and consulate staff; rifling through USIS materials sent by diplomatic pouch; surveilling the USIS reading room, inside and out; and banning war films and any films not in English from being shown.

For instance, in his May 9, 1946, report to the State Department's Southeast Asia section of the Office of Information and Cultural Affairs, USIS Director Robinson describes how the French refused his explanation of the desire for independence: to maintain good relations with both the "Annamites" and the French. Later, in Robinson's July 1946 "Special Survey Report," he reports the French feared that independence would lead to "a 'propagandizing' of native peoples still in a state of unrest" and explains further "that there are certain aspects of American policy, particularly in regard to colonial peoples and to China, which are considered inimical to French interests in Indochina." Presumably the author of monthly USIS-OIC reports, Robinson repeats this mantra in September, October, and November of 1946: the French resent the independent reading room because it promotes allegedly uncensored storytelling and is available to all. September's report says the USIS reading room's openness to all inhabitants, native and European, repudiates the exclusivity and perceived colonialist racism of the joint French/British reading room and advocates the exceptionalism of American culture. This repudiation (and subsequent divide between ostensible allies), says the report, "probably carries more weight than the content and objectives of the USIS program." October's report notes that French secret police surveillance of the reading room is producing further declining attendance of Vietnamese readers and, though printed materials have been chosen by USIS to avoid controversy, French authorities are withholding books sent by the State Department to the reading room on the grounds that they are "subversive literature." November's report describes an even sharper decline in attendance, with "police agents" inhabiting the reading room and still no delivery of books.

Though the December 1953 report previously cited does not explicitly refer to harassment or accusation, its "French sensitivity to American ideological and cultural penetration" insinuates that the French continue to be uneasy about American challenges to their masculine dominance (State Department). Several factors in addition to those already discussed—a history of French insecurity about masculinities, including worries about urbane effeteness and the disappointment that recolonizing Vietnam does not offer the compensations colonialism traditionally had—undoubtedly impact the U.S. and France competition for masculine hegemony. These factors include, as of January 1950, the recognition of and military support for the DRV by the Soviet Union and the People's Republic of China, the United States funding the majority of France's war efforts, and also the failure of France by 1954 to defeat the Viet Minh in the nearly eight years they had been at war (Cain 127). As Jacques Dalloz puts it, though the French at the war's end were traumatized by their loss, saying "never again," and wanting to avoid "putting them [the Viet Minh] into the hands of the Americans," still, "American hegemony had to be accepted in South-East Asia" (169, 185, 195). Meanwhile, according to Mark Philip Bradley, American contempt for French practices and exceptionalist confidence in its own were amplified with the provision of U.S. dollars and matériel: "As increasing amounts of U.S.

military and economic aid entered Vietnam, American scorn for French colonial methods and the assurance that U.S. models would best guide the construction of the Vietnamese state also intensified and provoked bitter disputes between French and American officials on how U.S. aid dollars in Vietnam would be spent" (*Imagining* 185). One might conclude that the French resented losing their hegemonic position not only to the already marginalized Vietnamese of north and south but, more bitterly, to the Americans.

EXCEPTIONALISM IN VIETNAM

Noteworthy as the contest for masculine hegemony is in regard to USIS, and as sensitive to the contest American State Department officials appear to be, the American archival record during the French war, especially during 1946–1947, does not suggest that these same officials had any doubt about the impartiality of their mission to inform, of the sharp distinction between "information" and "propaganda," or of their superior abilities to practice masculinist colonialism.[22] Despite a long American history of a masculine state of crisis, using words invoking male virility and citing instances of harassment and obstruction, the American officials position the French as undemocratic authoritarians and insecure performers of masculinities. With this positioning, the American officials exhibit exceptionalist assuredness in the United States' version of masculinist colonialism, assuredness that could be seen as hubris—or disingenuousness—motivating its constant engagement in Vietnam. Thus, the Americans repeatedly indict the French for injudicious if not despotic exertion of force/censorship/repression primarily driven by fear of humiliation or loss of masculine dominance, with a concomitant implication that the American unrestricted sharing of "information" displays secure, proud masculine dominance that can perform colonialism justly.

Stories of the period after the 1954 French military's departure from Vietnam indicate fractures in the American confidence, when the United States publicly assumed the hegemonically masculine position by more visibly propping up South Vietnam and the

Americans no longer had a Western ally against whom they could compare themselves (and privately subordinate) in the masculine hierarchy. With the French military gone, not only was there no apparent contender, given the marginalized status assigned to the Vietnamese, north and south, signs are that American confidence in its superiority led officials complacently to believe what R. W. Connell and J.Messerschmidt caution against: that once achieved, hegemonic masculinity would continue, regardless of context. Therefore, abiding by the 1954 Geneva Accords that called for a temporary division of the country into North and South but ignoring their call for free elections that might unite the two parts, in its complacency the United States repeatedly sponsored what turned out to be ineffective South Vietnamese leaders. This faulty judgment and thereby test of its masculine hegemony paradoxically led the United States to an unnerved reassertion of its dominance by pouring more and more resources into a futile situation, resorting to intemperate military measures resonant of some of the worst French practices, and remaining committed until 1973, when all combat troops were withdrawn, POWs returned, and monies halted by Congress.[23]

Two stories that occurred during what is called by Americans "the Vietnam War" underscore the United States' fear of losing dominance. First, in March 1965, simultaneous to the first-time commitment of entire American combat units to Vietnam, the assistant secretary of defense for international security affairs and "chief civilian aide to Secretary of Defense Robert McNamara," John McNaughton, claimed that 70 percent of the reason for continuing and heightening U.S. engagement was to "avoid a humiliating defeat" (Harrison and Mosher 505; Nashel 146). This refrain echoes French general Jean Sainteny's reported concern about "a loss of face" when, in 1945, he was required to clear all his interactions in Vietnam with the Americans (Patti 229). The second story is John Kerry's 1971 testimony before the Senate Foreign Relations Committee, alleging, "Each day . . . someone has to give up his life so that the United States doesn't have to admit something that the entire world already knows . . . [that] we have made a mistake.

Someone has to die so that President Nixon won't be, and these are his words, 'the first President to lose a war'" (Kerry). Thus, both warring Westerners, the Americans and the French, were concerned about and motivated by the potential humiliation of losing their position as the masculine hegemon, and they responded with violent measures to establish (and reestablish) their dominance. The American war's futility and its motivations were made public when the top secret *Pentagon Papers*, commissioned by Secretary of Defense Robert McNamara to chronicle American engagement in Vietnam from 1945 to 1967, were published only months after Kerry's testimony. They revealed that American and other Western officials knew since World War II's end that the cause in Vietnam was unwinnable, and yet American involvement never waned.

Using R. W. Connell and J. Messerschmidt's theory of masculinities as Mark Philip Bradley's "novel interpretive framework," and attending to the gendered "odd things" Andrew Rotter recommends, the story of American involvement in Vietnam from 1945 to 1973 reveals an exceptionalist desire to deny masculinity's instability and its perpetual state of crisis, to believe in a zero-sum game of singular masculinity, not a plurality of masculinities, and to think that once this singular masculinity is achieved, it always is held, at whatever cost. Because of their country's victory in World War II, American officials in Vietnam privately may never have considered that the French could occupy the hegemonic masculine position; the archival record for the Saigon consulate and USIS in 1946–1947 suggests as much. Certainly the cementing of beliefs in American exceptionalism, manifest destiny, the Truman Doctrine, and policies of containment emerging from the World War II era would have suggested to many, including the French, an unshakeable American dominance. The historical record suggests that this dominance may not only have led the French resentfully to attempt undermining American influence in the Indochina context, but it may also have led the United States into thinking it alone had the exceptional qualities to bestow—not encourage—democratically influenced peace to Vietnam. The archival record further intimates that French resentment and American confidence may have arisen from their relative positions within the masculine hierarchy Connell and Messerschmidt outline, leading the subordinated French to leave Vietnam for good and the hegemonic United States, certain of its exceptionalism, to persist in its delivery mission for nearly another two decades.

Concluding that the United States might have been motivated by gender as much as by geopolitics in Vietnam makes it no simpler to answer this chapter's opening question: When was the beginning of the American war in Vietnam? Moreover, the conclusion raises questions about motivations for current American warring in the Middle East—Iraq, Afghanistan, and Syria—and in the so-far-rhetorical provocations between leaders of the United States and leaders of North Korea and Iran. Afghanistan has been the site of the United States' longest military conflict, having begun with U.S.-led bombing in October 2001 following the 9/11 attacks; the beginning of the conflict in Iraq occurred more than a year later, on March 20, 2003. In 2019, tens of thousands of U.S. forces still occupied both countries. Have those "forever wars" been perpetuated by gendered influences similar to those impacting the long American engagement in Vietnam?[24] Was the commander in chief who initiated both of these forever wars so stung by the literal penetration of American bastions of masculinity—the World Trade Center and the Pentagon—that he took the country to war and kept it there for years?[25] Have the two subsequent commanders in chief resisted ending the wars, perhaps fearing, as Richard Nixon did, the ignominy of being the first president to lose a war? Will the 2016–2020 commander in chief wreak "fire and fury" in his zeal to hegemonically dominate a much smaller North Korea or Iran?

2

Staging War

Stories of Collectivity at, by, and through
the Vietnam Veterans Memorial

A photograph of a helicopter atop a building in Saigon, taken on April 29, 1975, commonly is identified as an image of Americans evacuating the U.S. embassy as the North Vietnamese invade. Taken from a distance, the photo depicts people patiently climbing up stairs to the man who will help them into the waiting helicopter, and it has become one of the iconic photographs telling the story of the United States' involvement in Southeast Asia. This identification—of Americans, of the U.S. embassy—is a mistake, however, because the image depicts escaping Vietnamese, not Americans, climbing stairs and into a helicopter atop a Saigon apartment building, not the U.S. embassy. As UPI photographer Hubert Van Es explains it, despite his accurate caption, his editors "took it for granted" that these were Americans and that this was the U.S. embassy, and the inaccurate identifications endure despite his efforts to correct them.[1] Though a single example, this wrong assumption and its persistence reveal both the American-centricity of most Western stories of the war, and also why the American war in Vietnam influences to a great extent the American ethos now. Like so many other at best half-truths concerning this conflict, only the assumed, heroic evacuation story was told in 1975, fitting as it would into what Andrew Bacevich says is "an apparently seamless historical narrative of American soldiers as liberators, with Operation Iraqi Freedom in March 2003 becoming a sequel to Operation Overlord in June 1944" (*New American Militarism* 98). At the same time, like a repressed memory whose reemergence cannot be predicted, well into the twenty-first century the Vietnam War story continues to surface, to haunt, to appear frequently, sometimes at the most unlikely and unwelcome moments, suggesting the story has not yet been adequately told.

A central chapter to that story is narrated by the Vietnam Veterans Memorial (VVM) on the National Mall in Washington, D.C. The Mall itself didactically constructs a story about the nation and its values, a story that binds citizen visitors to the nation with its highly codified commemorations, staging of rituals meant to "reinforce and extend national meanings" (Savage, *Monument* 4–11), concealment of "the violence of the nation-state itself," and "justification of the organized violence of war" (Stevens 39, 60).[2] Within this already deliberately crafted National Mall narrative, the VVM, including the original 1982 "Wall" and its numerous added components—the Wall's inscriptions, the 1983 flagpole and its dedicatory plaque, the 1984 figurative statue of men, the 1993 figurative statue of women, the 2004 plaque honoring veterans who died after the war, and the as-yet-unbuilt education center approved in 2001—tells a story that has been revised with each addition and with each federal administration.[3] The VVM's founders' aims were to restore justice to the war's ostensibly derided (American) combat veterans and thereby heal the Vietnam War era's national rifts. It was imagined that this healing, by invoking the core American value of collectivity, would bring an end to the rancor and division engendered by the conflict and permit the nation to move on. Instead, like the following chapter, this story illustrates the conflict between two core values, individualism and collectivism, in American war stories. Consequent to the VVM's multifaceted purpose and in its repeated attempts to conclude the story of the war with collective additions to the Wall, the memorial, figuratively acting as a staging site for war, has papered over some of the most serious wounds to the national ethos and literally has been used as a stage to promote American warfighting. After discussing the role of memorials generally and the lore about the Vietnam War and the Vietnam Veterans Memorial, this chapter first explores the memorial's figurative papering over and then the literal staging of American war.

"Staging War" proposes that the VVM exemplifies how the invocation of individualism and collectivism may contribute to an unresolved national trauma, when some stories are told and others are not, or when stories like those of the helicopter in Saigon are reframed to fit into what Tom Engelhardt and Andrew Bacevich both describe as a narrative of American triumph and heroism.[4] The additions to Maya Lin's original Wall design, a design judged as "antiwar" by critics and admirers, over the course of decades demonstrate the impulse to tell and tell again a conclusively heroic story about the American war, as though these repetitions never are finally able to make amends to the "veterans" or to the nation at large.[5] The repetitions also demonstrate how individualism and collectivism often are at odds with one another. Nonetheless, these retellings at, by, and through the VVM have framed the story of the war, normalizing a heroic version that obscures the complexities of that era.[6] Two recent instances illustrate the effectiveness of this revision, beginning with the assertion by Ronald Reagan—which he made both as a candidate and as president—that the war was a "noble cause," and intensifying since 9/11.[7] The first instance, an example of figurative staging, are the results of a 2013 Gallup poll that found older age groups continue to consider U.S. involvement in Vietnam's civil war a blunder, but eighteen- to twenty-nine-year-olds, who were raised and educated over the course of the VVM's life span, think American engagement in Vietnam was not a mistake (Favorite 197). This age-group difference suggests that the younger group has been educated to think differently of the American war in Vietnam during the United States' Afghanistan and Iraq wars of their own formative years.[8] The second, an example of literal staging, is one of the hundreds of thousands of objects left at the VVM. As the United States committed in 2001 and 2003 to more "forever" wars in Afghanistan and Iraq, the VVM became a location for veterans of these recent wars to commemorate their service, creating there a bonding site for veterans of the three wars.[9] Clarifying this bond is one object—a pair of desert combat boots and a letter addressed to "Brothers"—left at the Wall in 2009, archived by the National Park Service, and featured on the Vietnam Veterans Memorial Fund (VVMF) website. Someone in the Gallup poll's younger age group and claiming to have served two tours in Iraq as a junior Marine officer submitted the letter, summarized as saying "the nation at large owes the Vietnam generation of U.S. Marines a great deal." The website then quotes the letter directly: "IF YOUR GENERATION OF MARINES HAD NOT COME HOME TO JEERS, INSULTS, AND PROTESTS, MY GENERATION WOULD NOT COME HOME TO THANKS, HANDSHAKES, AND HUGS."[10] This sentiment, championed as it is by the VVMF, implies a cause-and-effect relationship among the wars, that without the therapeutic and revisionary story told by the VVM, those returning from the post-9/11 wars would not have had the "support the troops" and "thank you for your service" experience ostensibly denied the Vietnam War veterans. Thus, the VVM can be regarded as the stage on which both the Gallup poll results and the "Brothers" testimony appear.

This use of the memorial to tutor its spectators about war is not peculiar to the VVM but is inherent to war memorials. To persist as a boundaried entity, the United States relies on its capability to go to war. To go to war, the United States must convince its citizens that war is a worthy venture and that militarism is the primary way to define and secure the nation-state's boundaries. To attract recruits for its all-volunteer force, the U.S. government needs to persuade residents that war is the most appropriate venue for validating one's personal merit. Thus, the U.S. government promises citizens that in serving their country during war, they will be lauded as honorable, heroic, model patriots.[11] One medium for the promise includes memorials, which, Erika Doss explains, "create and celebrate an imaginary citizen: the representative

American, the 'good' citizen that all American citizens aspire to become" (56). War memorials, designed to solicit recruits, posit the "good citizen" as one willing if not eager to go to war for the country. "There is no better way to prepare for the next war," commented Daniel Sickles at the 1891 dedication of a New York monument to Union warriors in the Civil War, "than to show your appreciation of your defenders in the last war." He continued: "No nation can long survive the decline of its martial strength. When it ceases to honor its soldiers, it will have none" (Linenthal 105–106). Sickle's comments indicate that war memorials inherently are designed for political purposes, to produce subsequent generations of warriors explicitly by posing them as good citizens but also implicitly to support "martial strength" generally. Though the founders of the VVM sought an apolitical memorial by separating the warrior from the war, as a memorial to commemorate the dead of a particular war, the VVM inherently cannot resist telling stories and writing scripts that tacitly extol, and therefore stage, war.

Figurative Staging: "Tiny Mistakes" and Lore

The VVM-related scripts about the war are extensive and far-reaching. As Patrick Hagopian notes in his discussion of the 1980s-era discourse of healing and reconciliation developed through the VVM, the dominance of a narrative relies "not on a simple logic of repetition and dissemination, but on a million tiny—or huge—mistakes . . . whose cumulative effect is to crowd out alternative ways of seeing the world" (*Vietnam* 369).[12] This chapter identifies four of these Foucauldian "tiny mistakes," including, first, as chapter 1 already elucidated, the difficulties of establishing the duration of the U.S. involvement in Vietnam without a formal declaration of war. These dates influence which war stories can be told and which stories can be counted as concerning war.[13] By focusing on the core value of exceptionalism, chapter 1 challenges received notions that the American war originated in the early-1960s Kennedy-era commitment of military advisors, the 1964 Gulf of Tonkin incident, or the 1965 commitment of whole combat units, and concludes that the U.S. military commitment may have been kindled in the French-American competition to be the masculine hegemon immediately following World War II. Moreover, though April 1975 repeatedly is cited as the Vietnam War's close, the ending of the American war in Vietnam is more clearly dated to 1973: the January Paris Peace Accords, the February return of American POWs, the March withdrawal of all U.S. troops, and Congress's reduction of monies for the ongoing civil war. "Peace with honor" is how President Richard Nixon characterized the Accords (Nixon). Just as the origination of American involvement in Vietnam is consequential to the stories that can be told of its war there, so too is the American war's conclusion. The story that the "Vietnam War," a nomenclature applied only by the United States and its Western allies, is said to have ended in April 1975 seems aimed at refuting accusations that the United States dishonorably abandoned its ally by withdrawing its troops and treasure well before the civil war's ending. Its purportedly staying fully engaged until the Democratic Republic of Vietnam tanks crashed through the embassy gates aligns with the heroic narrative Engelhardt and Bacevich each describe. This narrative is reinforced by the VVM, which, though it cites 1959 as the year of the first American death in Vietnam and 1975 as the last, is interpreted as representing the war's duration.[14]

A second set of repeated "tiny mistakes" concerns the geopolitical status of the northern and southern parts of Vietnam, a status framing motivations of U.S. involvement in Vietnam. The two parts were not "sovereign nations," as presidential candidate Ronald Reagan averred when he insisted that the American war was a noble cause, but instead two entities temporarily divided in the 1954 Geneva Agreement following the French war in Vietnam, a division pending national elections in 1956.[15] Reagan's "noble cause" story hinged on this alleged sovereignty; otherwise, as Patrick Hagopian makes clear, the United States did not selflessly come to the aid of a beleaguered ally but instead invaded Vietnam. "A foreign power cannot justifiably install a friendly government in another country as a pretext for going to its defense," Hagopian explains. "A war fought on behalf of such a client is no less unjust than a blatant invasion" (*Vietnam* 424).[16] Reagan's rhetoric of one sovereign nation selflessly coming to the aid of another constructs the United States as a liberating, not invading, nation.[17] This narrative of altruistic liberation is reinforced by the VVM, honoring as it does only American warriors.

A third set of "tiny mistakes" has to do with the treatment of veterans both following the war and since then, a narrative dominated by what Jerry Lembcke calls the "spitting image," or the notion that on their return to the United States all veterans were spat upon by other Americans. The VVM was founded on the supposition that veterans had been ill-treated and that once there was a national memorial to reframe their service as honorable, they would be treated well. While there is contemporary evidence to suggest that Vietnam War veterans suffered high rates of unemployment, mental illness, drug addiction, poor health due to Agent Orange exposure, disability, and negative portrayals in popular media, there is little evidence to support the most common story—that veterans routinely were spat upon or accused of being "baby-killers."[18] Furthermore, while veterans of the wars in Vietnam, Iraq, and Afghanistan now are appreciated routinely with thanks for their service and what Jennifer Mittelstadt calls the "military welfare state," they still suffer disproportionately high rates of divorce, mental illness, homelessness, and health disorders such as traumatic brain injury, moral injury, and suicide (*Rise*).[19] One would be hard-pressed to declare that these postservice challenges primarily are traceable to being spat upon or to one's service being underappreciated. Nonetheless, the VVM reinforces the conflicted (and possibly contradictory) narrative of veterans simultaneously as self-sacrificing ("who gave their lives") and victims ("they were taken from us") in its inscriptions at the Wall's apex:

[Top] In honor of the men and women of the armed forces of the United States who served in the Vietnam War. The names of those who gave their lives and of those who remain missing are inscribed in the order they were taken from us.

[Bottom] Our nation honors the courage, sacrifice and devotion to duty and country of its Vietnam veterans. This memorial was built with private contributions from the American people.

A fourth set of "tiny mistakes" is related to the first one, about the duration of the American war. This has to do with the stories told about why the war was lost, most of which has the effect of exonerating American combatants.[20] The most common stories begin with blaming the print and visual media, whose access to combat was relatively unlimited and whose graphic footage appeared on the nightly news of one of the three network television stations.[21] Relatedly, the domestic antiwar movement was blamed for losing the war, disrupting as it did the unquestioning support for war on which the U.S. government relies. Other stories explaining the loss complain that the military was prevented from winning, either because the soldiers had to "fight with one hand tied behind their backs" due to restrictive rules of engagement, because of limits on bombing the northern part of Vietnam, or because Congress would not appropriate the funds necessary to conduct the war decisively.[22] Conversely, it is said that although the war may have been lost, every battle was won. The least dominant story is that the war always was unwinnable and was a futile waste of American lives. Whatever the cause of the war's loss, the stories avoid the "long, complex history of the war" and its devastating effects on Vietnam and the Vietnamese to cast American veterans as the Vietnam War's "primary victims" (Appy, *Reckoning* 241).[23] The VVM's commemorating the participants in a lost war contributes to the war's being regarded as the United States' most tragic conflict.[24]

The outcome of these mistaken stories constitutes lore about the Vietnam War that both undergirds and is propagated by the VVM. While the story told by the VVM publicly was intended by its founders simply to "recognize and honor those who served and died," several understandings related to the "tiny mistakes" accumulated in the simple story as it has evolved over decades

(Doubek 91).[25] In that time, "recognize and honor" became "heal and reconcile," a rehabilitative tale that says this: the particulars of the American war in Vietnam do not need to be understood or critically examined; the U.S. government, especially the Department of Defense, should be trusted to foreground U.S. citizens' security and well-being as it nobly promotes liberty abroad; American warriors and veterans always must be viewed and treated as model citizens; and though this war is the nation's most tragic in history, it nevertheless is part of a liberatory trajectory. As Christian Appy asserts in *American Reckoning*, "The most searing evidence of the damage the United States had done in and to Vietnam largely disappeared [in the 1980s] from public view and consciousness. In its place, a new mainstream consensus emerged around the idea that the Vietnam War had primarily been an *American tragedy* that had badly wounded and divided the nation" (xvii).[26] In trying to separate the war from the warrior, the VVM has propagated this lore and rehabilitated American war generally, thereby staging it.

The founding of the VVM has itself entered lore and contributed to the rehabilitation of the Vietnam War. Similar to chapter 3's contention that the film and memoir renditions of *Lone Survivor* and *American Sniper* reveal the tensions between American individualism and collectivism, the story about the VVM begins as a populist American myth of the self-made common man who through his own volition and inspiration pulls up his bootstraps to fight for liberty, and ends with the exceptional power of collective action to honor thousands of common people:

- A politically naive and working-class enlisted man who had served in Vietnam, Jan Scruggs, saw *The Deer Hunter* in 1979 and was inspired to do something for Vietnam veterans;
- single-handedly, Scruggs made the memorial happen;
- except other veterans also contributed to making the memorial happen, so veterans ultimately were entirely responsible;
- and those veterans were a homogenous group who agreed that recognition of service was their paramount need;

- and that recognizing service in war as honorable could be distinguished from recognizing the war as honorable;
- and, acknowledging that Vietnam veterans were due some honor, through their small donations private citizens provided the funds to build the memorial.

Not only does this myth attempt to resolve the tension between individualism and collectivism, but it also relies on a version of each that is insupportable. The portrayal of Jan Scruggs as a political naïf, for instance, is not accurate, since on his return to the United States from Vietnam and well before his claim of being inspired by *The Deer Hunter* he completed undergraduate and graduate work that focused on the welfare of Vietnam veterans, testified before a congressional committee exploring a veterans' center program, and formulated the idea of a thanks-giving memorial during his graduate research.[27] Another element of the myth, that Vietnam veterans alone were responsible for making the VVM happen, discounts all of the nonveterans in the federal government who lobbied on behalf of the first national war memorial on the Mall since 1936, all of the members of federal institutions who made decisions about the memorial's location and siting and components, all of the people who entered the competition and the jurors who judged it, and other nonveteran members of the VVMF. Finally, an element of the myth that is central to a collectivist argument is that the VVM was funded by the small donations of private citizens. So many ordinary citizens registering approval of the memorial by donating, the story implies, must reflect a truly popular, nationwide sentiment. However, as a cofounder in its earliest days who as an attorney filed the legal paperwork to form the VVMF as a nonprofit and who was responsible for the organization's finances periodically, Robert Doubek asserts not only that the private citizens solicited via mailings were more conservative than liberal (33), but also that the VVMF targeted corporations, especially defense contractors, for donations (35, 49, 98–104, 106, 112, 124, 156, 168, 182). In the end, he claims, nearly half of the funds came from private citizens (many of whom were wealthy), and the remainder was contributed by military organizations such as the American Legion and Veterans of Foreign Wars and by petroleum companies such as Sunoco (297). This funding history involving corporate monies, of course, tells a very different story from the one claimed by the VVMF website: that "individual Americans donated the majority of the money needed to build the Memorial."

The impetus to tell an inoffensive collectivist story that separates the warrior from his war is evident from the VVM's inception, given the lore engendered by it. As Harriet Senie comments, though "memorials are at least as much about trying to forget as they are about remembering" (2), they ought to "remember those who died <u>and</u> the circumstances that led to their death" (174). But like the history textbooks studied by Loewen, the impetus not to offend has led to a memorial that, at best, does only the first half of what Harriet Senie says a memorial should do. One of the problems with the VVM is that it focuses intensely on remembering those Americans who served and those who died, but only obliquely if at all addresses the circumstances of their service and deaths.[28] The names inscribed on the Wall and some of the memorial's additions appear to diversify this remembering—of male combat soldiers, of women who served, of those who died after the war era but consequent to it. Other additions—the flagpole, the inscriptions on the Wall, and the hoped-for education center—actively obscure the circumstances Senie prescribes, however. Such cross-purposes characterize the history of the VVM's founding, starting with President Jimmy Carter's July 1, 1980, Rose Garden signing of the bill authorizing the memorial, where he both argues to separate the warrior from the war and also honors the war.[29] Accounts of the process from the Rose Garden to the November 1982 "Salute" (a ceremony short of a formal dedication) make clear that the struggle to commemorate was eminently political.[30] All of the additions to Maya Lin's competition-winning design of the Wall, even those diversifying remembrance, illustrate the impetus not to offend, to avoid political statements which, Patrick Hagopian says, led not to the avoidance of political statements but only to the avoidance of "political reasoning" that left unexamined floating signifiers like "freedom," "honor," and "sacrifice" (*Vietnam* 90). In effect, the absence of "political reasoning" thwarts a serious encounter with Senie's "circumstances" and in the long run sets the stage for initiating war. Thus, not only are memorials always already political, but VVM was revised to be a stage as soon as additions were made to Maya Lin's original design.

Literal Staging: Tropes, Presidential Obligations, and Education

Though alone the black, reflective granite wall with names inscribed might have achieved the VVMF's singular aim to erect an apolitical memorial to the American warriors who died during the American war in Vietnam, the additions demanded by the Wall's various detractors evoke the nationalism that sets the stage for war, turning the memorial from one to commemorate those who died to one commemorating the war in which they perished. Even before the additions, nonetheless, the trope of stage had arisen in the plans for the memorial. For instance, the designer Maya Lin says that her aesthetic is to design staging areas: "I don't make objects; I make places. I think that is very important—the places set a stage for experience and for understanding experience" (Doss 51). More ambivalently, Lin has said memorials were not "stages where you act out, but rather places where something happens within the viewer" (Savage, *Monument* 270). Lin was not alone in envisioning the VVM's use as a stage. Robert Doubek, whose position on the VVMF required him to oversee the memorial's construction, lamented as the Wall was being constructed that it likely would be used as a stage, a use that needed to be regulated discriminatingly: "We didn't want the memorial to be exploited as a backdrop for every cause on earth" (Doubek 229).[31]

Furthermore, many of the article-length critiques of the memorial published within a few years of its celebratory opening, or "Salute," insinuate the VVM may function as a stage. Some of these early analysts remark on the commingling of nontraditional and traditional commemorative aesthetics (Abramson) but typically comment on the memorial's political qualities, especially in relation to its location on what is a highly politicized National Mall that itself "stage[s] power" (Savage, *Monument* 152). The four critics discussed below fall into this category, of seeing the VVM as the medium for a political, national narrative. First, in 1985, Arthur Danto disputed the possibility of a commemorative structure being apolitical and drew a distinction between memorial and monument that often is quoted: "We erect monuments so that we shall always remember, and build memorials so that we shall never forget." The usually unquoted portion of his distinction is equally remarkable: "The memorial is a special precinct, extruded from life, a segregated enclave where we honor the dead. With monuments we honor ourselves" (152).[32] Though Danto thought the circularity of the names inscribed on the Wall suggests not the beginning and end of war that Lin intended but the unendingness of it, he found the memorial extraordinarily moving (154). A second pair of early critics, Charles L. and Stephen S. Griswold, in 1986 suggested that the VVM is best understood in the context of its siting, both on the National Mall and in proximity to other memorials. The Mall, they claimed, "is made to educate and edify the citizens of the present as well as form those of the future by persuading them to live out the virtues of the past" (691). The VVM is a "living monument" to veterans because it offers "an occasion for therapeutic catharsis" (706), it asks viewers "to think about whether the sacrifice was worthwhile and whether it should be made again" (711), and, if it is a stage, it is not "a rallying place for unreflective and unrestrained exhibitions of a country's self-love" (713). A third early critic, Michael Clark (1986) made the case that the media, often blamed for the war's loss, is what unifies and divides Americans, but also is what makes the United States a nation. The memorial is one component of "the media" having "healed over the wounds that had refused to close for ten years with a balm of nostalgia, and transformed guilt and doubt into duty and pride" (49). Presciently, Clark concluded from his survey of novels, TV shows, and movies that the once-psychopathic-but-now-rehabilitated veteran depicted in these texts and by the memorial "embodies an ideal of historical continuity that turns Vietnam into just one more chapter in the epic narrative of the American dream" (77). Hinting at the memorial as stage, Clark concluded that "the memory of Vietnam has ceased to be a point of resistance to imperialist ambition and is now invoked as a vivid warning to do it right the next time" (78). A fourth early critic, Peter Ehrenhaus (1989), disputed the idea that a memorial can be apolitical. Instead, he argued, the VVM's appearance on the National Mall means it is sanctioned by those who both wield power and who gain more power from its sanctioning (97). Though those in power are expected to commemorate war-making, such commemoration calls attention to their own complicity and that of the population. According to Ehrenhaus, then, the VVM effectively diverts attention from these complicities by exonerating all—those in power and the public who sent soldiers to war.

Recent critics more overtly evoke the trope of the stage and staging. In both her 1991 article and 1997 book, Marita Sturken reads the Wall as a "screen," one that operates both as the surface onto which viewers project their personal interpretations and memories, and as a curtain that conceals information about the war, the treatment of veterans since the war, and the possibility of failure in future wars. In an overt evocation of stage language, Sturken contends that the memorial is an "integral component" of a "Vietnam War nostalgia industry . . . [that practices a] very active scripting and rescripting of the war . . . [so as] to rescript current political events and to reinscribe a narrative of American imperialism" ("Wall" 134). This rescripting "catalyzed the writing of a particular narrative of the war" and "allowed the discourse of heroism, sacrifice, and honor to resurface" (136). This whole-cloth new narrative about the Vietnam War, she intimates, makes the United States not only receptive but prone to new wars.

Several other recent critics in book-length analyses note the bifurcated scripts of the VVM and in these scripts recognize how visitors are encouraged to think that by bringing their memories and interpretations to the site, they will determine the meanings of the war. As even the early critics suggest, however, the memorial by definition always is political and didactic, as it tells stories about the war that evoke more emotional than logical responses. One of a memorial's lessons, Erika Doss explains, is that "we learn how to feel, we learn how to be emotional" (59), making clear that visitors to the memorial are taught how and what to feel about the Vietnam War through being taught how and what to feel about its American dead. Historical understanding is not needed to fuel these responses. In this sense, then, the memorial interpellates its visitors, simultaneously evoking and teaching feelings, beckoning with its scripts about how one should respond emotionally to the Vietnam War. Patrick Hagopian explains that while visitors arrive at the memorial with expectations and predispositions, they none- theless are cued to respond with patriotic feeling given the National Mall context in which the VVM is sited. Signifiers "of the nation, the state, the armed services, institutions of govern- ment, and ideologically inflected causes [are] fluttering nearby *and beckoning the audience*," Hagopian details, providing a "cultural script of responses to the memorial" (*Vietnam* 280, 386; emphasis added). Kirk Savage agrees that memorials on the Mall present a complex exchange for predispositions and pre-interpretations but that because "therapeutic" memorials like the VVM especially are didactic, they provide a script for affective responses (*Monument* 267, 283). Meanwhile, in Kenneth Foote's discussion of American memorials as "shrines" that "outline a carefully filtered vision of the national past and present a heroic vision of American history," he insists enshrinement is no "passive projection of sacral myth" but actively "forces people to grapple with the meanings of the past in ways they might otherwise avoid" (292). Though Foote's "forc- ing" is less subtle than Hagopian's "beckoning" and Savage's cathartic "therapy," they all implicate the VVM's didactic inter- pellation to feel—staging—that leads to war.

The most overt and literal way in which the VVM acts as a venue for staging war has to do with who is permitted to speak at the site and who is not, the regulation of which Robert Doubek expressed concern in the memorial's founding days.[33] Harriet Senie cites the memorial as a "national public forum" (30) that provides a voice to the populace, "albeit a silent one" (33), via the objects visitors are permitted to leave at the memorial.[34] With this permission, visitors may think they are able to influence if not determine the memorial's meaning. In most respects, however, formally delivered, verbal free speech is limited at the memorial, with access typically afforded only to those speakers who do not dissent from what now has become the orthodox view about the Vietnam War. If the memorial alone has been unable fully to evoke the patriotic feelings that enable the nation's ability to go to war, the Wall literally has been used as the backdrop to presidents' speechmaking that appreciates veterans and thereby encourages war.[35]

While what has become orthodoxy can be deciphered in the revisionary additions to Maya Lin's wall, its components were explicitly instituted on the stage of the VVM in President Ronald Reagan's 1984 and 1988 Veterans Day speeches, components of which have been echoed by nearly all subsequent U.S. administrations. In these two speeches, Reagan codified the faithful patriotism of American Vietnam War veterans as he set out a number of assertions that persist in the circular logic of the revised/now-orthodox narrative:

1. Good citizens do not question their country's use of military force.
2. Good citizens serve in the military.
3. The service is sacrificial.
4. The sacrifice is noble.
5. The nobility is heroic.
6. The nobility and heroism of troops' sacrifice means their cause is noble.
7. To be good, nonserving citizens must laud the sacrificial and noble heroism of the warriors.
8. Good citizens need not question their country's use of military force because the sacrificing troops are noble and heroic, and the cause of the conflict therefore is just.

In his 1984 speech, Reagan said (with emphasis added to highlight echoes of the assertions above), "Today we pay homage not only to those who *gave their lives* but to their comrades present today and all across the country. You didn't forget. *You kept the faith.* You walked from the litter, wiped away your tears, and returned to the battle. You fought on, sustained by one another and *deaf to the voices of those who didn't comprehend.* You performed with a *steadfastness and valor* that veterans of other wars salute, and you are *forever in the ranks* of that special number of Americans in every generation that the Nation records as *true patriots*" ("Remarks at Dedication"). Reagan's 1988 speech uses similar language, this time emphasizing the love the United States has for its veterans and "*the devotion and gallantry with which all of them ennobled their nation as they became champions of a noble cause.*" He also repeats a refrain common now in the story told about the American war in Vietnam, namely, that its protectors were prevented from winning: "It was, after all, however imperfectly pursued, the *cause of freedom*; and they showed *uncommon courage* in its service. Perhaps at this late date we can all agree that we've learned one lesson: that young Americans must never again be sent to fight and die unless we are prepared to *let them win*" ("Remarks at the Veterans Day").

As Andrew Priest avers, "No commander in chief can escape the Vietnam analogy when he commits troops to an overseas conflict" (539). Despite this inability to escape the contentious legacy of the Vietnam War, most presidents following Reagan—none of whom served on active duty during that conflict—understood the peril of appearing at the VVM, given the ongoing national irresolution about the war. Available reports suggest that though the representatives of most of the commanders in chief may have delivered formal addresses at the memorial, only Presidents Clinton and Obama appeared there themselves. Despite his own complex relationship with the war and "braving jeers of 'coward' and 'draft dodger,'" President Bill Clinton delivered a 1993 Memorial Day speech at the VVM (Marcus). In his brief oration, Clinton recited Reaganesque, newly orthodox tropes of honorable and sacrificial service to the country, heroism as the obvious outcome to what was a fight for freedom, unquestioning gratitude from other citizens, and certainty that the U.S. military lost the Vietnam War because it was not permitted to win:

- "These men and women fought for freedom, brought honor to their communities, loved their country, and died for it."
- "No one has come here today to disagree about the heroism of those whom we honor."
- "If the day should come when our service men and women must again go into combat, let us all resolve they will go with the training, the equipment, the support necessary to win, and most important of all, with a clear mission to win."
- "Let us resolve to take from this haunting and beautiful memorial a renewed sense of our national unity and purpose, a deepened gratitude for the sacrifice of those whose names we touched and whose memories we revere and a finer dedication to making America a better place for their children and for our children, too." (Clinton)

Priest points out that although all presidents since the Vietnam War have had to "appeal to public sentiment about Vietnam to garner support for their own military ventures" (539), no presidents have been more influenced by the Vietnam War in their rhetoric concerning foreign policy than the two following 9/11 and the subsequent wars in Afghanistan and Iraq: George W. Bush and Barack Obama. In his analysis, Priest finds that both Bush and Obama used similar appeals, appeals that echoed those articulated by Reagan decades earlier and indicate a cementing of the new story being told about the war:

Early in their presidencies, both Bush and Obama often attempted to avoid discussing the Vietnam War as much as they could. The implications of their wars becoming associated with such a lengthy, unpopular, and ultimately futile conflict made this a necessity. When this rhetorical strategy did not work because their wars were going badly, which then meant that more reporters asked them to address the parallels with Vietnam, both presidents accepted that there were some comparisons and lessons but argued that Vietnam was essentially like all other American wars in that the troops who had fought there had been noble in their intentions, as had, by implication, those policy makers who had made the military commitment. (556–557)

This new story, one that exonerates combatants and policy-makers both, is evident in President Obama's May 28, 2012, Memorial Day address, when he launched with a "Presidential Proclamation" a thirteen-year commemoration of what would be the fiftieth anniversary (2025) of the American war's ostensible ending (1975) (Obama "Presidential Proclamation").[36] This years-long commemoration would counter the story that the United States had ignobly betrayed South Vietnam by withdrawing its forces and monies early in 1973. The commemoration would instead reinforce and solidify the story—implied by the inaccurate caption to Hubert Van Es's iconic photo discussed at this chapter's outset—that the United States nobly supported and fought with South Vietnam until the very end, when North Vietnam invaded in 1975. The program was authorized by President Bush in 2008 when he signed the U.S. National Defense Authorization Act of 2008, legislation that was cosponsored by then-Senator Chuck Hagel (and Obama administration secretary of defense) and then-Senator James Webb. Both are veterans of the Vietnam War, and Webb especially had been vocal in his disapproval of Maya Lin's design. Webb's concerns led to his leaving the VVMF and airing in the *Wall Street Journal* his objections to the "nihilistic statement that does not render honor to those who served" (quoted in Hagopian *Vietnam* 107). Hagel, a member of the Vietnam Veterans Leadership Program, whose 1980s mission was to counter the poor image of veterans by "disseminating stories about proud and happy Vietnam veterans" publicly voiced a contentious (because it ignores moral implications) opinion about the conduct of the war: "If this war taught us anything, it is that our nation must make a total commitment to victory whenever we commit our fighting men and women" (quoted in Hagopian *Vietnam* 203, 411). Thus, with the 2012–2025 commemoration of a war's ending that was not the American war's ending, Americans were returned to the Reagan-era rhetoric of the Vietnam War as a "noble cause," as though the lessons of the wars in Afghanistan and Iraq never were learned.

It is no small irony, then, that Obama resolutely launched the thirteen years of commemoration in his May 25, 2012, proclamation at the VVM, the site of the nation's irresolution about the war.[37] In his speech, Obama recited what has become the common story: patriotic citizens dutifully and sacrificially heeded the call to service; they served with valor because they "never turned [their] back on America"; as "true heroes" they are "among the greatest generations"; and that, still, lest anyone doubt the force of the new orthodoxy, the thirteen years of events will "set the record straight." The latter appears to be a charge to citizens who did not serve to tell the story—the "straight record" Obama subsequently outlines—of the war and its American warriors: "This [program] is the story of our Vietnam service members—the story that needs to be told. This is what this 50th anniversary is all about. It's another opportunity to say to our Vietnam veterans what we should have been saying from the beginning: You did your job. You served with honor. You made us proud. You came home and you helped build the America that we love and that we cherish."

The revised, now-orthodox story of nobility was not expected to be left to the exclusive domain of presidential orations on the VVM stage, however, but instead was to be cemented by the Vietnam Veterans Memorial Education Center. First proposed in 2000 as a small, temporary 1,200-square-foot "visitors center" costing about $2 million to construct, the structure that finally was approved shortly after 9/11 had ballooned first to a 20,000-square-foot underground structure costing $75 million to $100 million to build and second, by 2017, a 37,000-square-foot "multimedia complex" costing approximately $125 million (Favorite 188).[38] All signs suggested that the underground Education Center was aimed less at "education" and more at resolving the ambivalent, individualist/collectivist story told by the above-ground memorial, aligning the memorial site more unequivocally with the ahistorical story told by presidents since Reagan. Military historian Meredith Lair and art historian Jennifer Favorite vigorously challenged the Center's tactics, claiming its resolution was no more based in the historical record than the VVM itself was. Lair notes in her 2012 critique that the Center's "proponents seek to advance a sanitized, seemingly apolitical narrative of the Vietnam War and an idealized, militarized version of citizenship" (35).[39] This will be accomplished, she remarks, with the preponderance of the space being committed to evoking emotional responses from visitors via the display of left-at-the-Wall artifacts juxtaposed against photos of the people whose names appear on the Wall. Consequently, the Center's "educational priorities lay not with the history of the Vietnam War but in conveying positive messages about wartime military service" (48). Lair concludes that the Center's alleged focus on educating young people sounds more like "indoctrination" (52), as it obscures many of the war era's historical complexities. By 2016, Favorite notes significant changes to the Center's Content Advisory Committee and what might subsequently be a more nuanced use of the historical record than the one Lair perceived.[40] Nonetheless, like Lair, Favorite reads the Center as an underground rejoinder to the ambivalent VVM site above, constituting "a counter-experience to the Vietnam Veterans Memorial, reframing the Vietnam War as a 'noble cause' and recasting those who died as a result of the war as emblems of military might." More problematically, despite the new emphasis on historical verifiability, Favorite comments, the Center's plans treat "personal memory as history," an exchange that will create "redemptive narratives for war as a national undertaking" and "canonize the dead" (187, 191).[41] If all were to have gone according to plan, Kirk Savage summarizes, the Center's effect would be "to turn the war into a war like any other, and the Vietnam Veterans Memorial into a war memorial like any other." He continues: "War memorials everywhere turn soldiers into martyrs sacrificing themselves for the noble cause of the nation. It doesn't matter whether they are fighting for or against slavery, for or against fascism, for or against communism, or for or against poor countries halfway across the globe struggling for their national independence. In the end it's only the willingness to wage war that matters ("Education Center").

In effect, rather than being a departure from the aboveground VVM stage, the planned subterranean Education Center instead was going to be the culmination of the ongoing national debate about the Vietnam War: disputes about the memorial leading to additions to the Wall, the "tiny mistakes" narrated often enough that they have become received knowledge, the mythmaking about the VVM's birthing, and the speeches using the reflective black granite wall as a stage for war. While the VVM only implies its usefulness as a war-staging site, the planned Education Center— the plans for which were discontinued in 2018 because funds could not be raised—made that use explicit as it scripted a story about the Vietnam War that even in 1982 Jan Scruggs objected to vociferously: "They [a small group of far-right critics] wanted to take an undeclared war that had oozed on and off the center stage of American life and transform it into a John Wayne movie. They wanted the Memorial to make Vietnam what it had never been in reality: a good, clean, glorious war seen as necessary and supported by a united country" (Scruggs and Swerdlow 93–94). That movie's story is what the memorial has been in the process of telling since its founding.

3

Lone Wolf Family Man

Stories of Individualism and Collectivism in
American Sniper(s) and Lone Survivor(s)

The part played by the single military male is fundamental to U.S. war narratives of the last half-century, narratives that play a significant role in formulating what it means to be American. Stimulated by American celebrity culture, memoir publishing, and the encouragement in creative writing programs of what Mark McGurl terms "autobardolatry," narratives concerning U.S. wars in Iraq and Afghanistan perpetuate this focus on the individual (*The Program Era*).[1] The single military male's centrality is problematic, however, as it emphasizes only one American core value over another: individualism over collectivism. In a 2015 *Harper's* review of veteran-authored fiction about the most recent wars, Sam Sacks notes the homogeneity of this single perspective among authors and their characters, citing the "confined viewpoints of individual soldiers who can't comprehend what they've experienced" (85). Nonetheless, Sacks observes, readers and publishers engage in the "fetishization of authenticity" and celebrate most "books that conform to our preconceived expectations about suffering and heroism" (87). Sacks concludes that these expectations "create a pitiable image of American soldiers that generates a condescending kind of sympathy but rarely any respect" (87–88). The simultaneous fetishization of and condescension toward the individualist warrior dangerously obscures the second core American value discussed in the previous chapter—collectivism (Marty). The paradox of privileging individualism in what fundamentally is a collectivist endeavor is especially troublesome in a post-9/11 "support the troops" environment that demands unquestioning valorization of American soldiers and veterans (Linehan).[2] Most importantly for this chapter, the privileging reveals the role of gender in how war narratives construct individualism and collectivism in a largely homosocial military culture. American war narratives influence U.S. culture of the post-9/11 era in numerous ways; this chapter focuses on their fabrication of its preferred gender behaviors.[3]

In American culture, individualism is coded largely as masculine and collectivism largely as feminine, with a preference for masculine individualism (Hofstede).[4] War narratives propagate that coding and rely on a pair of reductive equations: male body equals masculine behavior and female body equals feminine behavior.[5] For instance, in American Westerns (essentially war stories about manifest destiny) the male and thereby masculine individualist cowboy riding alone across the plain is prized over the female and thereby feminine collectivist pioneer developing a frontier community. Or, in a conventional American war story, (ostensibly masculine) males leave to fight heroically at the combat front, while (ostensibly feminine) females remain pitiably at the home front. The primary value heralded in American war narratives, then, is masculine individualism. This reductive view, however, cannot account for the multiple ways by whom and in which genders are performed. Female bodies frequently perform masculine behaviors, and male bodies frequently perform feminine behaviors (Halberstam), and, as Judith Butler argues in *Gender Trouble*, gender performativity is a complex undertaking, not a condition into which one is born. Thus, what is termed "manhood" is not synonymous with masculinity but is a particular form that masculine gender performance may take.[6] The purpose of this chapter is to scrutinize several recent stories—two memoirs and their film renditions—about the U.S. wars in Iraq and Afghanistan to explore how they construct masculinities as they negotiate the tensions between the American core values of individualism and collectivism.

A single person has not always been central to U.S. war narratives. According to Jeanine Basinger, this centrality differs from the melting pot storyline typifying American World War II–era combat films. Using *Bataan* (1943) as her template, Basinger describes the collective:

> Thirteen men are trapped in a situation. They come from different parts of the United States, and from different branches of the service. They are different in age, background, experience, attitude, and willingness to fight. . . . In establishing such a collection of misfits . . . the film confirms and makes specific the foundation of the combat patrols to follow. These men obviously represent the American melting pot, but the representation is not a simple-minded one. Our strength is our weakness and vice versa. We are a mongrel nation—ragtail, unprepared, disorganized, quarrelsome among ourselves, and with separate special interests, raised, as we are, to believe in the individual, not the group. At the same time, we bring different skills and abilities together for the common good, and from these separate needs and backgrounds we bring a feisty determination. No one leads us who is not strong, and our individualism is not set aside for any small cause. *Once it is set aside, however, our group power is extreme.* (31; emphasis added)

The melting pot storyline's emphasis on collective action and power shifted with filmic and prose narratives of the Vietnam War, however. Tony Williams makes this case about 1980s Vietnam War movies, asserting, "Many films tend conveniently to focus on a predominantly individualized personal tragedy or adolescent bildungsroman," thus direly "ignoring any accurate depictions of the broad social and historical picture" (114–139). Similarly, Susan White contends that *Full Metal Jacket* features the "timeworn combat-film formula—the adaptation of the individual to the demands of a ritualistic male group" and his subsequent failures to adapt (205). In his comparison of two films depicting World War II but produced during and after the Vietnam War—*Patton* (1970) and *Saving Private Ryan* (1998)—Andrew Fiala argues that American war narratives focus on individuals because war itself must not: "In ethics and in the narrative of war films, the individual matters. But war runs counter to individualism: it is a collective effort involving armies aimed toward defending public goods. In war, private individuals are viewed as mere parts of the larger whole" (338). Fiala notes how a narrative focus on the collective raises suspicions that the narrative is propagandistic, and the "reality" of war is reflected best by the supposedly earnest and nonideological viewpoints of individual participants. However, Fiala reminds his readers, "the 'reality' that is portrayed in such films is . . . a reality shaped by the needs and interests of the military" (340). We spectators may ask, then, what needs and interests are served in focusing on an individual serviceperson, especially during unpopular wars? How do mainstream American war texts negotiate the tensions between the core values of individualism and collectivism?

Four narratives concerning recent U.S. wars in Iraq and Afghanistan exemplify this tension between gendered conceptions of individualism and collectivism: the memoirs and films *American Sniper* (Kyle, McEwen, and DeFelice 2012; Eastwood 2014) and *Lone Survivor* (Luttrell and Robinson 2007; Berg 2013).[7] The parallels drawn in the two memoirs—between individualism, collectivism, and, thereby, Americanness—center on their conceptions of male masculinities, or manhood. The film versions also indicate this tension but in ways notably different from the memoirs. The memoir genre dictates its subjects be singular: they are written by the authors about themselves, registering their intentions directly. Meanwhile, the films distance themselves from the memoirists' authorial intent, sometimes heightening and sometimes downplaying events featured in the memoirs but usually serving the needs of a post-9/11, "support the troops" spectating public whose "preconceived expectations about suffering and heroism" include men who self-sacrifice for the group, but not so selflessly that they are perceived as unmanly (Sacks 87). Furthermore, the memoirs do not provide the story arc expected of a conventional combat film and so are altered to suit filmic storytelling (Basinger 46–52). Thus, while the U.S. military's "needs and interests" for support of the unpopular wars in Iraq and Afghanistan may be implicit in the memoirs, they are patent in the film versions of *American Sniper* and *Lone Survivor*. The films do this by negotiating the tensions between collectivism and individualism, thereby creating a composite military masculinity, what this chapter terms the "lone wolf family man."[8]

Echoing the nation-founding myth that Tom Engelhardt's *The End of Victory Culture* outlines, the "lone wolf family man" is an individual man who is victimized and oppressed by unmitigated evil, whose cause is thus moral and correct, and who has no option but to oppose such evil. He is a reluctant warrior, but his abhorrence of evil, evil which he naturally is able to identify, compels him to defend his family, however family is defined. Consequently, he is simultaneously individualist freedom fighter, or "lone wolf," and collectivist trooper, or "family man." This mythical man denotes the nation in its relationship to individualism and collectivism, as war narratives make sense of war and its place in the national ethos for the nation's constituents. Thus, just as the beleaguered "lone wolf family man" depicts the preferred position for U.S. combatants in recent American war narratives, he also influences American narratives of war, dangerously justifying U.S. wars as loathsome but necessary interventions by good against evil.

The Memoirs

Chris Kyle's *American Sniper* (2012) memoir covers the years before his enlisting to his leaving active duty (1997–2009). He says he grew up in Texas "with a strong sense of justice," tried life as a rodeo cowboy, then as a college student and a ranch hand, and finally left college to join the U.S. armed forces (8). Though initially the Navy medically disqualified him for pins in his arms due to rodeo injuries, Kyle joined the SEALs in 1997 at the age of twenty-four (9–30). To his great disappointment, he was not deployed to Afghanistan following 9/11: "That's about the worst fate a SEAL can imagine" (57). All four of his deployments after 9/11 were to Iraq: during the invasion of Iraq in March 2003, in September 2004 to Fallujah, in April 2006 to Ramadi, and in April 2008 to Sadr City. Angry as he was about the cautious "head shed . . . pussies" who prevented his "get[ting] out there and kill[ing]" during his first stint in Iraq, Kyle considered leaving the SEALs (103, 94, 104). But one incident, which serves as the prologue to his memoir—when, during his first deployment, he shot and killed an Iraqi woman armed with a grenade—satisfied his individualistic drives, leading him to sniper school, 160 officially confirmed killings, and the memoir's subtitle, "most lethal sniper in U.S. military history" (3–4). Kyle recounts many of his kills throughout the memoir, crowing, "I love killing bad guys," and reiterating that it was his serendipitous location on city rooftops that facilitated his record-setting, his being nicknamed "the Legend" or, alternatively, "the Devil of Ramadi" (251, 205). Moreover, Kyle implies he was fated to be in the right place at the right time to kill the right person. "Everyone I shot was evil," he vows at the conclusion of his memoir. "I had good cause on every shot. They all deserved to die" (430). In the memoir's rendition, Kyle is the quintessential individualist "lone wolf."

Marcus Luttrell's *Lone Survivor* (2007) memoir intersects with Kyle's because both were SEALs during the Global War on Terror; Luttrell's first deployment also was to Iraq in the spring of 2003, and both proudly hailed from Texas. Unlike Kyle's haphazard route to SEALdom and notoriety as a sniper, though, Luttrell says he and his twin brother were raised to be SEALs, told by their father that SEALs "were all that is best in the American male— courage, patriotism, strength, determination, refusal to accept defeat, brains, expertise in all that they did" (59). Living on a ranch, Luttrell's father taught his twin sons "how to survive": shooting rifles, building shelters, fishing and hunting and growing food (56–57). SEAL-specific training began in their teens, and, after acquiring a bachelor's degree in international business in 1998, in

1999 Luttrell enlisted in the Navy to become a SEAL. Luttrell's first deployment was to Iraq in April 2003, where he stayed for several months, mostly working in small, four-person SEAL teams. Unlike the lone sniper Kyle, who felt constrained by collective efforts led by inept "head sheds," Luttrell saw his primary obligation as being to the team: "In the SEALs, it's *always* your teammates" (29). Most of Luttrell's memoir concerns the June 2005 reconnaissance mission in Afghanistan when, of his four-person team, only he survived. An American rescue crew, sent to extract the team under siege by Taliban forces, failed when its helicopter was downed by those forces (285). Though Luttrell insinuates the prayer vigils held by his family and friends in Texas are what saved him, he also says he survived because Afghan villagers, whose cultural practices included protecting people in trouble, at great personal risk and for many days offered him a safe haven against the Taliban and identified him to U.S. forces who eventually recovered him. In either case, unlike Kyle, Luttrell's allegiance is to the collective, whether a group of praying Americans or protecting Afghans. Accordingly, in the memoir Luttrell is the consummate collectivist "family man."

Despite their different allegiances, both authors claim to have the final word on what is proper warring behavior, aligning their authority as service members with their masculine behaviors.[9] Both Kyle and Luttrell insist their authority on war derives from their authentic experiences as Navy SEALs and thereby implicitly discount authority derived otherwise. "Until you actually experience something," lone wolf individualist Kyle asserts, "you just don't know," and "warriors need to be let loose to fight war without their hands tied behind their backs" (31, 342). Meanwhile, family man collectivist Luttrell says, "Only men who have gone through what we [SEALs] went through can understand the difference between us and the rest" and resents "ever-intrusive rules of engagement . . . that represent a danger to us [combatants]" (86, 41–42). Each memoirist blames and resents the "liberal media" for this intrusion, both from reporters embedded in U.S. military units and those on the home front. Equally importantly, both claim authority based on their Texan manhood: sometimes a collectivist value and sometimes an individualist one, but always by definition embodied by males. After experiencing failure, "real men," asserts Luttrell, "get back out there, take risks, and when they hit it big, they just want to hit it bigger" (55). Luttrell says this in view of his parents' loss of their horse farm in 1986, but he also cites as real men the Count of Monte Cristo and another Texan, President George W. Bush, a "tough man in the White House" and "a real dude" (83, 24, 431). About Lieutenant Commander Kristensen, one of the men killed in the downed helicopter, Luttrell cites manhood as his motivation to rescue: "But more than that, he was a SEAL, a part of the brotherhood forged in blood. Even more important, he was a man" (284). Kyle's initial and only direct invocation of manhood is equally explicit: "In the end, my story, in Iraq and afterward, is about more than just killing people or even fighting for my country. It's about being a man" (Kyle 7). Thus, while both employ similar bases for their authority, their conceptions of male masculinity differ. While Luttrell peppers his narrative with definitions and models of manhood, Kyle's invocations subsequent to this early one in the memoir are more misogynistic than androcentric. Male combatants—Iraqi and American—of whom he disapproves are "pussies," "cowards," and "fanatics." "I would rather get my ass beat," Kyle claims, "than look like a pussy in front of my boys" (356). Collectivist Luttrell defines manhood with exemplars; individualist Kyle defines manhood by what it is not.

These starkly different references to manhood suggest that though the two memoirists are both male and Navy SEALs, their stories highlight variations not only in masculinities but also in what it means to be American: individualist or collectivist. Collectivist survivor Luttrell refers directly and obliquely to being a man, claims that what enabled his survival are his membership in collectives additional to his SEAL team—Christianity, family, Texans, twinship, Afghan culture—and also occupies the gendered position of survivor, of endurer, of passively being the rescued instead of actively being the rescuer.[10] Luttrell's most remarkable refrain is that during the many tumbles down the mountainside and then with his Afghan protectors, it was not his military training but God who always ensured his rifle would stay with him. After his first tumble when his rifle ends up beside him, he ruminates, "I'll always know it was guided by the hand of God" (Luttrell 217). After the third tumble, Luttrell supposes it could not be otherwise: "If He had been indifferent to my plight, He surely would not have taken such good care of my gun, right? Because how on earth that was still with me, I will never know" (261). To maintain the pretense with the Taliban fighters that Luttrell is an unarmed doctor, his Afghan protectors take his weapon away (334). They return it to him later, providentially: "This was the weapon God granted me. And, so far as I could tell, still wanted me to have" (369). Thus, Luttrell relied on a force other than himself to ensure his weapon—his masculine tool—was available to him. The collectivist, passive activities—as a survivor—for which he is remembered, then, could be seen to cast him as not-individualist, as not-masculine, as not-American, and as not-lone-wolf.

On the other hand, individualist sniper Kyle, a lone agent by occupation and described in the memoir's title as "American," rarely refers to being a man, implying that nothing more needs to be said about his masculinity: that Kyle is a male, a SEAL, and a sniper according to his memoir's logic sum up to his being masculine. The individualist activities for which he is lauded are thereby equated to what it means to be American. Kyle is American because he is a lone sniper, and he is a sniper because he is an individualist American. As the ultimate individualist, Kyle typically rejects collective action. He puts his desire to go to war, to "kill massive amounts of bad guys," before his obligations to his wife and children (Kyle 150). In fact, any "family" are his military mates, though he does not hesitate to disparage them when they display fear or to leave them when he is bored (207, 199, 182). Kyle is an individualist maverick: he resists being controlled, he chooses not to snipe someone only because it may land him in prison (177, 337), he sports a crusader cross tattoo, and he resents having to attend to his daughter's dire illness in lieu of being at war with "my guys" (250, 345).

Thus, the two memoirs center on notions of manhood but diverge in regard to masculinity's relationship to individualism and collectivism. R. W. Connell and J. Messerschmidt's schema of masculinities, deployed in chapter 1 to compare the French and Americans, is again useful, in this case to conceptualizing the differences between these two memoirists, both males and both SEALs yet whose performances of masculinity differ utterly. Connell and Messerschmidt's theory posits there is not a single form of masculinity identifiable across cultures and time (nor are the performances of masculinities limited to male bodies). Moreover, just as there is not a single form across cultures, there is not a single form within cultures, in this case, U.S. military culture. What does transcend time and culture, according to Connell and Messerschmidt, is a hierarchy of different modes of masculine behavior: hegemonic, subordinated, marginalized, and complicit forms (Connell and Messerschmidt). Understanding their distinctions within "masculinity" facilitates recognizing distinctions within military culture. As a reminder of the discussion in chapter 1, the hegemonic form is the dominant mode in any given culture. Second in dominance is the subordinated mode; it mimics and approximates the hegemonic form but is actively subordinated by the hegemon. The marginalized mode follows in the hierarchy of masculine forms, does not approximate the hegemonic form, and is actively marginalized by the hegemonic and subordinated forms. The fourth form is the complicit mode: "Men [or people generally] who received the benefits of patriarchy without enacting a strong version of masculine dominance could be regarded as showing a complicit masculinity" (832).

Connell and Messerschmidt's formulation is useful for comparing the two memoirs, even though both are by men serving in the same SEAL culture and in the same war era. Kyle as individualist sniper performs (and defines) the hegemonic form of masculinities in U.S. popular stories about the military, which is active and individualistic, or "lone wolf." Luttrell as collectivist survivor approximates and mimics the hegemonic form but is subordinated (or perhaps even marginalized) as passive and collectivist, or "family man." The hegemonic form as constructed by Kyle in his memoir actively subordinates "pussies," "cowards," "head sheds," and "liberal media"—that is, anyone who claims the perquisites of hegemonic masculinity without being a SEAL—but it also challenges/subordinates the passive survivor position Luttrell occupies. Furthermore, Kyle's hegemonic form marginalizes—as does the Luttrell memoir—male insurgents from Iraq or Afghanistan with a litany of simultaneously derisive and apprehensive descriptors: "fanatics," "savages," "whackadoos," "monsters," "maniacs," "wild men," "lawless," "hysterics," "thugs," "cutthroats," "barbaric." Those who could be regarded as complicit with this U.S. military hegemonic form include the Texans at home supporting Luttrell through prayer and Kyle's wife, whose voice periodically punctuates Kyle's memoir. She says that she loved her husband's willingness to sacrifice his life for his country, that he has her "unconditional support" for whatever he does in war, that she resents his leaving the family for war but wants to see it as out of his control, and that she finally concedes she was not "the most important thing in his life" (Kyle 49, 178, 348, 356). She does not, however, voice any objections to what might be called the Odyssean Siren system that simultaneously calls Kyle to war and reinforces the hierarchy of masculinities that dismisses her as an agent in her own life.

The Films

Comparing the film versions of these two memoirs, *American Sniper* (2014) and *Lone Survivor* (2013), spotlights how the relation between masculinities as individualist or collectivist constructs what it means to be American. This comparison is not to assert that the first stories—the memoirs—are true and that the films are deviations. Instead, the comparison illuminates differences in the stories told and so enables hypotheses about which are the preferred war stories constituting U.S. culture. As this chapter has just demonstrated, although both memoirs necessarily feature a single protagonist, neither characterization adheres strictly to the conventional individualist-and-collectivist war hero narrative

Jeanine Basinger outlines. Kyle's is a chronological sequence of vignettes about his lone wolf sniping (and visits stateside), connected only by their occurring in the course of his four tours of duty in Iraq; family man Luttrell's is mostly about the many days he spent protected by the Afghan villagers. Although the memoirs are the foundations for their film versions, each film tells a story more closely approximating Basinger's conventional World War II warrior narrative. In constructing the individualist/collectivist "lone wolf family man," these recently released films implicate Fiala's "needs and interests," not only of the all-volunteer U.S. military that is challenged to fill its ranks but also of a public that has been taught to expect of its warriors certain behaviors and attitudes.

The film titles retain the sniper/survivor binary, and their wildly different box office numbers suggest—after Chris Kyle's 2013 murder—a popular preference for the individualist sniper/martyr over the collectivist teammate/survivor. According to Box Office MoJo, *American Sniper* earned about $550 million and *Lone Survivor,* $155 million. Despite this box office difference, both films reshape the memoirs and moderate the binary opposition between the individualist sniper and collectivist survivor so that a military hegemonic masculinity is developed that includes both protagonists. *American Sniper* minimizes memoir-Kyle's individualistic roguishness and casts him as someone more religious, protective of family, and psychically wounded than a man who loves killing for its own sake. The film still includes Kyle's man-versus-man motivations, but it also depicts him as working in groups more than as a lone sniper killing people from rooftops. It also mitigates his singular role as a bloodthirsty sniper by fabricating his childhood family and spotlighting his adulthood family.[11] Conversely, *Lone Survivor* minimizes if not erases memoir-Luttrell's collectivist religiosity, his obligations to family, and his helplessness, and fabricates his actively resisting the Taliban in the village and his rescue by the Americans. According to the film, the only collective Luttrell belongs to is his family of SEAL brothers. This moderation of the gendered, individualist/collectivist differences between the two men produces the composite "lone wolf family man."

American Sniper is organized as the memoir is, chronologically, and follows Chris Kyle's four tours of duty in Iraq. Many of the scenes from the memoir are replicated in the film: SEAL training is hard, he meets his future wife in a bar and she initially dislikes him, once in Iraq he speaks with her on a satellite phone while on a rooftop and she overhears a battle, he elects to leave a rooftop to join Marines on the street, his marriage suffers from his devotion to war, and he laments not preventing more of his countrymen from being killed in Iraq. The film opens with the same scene that opens the memoir: in overwatch, Kyle spots an Iraqi woman approach a U.S. Marine convoy with a grenade concealed beneath her robes. In the memoir, Kyle kills the lone woman and comments it was his first killing and the only time he killed anyone not a "male combatant" (4). In the film, however, the woman gives the grenade to a boy who accompanies her, and it is he who runs with it toward the convoy. The film's apparent need to establish Kyle's ambivalent relationship with males (because of his father's lesson to him in childhood about helpless sheep, predatory wolves, and protective sheepdogs; see Grossman and Christenson 176–186) has him kill the boy and the woman both. His ambivalence extends throughout the film, from his retributive decision to enlist in response to late-1990s bombings of U.S. embassies abroad, through his and others' insistence that SEALmates are "brothers," to Kyle's competition with his two male nemeses, the Butcher and Mustafa, the Syrian sniper.

Two elements in the film combine to frame Kyle as the "lone wolf family man" and thereby reconstruct military hegemonic masculinity into a version that is more palatable to an American viewing public and includes both Kyle and Luttrell: one, Kyle's commitment to collective efforts, and two, his conquering the two nemeses as outcomes of collective action. Although Kyle is cast as a team player while pursuing these two "bad guys," it is his personal combat with them that serves as the film's foundation. In comparison, the memoir is an oddly impersonal and static account of Kyle's desire to kill, his enjoyment of killing, the various ways in which he killed, and the trouble his killing profession presented to his marriage and family life. The film version provides what the sniper's memoir does not: (masculine) action and humanizing faces for the inhuman enemies memoirist Kyle says deserved to be killed.[12] Moreover, because the film was produced shortly after Kyle's 2013 murder and presumably as an homage to his lethal service, it validates and lionizes his motivations for being in Iraq— and thus, in accord with Fiala's "needs and interests," validates and lionizes the United States' armed forces warring in Iraq.[13]

The first scenario of collective action has film-Kyle leading a team to dispatch the earliest of his nemeses, the Butcher, an Al Qaeda leader known for his butchering of Iraqis who do not comply with Al Qaeda's expectations. The collectivity of this mission implies that Kyle is not acting vigilante-style on his own judgment but is joined by other men equally compelled by the pursuit of justice against evil. While leading the team, Kyle talks with an Iraqi family who dread the Butcher, his having previously cut off a daughter's forearm. As retribution for the family's talking to Kyle, the Butcher kills the family's young son with a drill to his head and the father with a gunshot in the chest. Evidently, the film insinuates, the Butcher is the individualist predatory wolf Kyle's father had warned him about, and Kyle and his justice-seeking mates are the collectivist sheepdogs dutifully protecting the flock.

In a continuation of this scenario but in his second tour, film-Kyle resumes the collective effort to hunt down the Butcher. Mirroring the overwatch position of Kyle as sniper, his team settles into an apartment across the street from the Butcher's operations. Although the Iraqi family whose apartment they occupy are terrified by these hulking, armed American men, the man of the house invites the Americans to a shared meal, during which Kyle spots on the man the telltale reddened elbow of a sniper. Kyle surreptitiously reconnoiters the apartment and discovers a cache of weapons, which leads Kyle to demand the man help the Americans attack the Butcher's locale. They storm the site as the inhabitants flee. Should the film's spectators harbor doubt about the Butcher's monstrosity after his execution of the young boy and the older man, in this second episode of Kyle's collective action audience members are shown the Butcher's gory slaughterhouse where a whole human body hangs, waiting to be eviscerated, and already-dismembered body parts litter the shelves. Clearly, the Butcher as an archetype of the "savages" memoirist Kyle rails against is unequivocally evil and deserves to die. Kyle's causing the Butcher's fiery death in an exploding getaway vehicle is thereby justified, as one more monster is rightly dispatched.[14]

Film-Kyle's other nemesis, Mustafa, is also the bad to Kyle's good, Kyle's reverse image as a sniper. Not only are they physical opposites—with Mustafa slim and dark-skinned, and Kyle burly and fair-skinned—but their binary opposition is depicted by a pair of juxtaposed scenarios in the film. In the first, Kyle is at the brightly lit hospital where his baby has just been born. That is followed by a scene in their home where he and his wife are arguing about his returning to Iraq for a third tour. He protests that "[my comrades] can't wait [for me to return as their protector] and we [the family] can." This stateside conflict about which collective needs Kyle more is followed immediately by a parallel scenario in Iraq. Kyle drives down an Iraqi city street and is observed by Iraqis, who telephone Mustafa. He answers the call from a darkly lit room, where he sits with someone who appears to be his female partner, cradling a baby. He runs from the room immediately without saying a word to the woman; behind her, hanging on the wall, is a photograph taken at an Olympics ceremony, with a man who is presumably Mustafa on the gold-medal step. The juxtaposition of these two family scenarios indicates that Kyle has more to negotiate in a democratic, family-valuing nation than Mustafa does in his. These scenarios also compare the two men's motivations to war: Mustafa is motivated by steely/evil/unquestioning professionalism, whereas Kyle's motivations are reluctant/good/negotiated citizenship.

American Sniper the film builds on Kyle's and Mustafa's motivational differences. Kyle is adored as "the Legend" among U.S.

forces, something the memoir also notes, but he is notorious among Iraqis, who have offered a reward for his death. Mustafa, said to be from Syria and said to be an Olympic gold-medal winner, is represented as preying specifically on Kyle. Though Kyle opportunely targets Mustafa, he is not represented as the predator Mustafa is. This case again recalls the lesson taught by Kyle's father when Kyle was a young boy: preying (as the wolf) is evil and savage; protecting (as the sheepdog) is good and right. But this wolf/ sheepdog condition also problematizes the easy equation of action equals masculine on which U.S. military masculinities rely. As a suitable hero for American viewing audiences, film-Kyle occupies an uneasy position between collective, defensive sheepdog and individualistic, offensive wolf. Thus, once Kyle's teammate is killed by Mustafa, Kyle's desire to kill Mustafa can be perceived as righteous vengeance, not a blind will to kill. When film-Kyle the sniper finally kills Mustafa the sniper, it is, of course, not viciously point blank but from a righteously stupendous distance, Mustafa's death already having been justified by his murder of a member of Kyle's "family." Kyle's killing of Mustafa is represented as defensive retribution for an offense committed against the collective by an already-evil dark man, not an indiscriminately offensive act in and of itself. In the film's rendition of Chris Kyle, then, spectators find a composite of the individualist and the collectivist military masculine hero who enacts both American core values: the "lone wolf family man."

A similar composite of American individualism and collectivism can be seen in the film rendition of *Lone Survivor*. Even more than the *American Sniper* film, *Lone Survivor* stresses the collectivist band-of-brothers theme, especially in its opening montage of what appears to be actual footage from SEAL training. Though Luttrell's memoir also details the challenges of SEAL training, the memoir's primary frame—and the explanation for Luttrell's survival—is his belonging to several collectives, not least of which are the Afghan villagers, his family, his religion, and his Texan communities. However, as a film extolling the virtues of military masculinity, the band-of-brothers theme, explicitly stated at the film's opening, emphasizes only one collective that supports Luttrell's survival, the SEALs, and underscores Luttrell's individualistic agency in his recovery. Whereas the *American Sniper* film constructs a collectivist home-front storyline that minimizes memoir-Kyle's individualistic roguishness to formulate the "lone wolf family man," to formulate the same for *Lone Survivor* means conversely maximizing Luttrell's individualism by not providing any collectivist family context but that offered by his SEAL teammates. Film-Luttrell has neither obligations nor allegiances to anyone but his military "brothers." While his three teammates who perish in the mission—Murphy, Axe, and Danny—early in the film are humanized by images of their children, stories of their loves, and their playful and competitive edges, the film spectator is told nothing about Luttrell's background. Without this background, the film constructs Luttrell's survival as an act of personal will and strength, as agency, as individualism, not as the object of others' wills and strength. The film makes this happen in three ways.

The first way film-Luttrell's lone individualist agency is constructed is when the team has to decide how to treat the Afghan goat herders who discover the SEALs as they reconnoiter the mountain village. In both the memoir and film renditions of the story, though Murphy is the ranking member of the team, Luttrell's opinion dominates the team's decision to release the goat herders. In the memoir, he says it was his religious affiliation—his "Christian soul"—that led him to advise Murphy, "We gotta let 'em go" (236). After the deaths of his teammates, Luttrell reflects in the memoir that with that advice, "I'd turned into a fucking liberal, a half-assed, no-logic nitwit, all heart, no brains, and the judgment of a jackrabbit." He laments his influence on Murphy's decision: "I'll never get over it. I cannot get over it" (236). None of this moral concern or lamentation is evident in the film. Instead, Luttrell's voiceover at the film's opening invokes the internal strength of a single person, not the collaborative strength of a team or other collective: "You can push yourself farther than you thought possible."

This stress on film-Luttrell's individualism does not demand a parallel reduction of his teammates' efforts to resist the Taliban forces. But it does require a shift in focus, to the film's constructing survival as a hegemonically masculine position—that is, as heroic—not one that is subordinated or marginalized. One of the three goat herders released by the SEAL team, a young man who detests the SEALs, bounds down the mountain to alert nearby Taliban forces. Unlike the memoir, which spends twice as many pages on Luttrell's time with the Afghan villagers than on the mountainside battle, most of the film's latter half is spent on the team's chaotic battle with these forces. The second way the film makes Luttrell the individualistic and hegemonically masculine master of his fate is by focusing on him during the battle and by depicting the battle and his teammates from Luttrell's perspective. The camera treats Luttrell in close-up, a treatment that can make the other three SEALs seem almost interchangeable and Luttrell appear distinctly heroic. The storyline helps audience members forget that Luttrell is the team's medic, so his concern for the others' wounds seems like brotherly kindness and generosity, not his official role on the team. Furthermore, Luttrell's weapon stays with him throughout the battle and through many spectacularly violent falls down the mountainside. Because, unlike in Luttrell's memoir, no spiritual figure is cited as ensuring the weapon was always at hand, the film implies it was Luttrell's individual skill that ensured he retained his rifle.

The third way the film *Lone Survivor* frames Marcus Luttrell as a hegemonically masculine subject and not as a subordinated or marginalized object is how it treats his stay with the Afghan villagers. According to the memoir, Luttrell spends six days in the mountains, nearly five of those in sanctuary with the villagers. In those five days, the Taliban constantly threaten to attack and to seize Luttrell, but the Taliban's need to retain the respect and support of the villagers inhibits them for most of the time. Memoir-Luttrell is also terribly wounded from the battle and from his falls down the mountain, injuries compounded by his contracting a parasite from drinking contaminated water. He is a large man, and by the end of his six-day ordeal, according to the memoir, he has lost thirty-seven pounds (410). While in the village, then, memoir-Luttrell is weak, in pain, and immobile. Consequently, it is unlikely Luttrell would have survived without the protection and care of the Afghan villagers whose cultural values impelled their hospitality. However, just as the film attributes Luttrell's surviving the mountainside battle to his individual mastery, it also ascribes to his individual action his survival in the village and his recovery by the Americans. It is film-Luttrell who removes huge chunks of shrapnel from his own legs, whereas in the memoir it is an Afghan doctor who cares for his single bullet wound from the battle (333). It is film-Luttrell who fights off the brief beating by Taliban men, not a village elder who intercedes on behalf of memoir-Luttrell when on the first night the Taliban beat and interrogate him for six hours (336–341). With memoir-Luttrell spending several days in the village, and not what appears to be fewer than the twenty-four hours of the film, memoir-Luttrell depends entirely on the village men to conceal him from the Taliban, to protect him against the Taliban, and to make plans to carry him to the Americans who are two miles away. Thus, to have film-Luttrell enact American military masculinity currently sanctioned as hegemonic, his dependence on the Afghan villagers for survival is minimized and attenuated, and he fights his own way from the Afghans to the Americans. The film constructs this story of the "lone wolf family man" by prolonging the mountainside battle scene, abbreviating Luttrell's stay in the village, and making him physically capable of mending and defending himself.

The Lone Wolf Family Man

Plainly, the stories told by the Kyle and Luttrell memoirs and those of their film renditions differ dramatically. Why do these differences matter? Is it not enough to say these two media have different conventions and modes of storytelling, so readers and viewers should not expect the same stories to be told? This would be the case were the two media not integrally connected and equally reliant on what Sam Sacks names the "fetishization of authenticity" (87). That is, both memoirs rely on an American public's willingness to accept as truth the word of veterans, especially covert warrior forces such as SEALs. The films, too, rely on this same truth value, both insisting their basis is in the "true story." The fetishization is enough of a problem to note these differences and to provoke questions about how and why the stories might differ, aside from variance in genre. In an article entitled "Dispelling Myths about Special Operations Forces," former Special Operations Forces (SOF) officer Craig Michel says this about stories of SOF, a term that includes SEALs:

> The American public is usually exposed to [myths] through the media or Hollywood, and as a result, stories about SOF tend to focus on great successes, failures, or controversy. . . . Whether the tales are told by the community's heroes or by its disaffected, they are almost universally accepted as equal and expert testimony. But this does not make them equal in reality. As with any organization that shuns outsiders, SOF keep the most important details close to the vest and rarely see an upside to pushing back when their story is poorly told. Not surprisingly, misperceptions are common and often left to fester.

Given this myth propagation, one might ask why these stories— both in the memoirs and the films—are being published and produced now, and what is their resonance for American audiences? Which of the U.S. military's "needs and interests," according to Andrew Fiala, might be addressed by these popular diegeses? What activities and attitudes are normalized by these blockbuster films and popular memoirs? In *The Right Way to Lose a War*, political scientist Dominic Tierney comments that story is how we make sense of the complexities of war that are otherwise too difficult to comprehend. "A tale of conflict creates order out of an overwhelming mass of information," Tierney says. "The narrative is more than just a chronology of events. It provides a coherent representation of events that explains why we started the mission, what we achieved, the challenges we overcame, the mistakes we made, how we withdrew, the consequences that followed, and the lessons we should learn." This story, Tierney continues, is "never self-evident," nor is it static; it is "constantly being revised and reinterpreted based on battlefield events, media coverage, and political spin" (140). Moreover, Tierney cautions, "creating the illusion of success in wartime is dangerous if it prevents us from learning important lessons" (141). Although Tierney is discussing the narrative a nation's leader must construct for his constituents, he concludes that "war is fundamentally a contest to control the narrative" (143).

Tierney's comments suggest that war stories—issued by a commander in chief, a warrior, or a film director—are impactful as they vie to control popular conceptions of war. Those conceptions, this chapter's comparison asserts, are comprised not only by combat but also by national values such as individualism and collectivism. Furthermore, this chapter's comparison also reveals the criticality of gender roles in war-time narratives and how these roles can be manipulated and re-signified to tell stories about the nation. As U.S. military members enact the core American values of individualism and collectivism, they reveal not the stability but the mutability of masculinities, a mutability evident in the differences between the memoirs and the films. Because of their differing attitudes about individualism and collectivism, the Chris Kyle and Marcus Luttrell memoirs do not conform to Basinger's conventional war stories; however, their film versions more closely approximate the convention with the "lone wolf family man" trope, even when the wars being fought are unpopular.[15] Kyle's memoir reveals an individualistic man who loves killing, loves doing it alone, and neglects his family to pursue it. The film version, potentially addressing the expectations of a viewing public for heroic military masculinity, reconciles the killing and family life so that Kyle is more a collectivist man motivated to protect his family from evildoers, not to indulge bloodlust. Luttrell's memoir reveals a collectivist man who loves his teammates and consistently asserts that he does what he does as a SEAL for multiple groups: his religion, his family, and his country. The film version, again possibly addressing the expectations of a viewing public for heroic military masculinity, instead casts Luttrell as an individualistic man whose prime motivation is to be a self-sufficient warrior independent of any collective but the warrior "brothers" with whom he serves.

In its reconciliation of American individualism and collectivism, the filmic "lone wolf family man" not only might satisfy the needs of a U.S. military reliant on volunteers, who are recruited by advertisements simultaneously selling the U.S. Navy as a collectivistic "Global Force for Good" and the U.S. Air Force as individualistic with the exhortation to "Aim High," but it also offers assurances to a populace that sends its armed forces to war. In a nation that since the 2001 invasion of Afghanistan and the 2003 invasion of Iraq has been exhorted to "support the troops," these troops, the "lone wolf family men" who enact for spectators both the individualist heroics and the collectivist benevolence expected of hegemonically masculine U.S. warriors, are the ones Americans want to support.

4

Military Judgment in a Neoliberal Age

Stories of Egalitarianism and the All-Volunteer Force

The end of conscription did not change the army's purpose: the fundamental mission of the U.S. Army is to fight and to win the nation's wars. Combat, of course, is the means to this end. But the all-volunteer army had, quite purposefully and more powerfully over time, tried to recast the meaning of military service. It downplayed notions of duty and service and obligation; it sold itself to potential recruits and to the broader American public *as a source of opportunity.* Neither combat footage nor the reality of war fit well with the army's recruiting message about the "long-term attributes of Army service."

—Beth Bailey, *America's Army: Making the All-Volunteer Force*
(emphasis added)

The dynamics of the all-volunteer force call for professional military as well as business judgments in formulating military personnel policies. When a policy is formulated and its expected result is reviewed, military and operational considerations are paramount....Indeed, recruiting an all-volunteer force year after year...is big business.

—Melissa Wells-Petry, *Exclusion: Homosexuals and the Right to Serve*

A common story told about the U.S. military in the twenty-first century is that it is egalitarian, that as the natural outcome of democracy it is heterogenous, and that it provides the primary opportunity in a democracy for all Americans to justify their rights as citizens and for foreign nationals aspiring to citizenship to demonstrate their commitment.[1] This story of egalitarianism is evoked when military members try to mitigate charges of racism by claiming that the only color they see is green, when recruiting ads depict a visually diverse array of armed forces members, or when someone has not served but, perceiving the social and cultural benefits of a record of American military service, falsely claims heroic military involvement in a case of "stolen valor." The story is further reflected in national surveys registering the highest level of confidence in the U.S. military among all sizable American institutions. For instance, a 2017 "Confidence in Institutions" Gallup poll shows that confidence in the U.S. military has grown steadily since 1975, when 58 percent of those surveyed reported that they had a "great deal/quite a lot" of confidence, compared to 72 percent in 2017. Among the seventeen American institutions cited in 2017, only "the police" and "small business," at 57 percent and 70 percent, respectively, approach the level of confidence in the armed forces ("Confidence").[2] That confidence gradually has increased since 1975 though no wars have been won (or declared) and the military institution meant to ensure democratic egalitarianism, the draft, has ended in that time suggests the efficacy of the egalitarian story. The story of egalitarianism is further evoked semantically by use of the word "service" to characterize labor in the armed forces, "service" implying a vocational calling to sacrifice as opposed to fair employment that pays the bills.[3] The implications of this story of egalitarianism are that anyone can be employed by the U.S. military, anyone can succeed as an employee of the U.S. military, and, perhaps most significantly, anyone who loves this country should offer his services, if not his life, to the armed forces. It follows that if all may be employed in the U.S. military, all should take that opportunity. The less than 1 percent who have taken this opportunity, especially since the advent of the Global War on Terrorism, are widely portrayed as model citizens, nay, heroes.[4] Since the 1973 birth of the all-volunteer force (AVF), this unquestioning and growing public confidence in the U.S. military to do the right thing has granted it the authority to use its own reasoning—"military judgment"—to formulate its own rules, regulations, and practices.

Such reverence for the U.S. armed forces and subsequent accession of authority paradoxically can also challenge the very democratic institutions that are designed to safeguard egalitarianism. In a 2018 Brookings Institution report entitled "Military Worship Hurts US Democracy," its authors caution that such confidence may be warranted but is also "corrosive" to US national security, as it diminishes the role of civilian leaders in the national use of force, "a profound problem for a democratic system" (Karlin and Friend). In *Bring Me Men*, Aaron Belkin asserts that the current uncritical approach to the U.S. military, especially to its dominant culture of military masculinity, undermines democracy as "a straightjacket that constricts what it means to be free" (182). Furthermore, however democratically oriented its tellers believe or want the egalitarian story to be, it is contradicted by the limits on who in the conscription eras of U.S. history have been required to be available for employment and who, since the 1973 beginnings of the professional AVF, have been permitted to seek employment. Neither were all U.S. citizens required to offer their services, nor were all U.S. citizens allowed to offer their services during the twentieth century's conscription era. Conscription of younger men was enacted in World War I, for instance, but many eligible men were sidelined for being African American or exempted for being fathers to dependent children, having disabilities, being in college or graduate school, or doing work seen as valuable to the war effort (Flynn 9–43). Even during the World War II era of the "Greatest Generation," though approximately 50 million men registered with the Selective Service and the draft was received positively by the American populace, only about 20 percent of those men were actually inducted (Flynn 85). Though an even lesser percentage was inducted from the pool of eligible-aged men during the Vietnam War, it was an era notorious for the discriminatory methods by which the ranks of the U.S. armed forces were filled, not just the conscripting of only men but also the enabling of men of means legally to avoid the combat-heavy branches or even conscription altogether. Despite the armed forces currently populating its ranks with "volunteers" (while sustaining since 1980 the possibility of instituting conscription through required registration with the Selective Service), the vast majority of otherwise eligible volunteers are disqualified—disqualifications that conveniently have been adjusted when recruiting goals, especially in a time of conflict, cannot be met.[5]

What is most paradoxical is that although the story of egalitarianism cannot be substantiated, it is sustained by tales about several groups traditionally excluded from being drafted or volunteering.[6] To investigate why the story cannot be corroborated and on whom it relies nonetheless, this chapter examines in brief the integration history of African Americans, and more substantially those of women and people who identify as gay or lesbian in the largest of the five armed services, the U.S. Army.[7] Since June 12, 1948, when President Truman signed the Women's Integration Act, July 26, 1948, when Truman signed Executive Order 9981 mitigating racial segregation of the armed forces, and 1950, when the new Department of Defense for the first time formally banned homosexuals in the Uniform Code of Military Justice, the story of egalitarianism has been founded on the integration experiences of these three groups, experiences touted as exemplifying the forces' democratic leanings. However, the historical record of the last seven decades demonstrates strong resistance within and without the military to integrating all three of these groups and the calculated measures—overtly prior to the AVF and more obliquely afterward—taken to guarantee their inability to join.

This ongoing resistance to integration suggests not only that egalitarianism does not naturally evolve from or align with American democracy, but also that, according to prejudicial military judgment, members of these three groups are not preferable as soldiers to white, heterosexual, men. Including members of these three groups, particularly in the largest of the branches, the U.S.

Army, consequently is reluctant, provisional, and therefore revocable at any moment. It seems that their employment numbers since the institution of the all-volunteer army have grown primarily not because the U.S. Army is committed first and foremost to democratic egalitarianism, equal opportunity, or individual liberty, but to necessity: the all-volunteer army is not able to be populated by white heterosexual male recruits alone, and the military often is the only or at least best employment-with-benefits available to members of these three groups. Not only are white men's numbers as a proportion of the U.S. population shrinking, on average, 70 percent of all young men already are disqualified from military employment for reasons other than those of the conscription era: inadequate education, health concerns such as prescription and nonprescription drug use and mental illness, criminal records, certain tattoos or piercings, disabilities, and perhaps the most surprising disqualifier for nearly a third of potential recruits, obesity.[8] Another portion of this cohort prefers to go to college right out of high school.[9]

This shrinking cohort of eligible young men has become especially problematic for the Army since 1973 and the birth of the AVF, when the Army's ranks thereafter had to be populated with persuaded recruits, not mandated conscripts. Not only did the recruiting Army struggle to attract candidates under the weight of its ignominious reputation from the Vietnam War, but it also was pressured by the neoliberal thinking that fashioned President Nixon's decision to turn away from the draft and toward recruitment. Thus, simultaneously the U.S. Army had to rebuild its post–Vietnam War reputation, make military life attractive to potential recruits, adhere to the neoliberal notion that the market is the best way to affect freedom (the draft being akin to "slavery"), be responsive to the ongoing commitment of the nation to civil rights, and retain its final authority on all matters via military judgment.[10] This chapter unpacks the egalitarian story by exploring in tandem the influences of neoliberalism with the U.S. Army employment records of African Americans, women, and people who identify as gay or lesbian during the twentieth and twenty-first centuries.

Together the records illustrate the tenuousness of the full inclusion of these groups and thus the fragility of the story of a democratically egalitarian armed force.

Neoliberalism

The neoliberalist emphasis on individual liberty to do as one likes in the marketplace informed the 1973 transition from a conscripted to a recruited armed force. In *A Brief History of Neoliberalism*, David Harvey explains, "[Neoliberalism] proposes that human well-being can best be advanced by liberating individual entrepreneurial freedoms and skills within an institutional framework characterized by strong private property rights, free markets, and free trade. The role of the state is to create and preserve an institutional framework appropriate to such practices" (2). However, "entrepreneurial freedom" is not unequivocally positive for all concerned. In *How Did We Get into This Mess?*, George Monbiot voices a common critique of these "freedoms," namely, that these freedoms may be exercised by some against others: "Freedom of the kind championed by neoliberals means freedom from competing interests. It means freedom from the demands of social justice, from environmental constraints, from collective bargaining and from the taxation that funds public services. It means, in sum, freedom from democracy" (4). With neoliberalism's redefinition of citizens as consumers, spending becomes more important than voting. Under neoliberalism, what Monbiot calls a "zombie doctrine" because it is both pervasive and invisible, we all "internalize and reproduce its creeds" so that "democracy is reduced to theatre" ("Neoliberalism"). This conception of neoliberalism poses problems to a federal institution ostensibly egalitarian.

Beth Bailey's *America's Army* outlines the challenges of the military's transition to a neoliberalist institution, focusing especially on the U.S. Army because its status as the largest of the military services meant it was most impacted by and therefore had more adjusting to "the legacies of the social change movements of the 1960s" (xi). Bailey contends that in the nearly five decades since the inception of the AVF, the Army learned many lessons, chiefly about how to market itself, especially to members of the social change movements. In tracing the Army's marketing activities, Bailey not only records the substance and quality of appeals to potential recruits, but she also chronicles the Army's struggle to adhere to the neoliberal principles underlying the conversion to a recruited armed force. The early proponents of these principles "portrayed the decision [to abandon conscription] as part of America's ongoing debate about the relative importance of [individual] liberty versus [collective] equality as the nation's defining value," she writes. "Instead of framing the debate about the AVF around notions of citizenship and obligation, or around concerns about the shared burden of service and social equality, they offered plans based on conservative or libertarian doctrines of market economies" (4).

Bailey further characterizes the 1971 report submitted by the Gates Commission recommending ending the draft as ideological: "Although the report relied heavily on quantitative economic studies, it made its philosophical case around issues of individual freedom and liberty. It paid little attention to the question of fairness, simply suggesting that free-market forces would be fairer than government engineering" (31). Bailey notes how the Gates Commission ignored the "noneconomic recommendations," or military judgment, extended by the Army (39), subsequently forcing the U.S. military to face "laws of the market" against which it previously had been protected (68). The employment of members of the three groups examined later in this chapter therefore "was a byproduct of the move to the market, the shift from the powerful cultural traditions of military service to the structural imperatives of labor-market competition" (133). Despite the Army's efforts to skirt them, the pressures of this shift constantly arose as the all-volunteer Army evolved in the later 1970s with concerns about equal opportunity (117–118) and in the 1980s with debates about whether the military was a job or a vocation (127). Bailey reports that in the Reagan era, the Army "staked its future . . . on state-of-the-art econometric models and the details of market shares and media weight. It learned the lessons of corporate management and information economies" (175). A brief hiatus in this mostly economic orientation occurred during the 1990s, when "Army claims of inclusion and equal opportunity had much substance" (224). Because the valuing of individual liberty above all is incongruous to an institution predicated on collective efforts, however, the Army struggled against incorporating neoliberalism's primary focus on the individual. Nonetheless, with the turn of the millennium and recruiting challenges, the Army's emphasis on an individualistic "warrior ethos" (233) and its referring to enlistees as "consumers" (242) cemented its commitment to neoliberal individual liberty over collectivist egalitarianism. Like Monbiot above, Bailey cautions her readers about the discriminatory risks of this commitment: "The all-volunteer military allows most Americans the safety of distance not only from war but from the possibility of military service, even from their fellow citizens who have volunteered to serve" (255). She goes even further, concluding that "in a democratic nation, there is something lost when individual liberty is valued over all and the rights and benefits of citizenship becomes less closely linked to its duties and obligations" (260).

In *The Rise of the Military Welfare State,* Jennifer Mittelstadt also takes up the question of neoliberalism's impact on the U.S. Army, one of which is the option to invoke military judgment. She notes that a particular attraction of the AVF was the "elaborate social and economic safety net" offered by the U.S. military, ranging from subsidized healthcare, housing, groceries, clothing, moving costs, and family support, to "social services ranging from financial counseling to legal aid" (3). Without these benefits, military leaders contended they would be unable to attract enough volunteers to fill the ranks.[11] Though, as Bailey attests, a central element of the AVF's foundation in neoliberal principles was to free the individual from collectivist imperatives, Mittelstadt recounts how the military insisted on using its own judgment to contest for nearly two decades the neoliberal principles that demanded expunging these collectivist supports. While "fears of a feminized and overly African American army . . . fed anxieties that the army was transforming from a war-fighting institution into a social welfare institution" (8), outweighing those fears of social welfare were anxieties that cutting military entitlements would make service people just like any other employees who would demand to unionize and collectively bargain (46–72). The Reagan era's increased military budget combined with pressures by Army wives (120–147) and Christian evangelicals (148–170) to support military families delayed the neoliberal imperative to untether the military from social welfare. Mittelstadt points out that the Reagan administration still abided by neoliberal tenets when it created the GI Bill to attract white, middle-class young people to enlist while at the same time cutting federal educational loans and grants, thereby suggesting that only military employees deserved federal assistance (96). Reagan's policies "sought to recalibrate the meaning of deserving and undeserving in the realm of entitlements," marked "a championing of the military as the most legitimate function of government," and thereby fortified military judgment (113, 116).

Following the fall of the Soviet Union in 1989 and the first Gulf War in 1991, however, cuts to defense spending in the George H. W. Bush and Clinton eras meant less money going to corporations accustomed to profiting from the U.S. war machine. Here, Mittelstadt asserts, is when the neoliberal transition made itself evident in the U.S. military via privatizing: simultaneous to a change in attitude by military leaders about the military welfare system (173), "business interests close to the Pentagon, whose bottom lines also suffered from the drawdown, supported [the] outsourcing agenda to help them capture a new source of revenue from government contracts" (200). With the twenty-first-century start of conflicts in Afghanistan and Iraq, rhetorics of individualistic "self-reliance," independence, choice, and "resilience" were deployed to persuade troops of the superiority of private contracting over military-regulated support systems and of military members' personal responsibility for readiness, even when private contractors provided and continue to provide inadequate care (224). "Under the pretext of providing 'choice' to military personnel," Mittelstadt avers in a 2012 article, "the [privatized] programs decrease total benefits and increase private sector access to government funds and the money of military personnel" ("Neoliberalism"). According to Mittelstadt in *The Rise of the Military Welfare State*, demands for further privatization persist, specifically in regard to healthcare and retirement, changes that would "completely marketize the social provisioning in the army," boding ill for civilian social supports. "If soldiers, sailors, airmen, and marines can have their benefits outsourced and privatized—even while they are at war—what will become of the social programs that remain for civilians?" Mittelstadt asks (227).

Finally, according to Deborah Cowen, neoliberalizing of the U.S. military has a dire impact on American concepts of citizenship, the very thing in the story of egalitarianism that is supposed to be verified by service in the U.S. military. While many critics of the volunteer force have lambasted the dissolution of the American citizen-soldier, few overtly link it to neoliberalism as Cowen does.[12] Instead, she sees the military being populated largely by the working class and their progeny, a situation creating not only a "warrior caste" but also "a broader restructuring and polarization of citizenship in which the military is increasingly playing a core role—as the patriotic home of the deserving poor" (177).[13] Their sacrifice warrants even the diminished social services Mittelstadt cites, exemplifying to Cowen the neoliberal concept of "workfare." Military employment has become the "economically rational free choice" for a segment of the population for whom the benefits outweigh their costs (173). "Military service," disparages Cowen, "has become one of the primary normative means for the poor to practice their 'freedom' and 'protect' everyone else's. It is a means for people to actualize themselves by war-working for their welfare" (181). "They might do all this for a chance at the American dream—even if it costs them their American life" (180), Cowen concludes in painful irony. Thus, Cowen's formulation suggests that the AVF is conducting a campaign of neoliberal exploitation rather than democratic egalitarianism.

Still, neoliberalism's increasing hold on the U.S. military might suggest that the ranks are entirely open to individuals freely exercising their individual liberty. Just as in the quote above George Monbiot laments that "freedom" can mean at once self-actualization and the ability to oppress others, Deborah Cowen comments that the absence of force—the draft—does not equal freedom (181). That is, "freedom" is not a universal term that always means an unfettered state, egalitarianism does not flow naturally from democracy, and the U.S. military is most concerned with exercising its own judgment and filling its ranks—"readiness"—than with providing equal opportunities. Instead of alleged "freedom" to choose, however, the makeup of the current military's volunteer corps registers the transactional qualities bequeathed to it by neoliberalism.

Lastly, a crucial outcome of the 1970s turn to a neoliberal all-volunteer force is what is lamented by Bailey, Mittelstadt, and Cowen: that it precipitated the military-civilian divide that now means only about one-half of 1 percent of American citizens (and foreign nationals hoping to become citizens) volunteer for the armed forces. Equally importantly, and especially in the "support the troops" era since the turn of the millennium, this divide also has led to the post-AVF invocation of military judgment to justify rules and regulations sometimes at odds with the sensibilities—let alone laws—dominating American culture, and civilian willingness to accede to that judgment. As discussed at the end of this chapter, this invocation is most apparent in regard to the policy governing the employment of transgender people in the U.S. armed forces.

African Americans prior to the Vietnam War

Although African Americans often are used as primary evidence in the story of egalitarianism, the transactional condition cited above has been the case for them throughout American military history, not only since the neoliberal turn. Their experience throughout this period portends what ultimately would happen with women and gay and lesbian people following the AVF, however. Their employment has been less about egalitarianism and more about the institution's periodically using overt discrimination before the AVF and military judgment subsequently to ignore its systemic and sometimes institutionalized racism in order to suit the readiness needs of the service. Before the AVF's neoliberal turn, discrimination did not have to be obscured, a supposition confirmed by numerous scholars. In their collection of documents concerning African Americans' role in the U.S. military from the republic's beginnings through the American war in Vietnam, editors Bernard Nalty and Morris J. MacGregor claim in their introduction, "Progress from exclusion to full participation has proved uneven. . . . At one time, a need for manpower may have contributed to progress; at another, unreasoning prejudice may have turned advance into retreat, thus causing the nation to ignore a potentially valuable source of recruits" (ix). Douglas Walter Bristol outlines how black soldiers during World War II, rather than passively accepting their subordinated role in the military, together with African American civilians actively resisted discrimination against them. In this period, "they expected more, spoke out, and fought back" (22). In fact, says Bristol, more African Americans claimed to have enlisted during World War II because they were unhappy with racial conditions in the United States than did out of patriotism (28). Despite the African Americans expressing dissatisfaction and their motivations for enlisting, the white-dominated armed forces nonetheless were unapologetically free to employ African Americans according to their own will.

Moreover, because the different branches of the U.S. military prior to the AVF could actively and openly practice segregation and resist integration, military judgment did not need to be invoked. According to Richard Dalfiume about the period from 1939 to 1953, undoing segregation and its racist underpinnings in the U.S. military following World War II required a mandate from the government's highest reaches (4). Even then, as James Westheider points out, President Harry Truman issued Executive Order 9981 in 1948 only under pressure from black leaders threatening to defy a recently legislated segregated draft (101). While the order offered hope to African Americans that they would be treated equally in the armed forces and thus in American society at large, these hopes were abated through the American wars in Korea and Vietnam and finally were dashed by the post-9/11 American wars in Iraq and Afghanistan. Now, Kimberley L. Phillips avers, "the traditional model of black support for military service to further political and cultural agendas is no longer valid" (118).[14] In fact, like Nalty and MacGregor, Phillips counters the notion that these hopes ever were valid, that whether military judgment was invoked or whether racial discrimination was practiced openly, African Americans always have been employed transactionally: "Federal officials calculated African Americans' exclusions from economic and civic life into the episodic need for combat labor" (6). In an echo of the neoliberalist creed, Phillips claims, such exploitative calculations enabled the AVF: "The volunteer military emerged as much in response to the availability of large numbers of economically vulnerable men and women as it did in response to the nation's discontent with the draft during the Vietnam War" (277).

The primarily economic motivations of African Americans to enlist are indicated by dramatically raised enlistment rates after the 2007 recession.[15] But the calculations Phillips cautions are also evident in the disproportionate representation of African American men and women in today's active-duty military, where African Americans (who comprise less than 13 percent of the U.S. population) constitute 17 percent of the total, with disproportionately high numbers of enlisted personnel (19 percent) and disproportionately low numbers of commissioned officers (9 percent) (Parker et al.). The Army alone reports that in 2016, African Americans made up 43 percent of active duty members, up from 38 percent in 2006 ("Army Demographics"). This alarming overrepresentation suggests either that African Americans are exceptionally patriotic or that something is awry, as though the military is a "de facto jobs program" (Kimberley Phillips 277) or the "workfare" Deborah Cowen cites.

These numbers are especially remarkable because they differ dramatically from those of the first half of the twentieth century, when the armed services were intentionally and openly racially segregated and there were sufficient numbers of white men eligible to populate the ranks otherwise. During World War I, overtly racist attitudes in the U.S. military toward African American men prevailed and thus resulted in racial segregation (Dalfiume 5–24). These men were said to be unintelligent, lacking initiative, prone to rape, and cowardly, and so more often than not they were assigned to units that conducted support labor as opposed to combat (Dalfiume 15–16; Nalty and MacGregor 89). African American men rarely were made officers, even for all–African American units. Writing in 1969, during the Vietnam War era, Richard Dalfiume commented: "A common premise in the Army was that the Southern white noncommissioned and commissioned officers made the best leaders for Negro soldiers because they 'understood' them" (13). Of the nearly 5 million American men who served during World War I, about 380,000 blacks—or approximately 9 percent of the total—served in the Army.[16] Less than 10 percent of those African American service members served in combat, mostly with the French forces, with the remainder acting as "laborers in engineer, quartermaster, or pioneer battalions."[17] As Bernard Nalty and Morris McGregor conclude, "The reality of Jim Crow, enforced by American authorities, followed the [African American Ninety-Second Division] overseas and persisted after the Armistice" (87). One indicator of this persistently overt racism was the deliberate attempt after the war to reduce the size of black units in order "to permit the recruitment of more whites," largely to populate the new, all-white Air Corps (92).

The U.S. military continued its policy of overt racial segregation during World War II, insisting as it did in the previous war that African American recruits were best suited to menial labor and that their portion of the military should not exceed 9 percent (Kimberley Phillips 7). Despite evidence from the segregated units that these men were competent enough to fill positions across the service and the protestations of black leaders at the injustice of Jim Crow in the military, segregation continued (Nalty and MacGregor 108–109). To counter this discrimination, and to echo the victory campaign launched by the Office of War Information,

African Americans initiated their "Double V" campaign to fight fascism and Jim Crow, to "challenge a national visual narrative that refused acknowledgement of their participation in the War campaign, compelled them to accommodate segregation, and denied the violence of American segregation" (Kimberley Phillips 25).

Just as Truman's 1948 unilateral Executive Order 9981 promised the end of Jim Crow in the military, so did the unilateral decision by General Matthew Ridgway to integrate combat units in Korea mean the Army could claim late in that war that the vast majority of African Americans were fully integrated (Dalfiume 218).[18] Resistance to the integration was strong, however, and integration was precipitated largely by the need for manpower in combat units and not a commitment to egalitarianism. Kimberley Phillips notes the ongoing discrimination leveled at African American combatants in Korea, furthermore, with their being poorly armed and supplied (133), with disproportionately more accusations of cowardice (136), and even in the face of such discrimination, disproportionate rates of enlistment, re-enlistment, and drafting. This latter pattern "masked blacks' struggles to find work more generally, the protracted efforts to desegregate the armed services, and the establishment of an unequal draft system to meet the needs of a Cold War military" (146). Thus, the way African American men have been treated in the military, prior to the AVF and after—namely, overtly discriminated against and then not so overtly with the rhetoric of military judgment—can offer a way to understand how women and queer people are treated subsequent to the neoliberal AVF.

Women since the Birth of the All-Volunteer Force

Just as the twentieth-century history of African Americans in the U.S. military belies the story of an egalitarian armed force and presages neoliberal sensibilities, so does the history of women's military employment following that period. Many critics objected to women serving in the regular forces, let alone combat, even before the 1974 lifting of the 2 percent limit on women in the armed forces, the 1976 opening of service academies to women, and the 1978 end of the Women's Army Corps (WAC). Tanya Roth outlines this history since 1948's passage of the Women's Armed Services Integration Act, detailing how the inclusion of women on a permanent basis in the regular forces following World War II, to ensure readiness, was predicated on their remaining fit as future wives and mothers (75). "Respectability" was a premium value and was used as a code word to "assuage fears of lesbian activity" (76). In fact, Roth points out, a predominant recruiting tactic aimed at women was to depict the military as a rich source of husband material (79) and to stress "ladylike" clothing and behavior (82). Under these conditions—emphasizing becoming a wife and mother, and minimizing professional ambitions—well into the 1970s military women were trained more in grooming than combat drilling; limited to positions in administration, clerical work, and the health professions and to comprising no more than 2 percent of the total force; forced out of the service with marriage and pregnancy; and not permitted to achieve the highest ranks or to command men.[19] "For nearly thirty years," Roth concludes, military judgment "ensured that no woman would face a conflict between career and family; according to military leaders, family trumped everything else for women" (86).

Following the 1973 institution of the all-volunteer Army and the 1978 ending of the Women's Army Corps (WAC), the number of women in the armed forces escalated dramatically, from 2 percent of the total to 10 percent ("Population Representation" 32). As of 2016, with the services witnessing the decline of eligible males and taking "steps to attract more female recruits,"[20] women comprise more than 18 percent of a generally shrinking armed forces, and just over 14 percent of the Army enlisted personnel and 18.4 percent of commissioned officers ("Population Representation" 3, 32, 33–34; Parker et al.). Together, enlisted and officer women comprise 15 percent of the 2016 active duty U.S. Army and, when including the National Guard and Army Reserves, 17 percent ("Army Demographics"). Furthermore, according to a 2018 Council on Foreign Relations report, "In the army, there are nearly as many black women as white women," suggesting that the Army may be exploiting a civilian labor market that discriminates against women, black women in particular (Reynolds and Shendruk; Stachowitsch 3–4).[21] These numbers are often used to imply that women have reached equity in the military. However, in the midst of economic and cultural conditions that are not conducive to recruiting the preferred males, like African Americans, women have been targeted transactionally. As the Office of the Under Secretary of Defense, Personnel and Readiness admits, under the 2016 conditions the military must do all it can—including permitting women to occupy combat positions—to "increase interest in military service among young women" ("Population Representation" 4).

Nonetheless, there has been considerable objection to women in combat positions, objections that are as much about preferred gender roles than "readiness" or "cohesion," two concepts under the rubric of military judgment frequently used to found these objections. No critic has been so notorious or overt as James Webb in 1979's "Women Can't Fight," which he wrote after having spent one year instructing women at the U.S. Naval Academy.[22] Webb contends, "There is a place for women in our military, but not in combat," because men fight better, men are more naturally violent, and "men fight better without women around" (212). Furthermore, though the Naval Academy is a "horny woman's dream," at risk is women's "sexual identity" as heterosexual women who, of course, are naturally desirous of becoming mothers (221).[23] Though in 2017 Webb apologized for his 1979 "immaturity," as recently as 2013, the current commander in chief, Donald Trump, opined as a private citizen on Twitter about women in the military and sexual assault simultaneous to and within months of the January 2013 Department of Defense removal of the combat exclusion (Lamothe; @realDonaldTrump). On January 25, 2013, at 4:40 P.M., Trump commented, "Maybe I'm old fashioned but I don't like seeing women in combat." On May 7, 2013, at 7:04 P.M., Trump naturalized sexual assault as something that is bound to happen when men and women work together: "26,000 unreported sexual assults [sic] in the military-only 238 convictions. What did these geniuses expect when they put men & women together?"[24] Within days of blaming mixed-sex working environments for sexual assaults, on May 17, 2013, at 6:36 A.M., Trump excused sexual assault by military men as inevitable: "Unfortunately with some men when the poison kicks in (not me of course) there are no rules or guidelines in the military that will stop them." Though decades apart, both Webb and Trump promote the idea that differences between men and women are natural and cannot or must not be overcome, as though stemming (natural) aggression in their male comrades would dilute the comrades' aggressions against the enemy, and that egalitarianism between the two sexes is a pipe dream.[25] Lest it seem that men alone promote this ideology, note the position of Heather MacDonald of the Manhattan Institute, who warns that "eros" will erode cohesion: "The argument for putting women into combat roles has always been nonmilitary. . . . War isn't about promoting equality. . . . The claim that female combat soldiers will perform as lethally as men over an extended deployment entails a denial of biological reality."

These attitudes at the highest levels persist, often rationalized as military judgment, and continue to inform the roles women are permitted to play in the U.S. military. Though it has been regarded as the epitome of women's equal treatment, the January 2013 lifting of women's exclusion from combat has not ensured the egalitarianism of the U.S. Army. Instead, as many critics aver, rather than military culture reconceiving its aims and methods (as ordered by the secretary of defense in 2015), the Webb and Trump attitudes (women can't fight; men can't resist their natural sexual predation) prevail, manifesting in two ways (Secretary of Defense "Implementation Guidance"; Makeschin). First, women are pandered to in order to cement a promilitary stance that will encourage them to enlist, to seek officer commissions, or to support men's enlisting and seeking; second, women who do enlist or seek are expected to assimilate into a culture that continues to value and enact the masculine qualities traditionally ascribed to male bodies.[26] The first shows itself among critics arguing from a feminist viewpoint, who have concerns that women are being exploited primarily to fill the ranks of the AVF. Cynthia Enloe's argument outlined in this book's introduction is one example of such a viewpoint. Another is *Post-Feminist War*, in which Mary Douglas Vavrus echoes Deborah Cowen's argument about "workfare" by asserting that the media representations of women in the military, rather than bringing about egalitarianism, market militarism and war that "work together to maintain systems of inequality and oppression." This representation, Vavrus elaborates, "obscures the sexual violence, PTSD, racism, increased risk of suicide, and war violence that women are likely to encounter during active duty" (193). Noah Berlatsky presages Vavrus's argument when he points out the ambivalence of feminists to women being permitted to serve in combat, of "the acquiescence to war as a moral force and a moral standard" such inclusion requires, while leaving unquestioned and thereby naturalized male patriarchal values dominating the military and the conduct of war.

The second manifestation of the Webb and Trump attitudes prevailing shows itself among critics who challenge the values that continue to undergird—and may have been heightened in the post-9/11 era of the AVF—a masculinist military. Kacy Crowley and Michelle Sandhoff argue in their examination of Army women during the Iraq War that limits on the women's full participation in the military emerges from the ideology of male masculinity: "Regardless of how tomboyish they were or how much they defined themselves as different from other women, they were still seen [by the men] as women. In the masculine culture of the military, this femininity, which they could not escape, was also a source of violence and degradation in the form of sexual harassment" (232). Echoing African American men's experience of assimilation versus integration in the armed forces, Crowley and Sandhoff conclude, "As the U.S. military expands roles for women, including in combat, there is increased discussion of gender integration. What is demonstrated by these women [fighting in Iraq], however, is that these discussions are not really about *integrating women* into the masculine culture of the military but rather about *assimilating female bodies* into the masculine culture of the military. Women are not being welcomed as additions to the military force but rather accepted and tolerated as long as they abide by the masculine ideal" (235; emphasis added).

Anthony C. King affirms this conclusion in his assessment of the "honorary man" position conferred on some military women in place of the "slut-bitch binary": "The status of 'honorary man' has been ascribed to competent, respected female soldiers who are no longer seen in sexual terms; they are neither sluts nor bitches on this account. The concept of the honorary man is, in effect, a new category that has emerged in the past decade, partly displacing the slut-bitch binary" (383). King cautions that while this new identity may be the only way by which to integrate women into the military's masculine culture, serious drawbacks include not requiring a shift in gender privileging, "honorary man" being conferrable only by men, and the position's revocability (385). Both articles clarify the challenges women face in being integrated or assimilating into a masculinist culture.

In *Beyond the Band of Brothers*, Megan Mackenzie questions this culture in asserting that the combat exclusion of military women has been less about women's abilities and more about men's maintaining their privilege. Mackenzie contends that the "band of brothers" myth—or the story that men's connection to one another is vital to national security—is at the heart of justifying war as it "legitimizes male privilege, . . . represents war as the 'ultimate expression of masculinity,' and casts violence as a necessary political strategy" (4). Furthermore, women have been used to shape this band-of-brothers military identity, even after the removal of the combat exclusion policy.[27] In effect, the removal has only resulted in a revision of the myth to "a new, more equal and inclusive [patriarchal] family" (65), one deployed to distract from scandals like the sexual violence by male military members on female military members (66), the "groupthink" of incidents like that at Abu Ghraib (70), and the abuse of the bodies of dead enemies (71). Mackenzie further submits that arguments based on the "cohesion hypothesis"—that women will disrupt the allegedly natural cohesion of men on which combat performance depends—is illegitimately invoked by military judgment to position women "as subordinate outsiders in need of protection" (136), rather than the protectors themselves.[28] This band-of-brothers myth has become especially important to recruitment during the era of the neoliberal AVF as it has "revived enthusiasm for participation in, and support of, the military. Shifting the attention away from broader discussions of the ethics of specific wars and military strategy to the group level also made support for the military more attractive to the general public" (141). Mackenzie's assessment suggests the success of Army recruiting efforts outlined above. However, including women in combat only "serves to recover a battered military image, rewrite the history of women's roles in Iraq and Afghanistan, and falsely portray the military as a gender-inclusive institution." Mackenzie concludes: "Without the sheen of the band of brothers myth, war looks far less attractive, easy, clear, and just" (196–197).

To an extent, it is the band-of-brothers myth and its rhetorical linkage to military judgment that informs the attitudes of Webb, Trump, and MacDonald cited earlier. The trio's advocacy for a single-sex combat arms is based on beliefs in the supremacy of cisgender male masculinity, heteronormativity, and the imperative of cohesion, despite research confirming that the growing technologization and asymmetries of war no longer require the brawn or uniformity of troops associated with traditional warfare. In fact, in addition to women's numbers being essential to filling the ranks, evidence suggests that women are integral to peace processes, both as military personnel and as political negotiators ("Women's Participation"). Nonetheless, as Saskia Stachowitsch points out, representations of women in the U.S. military are used more to tell a story about an egalitarian nation than to ensure egalitarian armed forces: "Military women predominantly become an issue in the media when it serves the positive portrayal of the nation, the military, and the current war effort. They are portrayed particularly favorably when their images can be used for war propaganda" (132).

Although it was not until the 1950 service-wide Uniform Code of Military Justice's (UCMJ) prohibition against "unnatural carnal copulation" that certain sexual practices were prohibited and punished, people who act on same-sex desire or are alleged to be willing to act on that desire have been unwelcome in the U.S. military since its inception (Frank 9).[29] However, before the advent of psychiatry at the turn of the twentieth century, it was the conduct or act of sodomy alone that was punished; after the normalization of psychiatric diagnoses and during World War II, the conduct was interpreted as a personality disorder or sexual psychopathy leading to immediate discharge, an interpretation that meant due process through court-martial was not required and people could be disqualified before enlistment.[30] For most of the twentieth and into the twenty-first century, the U.S. military has grappled with these two interpretations: chosen practice or psychiatric disorder. As Timothy Haggerty points out, the medical and political discourses concerning same-sex sexual orientation shifted over the course of the twentieth century, requiring American institutions that normalize sexual behavior—including the military—"to discover and regulate both homosexual 'behavior,' or same-sex acts, and the homosexual 'personality,' or those that have adopted gay, lesbian, or other nonnormative sexual identities" (11).[31]

Despite understanding this distinction between behavior and personhood, and periodic sponsoring of evidence-based research on the issue by the Department of Defense, repeatedly the military has rejected and often concealed research outcomes that don't confirm its already-held beliefs. In doing so, the military asserts that its own judgment—exclusive, of course, to military leaders—is superior, thereby silencing any evidentiary-based arguments to the contrary.[32] An early instance of research outcomes being suppressed are those from the 1957 U.S. Navy–sponsored "Crittenden Report," which concluded that (1) homosexuals were no greater security risks than their heterosexual counterparts,[33] and (2) there was no evidence that homosexuals were sexually predatory

(Haggerty 22–26). The report was only released to the public by court order in 1977 with no apparent intervening changes made to policy (Frank 118). Additional research projects either suppressed or discounted by military judgment include two 1988–1989 reports sponsored by the Defense Department's Personnel Security Research and Education Center (PERSEREC), whose most remarkable findings were the "unit cohesion" argument used to exclude gays and lesbians from service was based on fear, not fact, and that people who identify as gay or lesbian are better suited to military service than people who identify as heterosexual (Haggerty 36–40; Frank 118–119).[34] PERSEREC was chided by the Defense Department in this case for "exceeding authority"—or presuming it could exercise military judgment—in assessing not only the reliability of people who identify as gay or lesbian but also their suitability. A third study was conducted by the General Accounting Office (GAO) in 1992 that reportedly included in an early draft a recommendation that the secretary of defense reconsider the gay exclusion; by the final draft, the recommendation had been excised. Subsequently, not only did the Department of Defense (DoD) dismiss the report, more importantly in an echo of its excluding African Americans and women, DoD asserted its legal independence from civilian society with its superior military judgment: "The courts, it said, 'have not required scientific evidence to support the Defense Department policy because the Military constitutes a specialized community, governed by a separate discipline from that of the civilian community'" (Frank 121). A fourth study nonetheless was commissioned in 1993 of the RAND Corporation by the secretary of defense. The study concluded that "sexual orientation alone was 'not germane' in determining who should serve" and that "gay exclusion" could be lifted if done systematically with the support of military leaders (Frank 114). This study, too, like so many before, was suppressed by the Pentagon and dismissed for exceeding its authority. Military judgment would be limited to only a select few military leaders, and it alone—without recourse to evidence outside of this exclusionary rationale—would determine who was permitted to volunteer for the ranks.

The "gay exclusion" policy of the U.S. military since the Cold War UCMJ prohibition did not preclude men and women who identify as gay or lesbian from being drafted or from volunteering, and with the pressures to populate the AVF ranks, their sexuality often was ignored or overlooked. However, after about a decade of the neoliberal AVF and the consequent pressures to fill the ranks, targeting of gays and particularly of lesbians began in the 1980s.[35] Consequently, what became the 1994 "Don't Ask, Don't Tell" (DADT) statute was intended by the Clinton administration to enable open service and to mitigate the disproportionate discharges levied against these service members. Instead, for eighteen years, DADT forced heightened concealment and led to further targeting of military gay men and lesbian women.[36] The 2011 repeal of the law and subsequent open service of gay and lesbian service members—"a civil rights triumph" (Hillman)—is often held up as a model tale of egalitarianism.[37]

Yet the occasion also illustrates how the U.S. military, especially since the birth of the neoliberal AVF, uses a military judgment rationale to justify its own rules and regulations, rules and regulations sometimes in conflict with federal and state laws and regulations.[38] Says U.S. Army apologist Melissa Wells-Petry in defense of DADT: "Clearly, the determination that homosexuality is incompatible with military service is not, strictly speaking, a determination of *fact*. Rather, it is an exercise of professional military judgment in making a broad policy choice. . . . The law clearly does not require proof of the factual merits of the [defense] secretary's exercise of judgment in making policy choices" (89–91; original emphasis).[39] This rationale declares that the U.S. military can be above or outside of the democratic processes that warrant egalitarianism and that the U.S. military is meant to defend. Even military leaders retired from active duty can employ the military judgment rationale, evidenced by the over one thousand retired flag officers who publicly objected to the repeal of DADT.[40] Not only did these former generals and admirals express in their letter the orthodox fears about loss of morale, unit cohesion, and retention should people who identify as gay or lesbian be free to serve openly in the U.S. military, but they also revealed the neoliberalist fundaments of their fears: that the repeal might "break the All-Voluntary Force" (Center for Military Readiness, "Policy Analysis").

Egalitarianism, however, is founded on the rule of law being applied equally and without discrimination. As Elizabeth Hillman cautions about the military's invoking military judgment in the 2011 DADT-repeal case, "For the first time in the history of U.S. civil rights, a federal law ending official discrimination [DADT] was allowed to take effect only after the military agreed to its terms." "In the past," Hillman explains, "progress toward integrating racial minorities and women into the military was sometimes halting and uneven. . . . But in the past, executive orders and legislative acts that reformed military rules and regulations did not require the acquiescence of military leaders before they became law" (178). Prior to the institution of the AVF and with it the need to appear nondiscriminatory, the military's discrimination against African Americans and women was sanctioned by U.S. law and practices. The endurance of DADT for eighteen years following the AVF's establishment and the need to gain military approval before passing its repeal, Hillman points out, indicates a costly civilian deference to military judgment that originated with the AVF (180), suggesting that the neoliberalist underpinnings of the AVF—which simultaneously heroicize service members while limiting access to that status—have become deeply embedded in both the military and civilian realms. As Hillman points out, and resonating Rosa Brooks's "vicious circle" outlined in this book's introduction, civilian deference to military judgment developed in parallel to the AVF and its neoliberal professionalist force, paradoxically generating the same civilian-military gap that then necessitated such deference.[41]

In hindsight, there is some consolation that although the Department of Defense had an oversized part in DADT's repeal and thereby exercised military judgment, DoD's influence was made to appear relatively transparent. It assembled the Comprehensive Review Working Group, and the public was given access to the group's lengthy report. The results were neither concealed nor suppressed nor ignored, as had so much previous research on the subject of gay and lesbian people in the U.S. armed forces. This seeming openness might suggest that the civilian deference paid to the military is lessening, that the neoliberalist AVF concedes it has a responsibility to be less about individual liberties and more about collective equalities. Except that in the case of transgender people—"the last unemancipated group of US service members"[42]—it appears that in 2019, military judgment once again was invoked to exclude a group of people from the U.S. armed forces, but according to many military personnel, it is being appropriated as a cover to discriminate.

In June 2016, after having commissioned a study by the RAND Corporation, the secretary of defense in the Obama administration issued a "Directive-type Memorandum" to the U.S. military that transgender people would be permitted to serve openly: "These policies and procedures are premised on my conclusion that open service by transgender Service members . . . is consistent with military readiness and with strength through diversity" (Secretary of Defense "Directive-Type"). The attachment to the secretary's memorandum addresses equal opportunity, making clear that this decision is not based solely on military judgment: "It is the Department's position, consistent with the U.S. Attorney General's opinion, that discrimination based on gender identity is a form of sex discrimination [prohibited by federal law]."

In July 2017, the new president, Donald Trump, rescinded the policy by invoking in a tweet what might be read as code for military judgment: after "consultation with my Generals and military experts," he concluded that permitting openly transgender people in the armed forces would come at too great a cost to readiness (@realDonaldTrump). This tweet was followed on August 25, 2017, with a presidential memorandum invoking his own authority as the commander in chief, ordering that the Obama policy would be abandoned and there would be a return to the previous policy of banning transgender service people (Presidential Memorandum, August 25, 2017). In a February 2018 memorandum for the president, Secretary of Defense (and retired Marine Corps General) James Mattis also cited military judgment to conclude that while a diagnosis of gender dysphoria in and of itself is not disqualifying, particularly if they "serve . . . in their biological sex," "transgender persons who require or have undergone gender transition are disqualified from military service" (Secretary of Defense, "Memorandum for the President"). Subsequently, the commander in chief signed on March 23, 2018, a presidential memorandum accepting the secretary's advice, citing the secretary's "independent [military] judgment," revoking his August 2017 presidential memorandum, and authorizing the secretary to "implement any appropriate policies concerning service by transgender individuals" (Presidential Memorandum, March 23, 2018).

Following this exchange of tweets and memoranda, an April 2018 letter signed by fifty bipartisan U.S. senators addressed to Secretary of Defense Mattis repudiated the judgment producing the new policy, saying that the judgment is "contrary to medical and scientific consensus and misrepresent[s] the most comprehensive analysis of the costs and implications of transgender service." Furthermore, the senators argued, numerous military representatives have testified to the Armed Services Committee that "open service [in the less than two years of the Obama policy] has had no impact on readiness or good order and discipline, and that transgender service members should be treated with dignity and respect and allowed to serve as long as they meet the standards." The letter also quoted fifty-six retired generals and flag officers: "The proposed ban, if implemented, would cause significant disruptions, deprive the military of mission-critical talent, and compromise the integrity of transgender troops who would be forced to live a lie, as well as non-transgender peers who would be forced to choose between reporting their comrades or disobeying policy. As a result, the proposed ban would degrade readiness even more than the failed 'don't ask, don't tell' policy" (Gillibrand).

In light of this contest over whose military judgment is more authentic and whose information is timelier, it is especially interesting that forty-one retired generals and admirals issued a statement in February 2019 warning that the military judgment being invoked by the president and his secretary of defense to issue the policy is being used as a disguise for outright discrimination, the sort openly levied against African Americans, women, and gay and lesbian people in the past. "Rather than being 'based on professional military judgment,'" write the retired generals and admirals, "this policy contradicts the actual judgment of both current and former senior military leaders, as well as medical research and the experiences of our own military and of other militaries. In truth, a solid wall of military sentiment opposes discrimination" ("Retired Generals"). The fear of the retired generals and admirals is that trying to defend a ban—the "result of [Trump] White House–driven politics"—with military judgment when so much professional medical and military evidence is arrayed against such judgment "will undermine the integrity of United States military judgment."

What is at stake in this debate about when military judgment can be deployed as the final authority is the autonomy delivered to the U.S. military by way of the neoliberal AVF. Research from across the world and in the United States repeats that there is no valid reason, whether medical or financial, to exclude transgender people from serving in armed forces.[43] As in the case of the three groups examined in this chapter, it has been fear, sometimes enabled by overt discrimination, sometimes using the guise of military judgment, that motivates their exclusion. But the neoliberal marketplace and stories of egalitarianism could be said to underwrite that fear: fear of the military's social welfare, fear of the military's overt political control, fear of the defense industry's waning influence. The exclusion of people identifying as transgender by way of military judgment signals the domination of the neoliberal market. As stated earlier in this chapter, Jennifer Mittelstadt questioned the security of social benefits to civilians if those afforded to military members are threatened (*Rise* 227). How soon, we might ask, before members of the three minoritized groups discussed in this chapter are excluded from the business of the U.S. warrior caste?

5

The Soldier's Creed

Stories of Warrior Patriotism in Visual Culture

Soldier's Creed

I am an American Soldier.

I am a warrior and a member of a team.

I serve the people of the United States, and live the Army
Values.

I will always place the mission first.

I will never accept defeat.

I will never quit.

I will never leave a fallen comrade.[1]

I am disciplined, physically and mentally tough, trained and
proficient in my warrior tasks and drills.

I always maintain my arms, my equipment and myself.

I am an expert and I am a professional.

I stand ready to deploy, engage, and destroy, the enemies of the
United States of America in close combat.

I am a guardian of freedom and the American way of life.

I am an American Soldier.[2]

(November 2003)

When in the fall of 2017 President Donald Trump continued his
campaign to demonize National Football League players who
expressed political dissent by not standing during the playing of

the national anthem prior to games, his presumption that the players' choice to exercise their democratic freedoms was illicit can be understood in a few ways. Not only was Trump a man known for relying on his innate intelligence as opposed to studying history, like many Americans, it is probable that Trump imagined the recent protocol—that NFL players should act as proto-patriots by standing at attention on the sidelines while the national anthem is played or sung—was long-lived. At this twenty-first-century point in the story of the United States, the playing of and standing for the national anthem at sporting events seemed ubiquitously normal patriotic performance. For all of Trump's seventy-some years, after all, the national anthem had been played prior to professional baseball, football, and ice hockey games.[3] Why shouldn't a male professional sports warrior stand for the anthem and the flag? Why shouldn't, for that matter, public school, college, and university athletes do the same? Why shouldn't they all, to some extent, abide by the Soldier's Creed?

In fact, although a nationalist tune had been played before NFL games since 1946, the stipulation that NFL players be present on the sidelines for the anthem only came into existence in 2009.[4] While this expectation publicly is said to have evolved for pragmatic and not propagandistic reasons, that the military, especially after 9/11, is so visible during football games tells a story that both naturalizes the alliance between sports teams and the U.S. military, and also stages the players as exemplary warrior-patriots and the spectators as warrior-patriot aspirants.[5] This production of American patriotism as fundamentally militaristic is neither coincidental nor organic, as the "Soldier's Creed" above exemplifies: "I am a guardian of freedom and the American way of life."[6] In their 2015 joint oversight report, "Tackling Paid Patriotism," then-U.S. Senators John McCain and Jeff Flake determined that although many of the 2012–2015 military spectacles before, during, and after athletic competitions may seem to be "pure display[s] of national pride" arranged and paid for by the teams, instead the teams were paid approximately fifty-three million dollars by the

Department of Defense to facilitate those displays (1).[7] "The DoD," wrote the two Arizona senators,

> paid for patriotic tributes at professional football, baseball, basketball, hockey, and soccer games. These paid tributes included on-field color guard, enlistment and reenlistment ceremonies, performances of the national anthem, full-field flag details, ceremonial first pitches, and puck drops. The National Guard paid teams for the "opportunity" to sponsor military appreciation nights and to recognize its birthday. It paid the Buffalo Bills to sponsor its Salute to the Service game. DoD even paid teams for the "opportunity" to perform surprise welcome home promotions for troops returning from deployments and to recognize wounded warriors. (6)

The report enumerates other beneficiaries of "paid patriotism": NASCAR, the Iron Dog snowmobile race in Alaska, Indiana University and Purdue University football and men's basketball programs, the University of Wisconsin football and ice hockey programs, Motor Sports race day events, and Comic Con. Noticeable in the report are the senators' financial qualms: the inauthenticity of these "tributes" because unsuspecting taxpayers simultaneously fund them and are targeted by them; the activities' "boondoggle" nature for DoD personnel; and "DoD's complete lack of internal controls for awarding, managing, and overseeing these contracts" (7). Furthermore, and most alarmingly to the senators, these funds are spent haphazardly: "DoD cannot accurately account for how many contracts it has awarded or how much has been spent" (8), and even if these activities are recruiting efforts, there are no measures in place to assess their effectiveness (9). Given their obligations as representatives of Arizona's citizens, McCain and Flake's preoccupation with the spending of taxpayer monies was reasonable.

But equally remarkable is McCain and Flake's unconcern for the military's appropriation of a core American value, patriotism, when men's athletics, nationalism, and militarism are so spectacularly combined: that in this story, the ideal form of American patriotism is militaristic.[8] The subject of this chapter's war story, "warrior patriotism," and its delivery system, visual/virtual culture, is especially reinforced, but not exclusively, by male athletes, which can explain why McCain and Flake's "paid patriotism" occurs almost entirely with male athletic teams and in visual/virtual texts that evoke the affective responses on which patriotism relies.[9] The dominant enactment by athletes of the warrior version includes: following orders; presenting a muscled body; standing erectly in a uniform and in a straight line; and being solemn in the presence of nationalist notes and the American flag.[10] The implication is that militarism is the answer to all national challenges, and that all Americans should unquestioningly support and emulate the ultimate warrior patriots, troops, and their activities.[11] The visible stance at the athletic competition's outset is complemented by the linguistic "combat," or "kinetic" warfare of the games themselves: the "kills," the quarterback's "rifle for an arm," being "in the trenches," sending "bullet passes" and "the bomb," being a "sharpshooter."[12] Team names reinforce their gladiatorial, ferocious, or pugnacious behavior: "Warriors," "Crusaders," "Redskins," "Trojans," "Spartans," "Timberwolves," "Bullets," "Warhawks," "Fighting Irish," "Patriots," and "Wildcats."[13]

Because civilian warrior-patriot aspirants need outlets for learning, developing, and performing their warrior patriotism, the story of warrior patriotism is told neither only about male athletic teams nor only in visual/virtual culture. "Patriot" names the laser-guided surface-to-air missile used by the U.S. Army since 1984 and titles the law enacted after the 9/11 attacks to enhance national security.[14] The story founds the all-volunteer force's hero-making of all U.S. service people, its "warrior ethos," and the civilian refrains of "thank you for your service" and "support the troops."[15] It underlies the integration of militarism into everyday American life: camouflage as fashion; Jeeps and Humvees on American roadways; the normalization of drones (large and small), surveillance, civilian access to military-grade weapons, and the social authority of the National Rifle Association; the prevalence of war themes in video games; the popular appeal of comic book heroes like Captain America and the Avengers, and the revision of Superman from Clark Kent the journalist to Clark Kent the Navy SEAL (Froeba); nostalgia for the World War II era and the "Greatest Generation"; and the militarization of local police and immigration forces.[16] The story of warrior patriotism also underlies Trump's indignation that kneeling or not standing while the anthem plays and the flag flies is inappropriate as American warrior-patriot spectacle. Furthermore, the story recounts and the "Soldier's Creed" affirms that this form of patriotism is embodied primarily by U.S. service people and secondarily by male athletes. Other citizens can only hope to be sutured into the label of "warrior patriot" with wearing of camouflage, support of elected officials who allot mammoth sums to the Defense Department and its corporate colleagues, and utterances of "thank you for your service." Instead of a range of patriotisms available to and applauded by U.S. citizens, warrior patriotism is naturalized as the most authentic form when the associations between American men's sports teams and American military forces are taken as genuine. As Flake and McCain conclude in their letter prefacing their "paid patriotism" report, "It is time to allow major sports teams' *legitimate tributes* to our soldiers to shine with national pride rather than their being cast under the pallor of marketing *gimmicks* paid for by American taxpayers" (emphasis added). Their asserting that there is a patent difference between "gimmicks" and "legitimate tributes"—the difference hinging on whose dollars pay for the event, not on the story told by the event—minimizes if not obviates why there is this relationship in the first place and what its effects are.[17]

Were it not that this consistent melding of (men's) sport and American patriotism is relatively unique to the United States, perhaps the issue of players paying proper homage to national symbols may not have been contentious. Enquiring minds might ask why an 1814 lyric celebration of martial victory—the War of 1812—seems the most apt celebration of the nation. These same minds might also ask: What was it that led the U.S. Congress in 1931 to decide "The Star-Spangled Banner" would be the national anthem, why is it played at the beginning of sporting events and not at other large gatherings such as movie screenings or concerts, why are players enjoined to be part of this display, and what is the effect of this visual conflation of sport and patriotism? This chapter asserts that the stories of warrior patriotism are most effectively cemented as the dominant narrative by way of visual texts: on stadium and arena surfaces, as already discussed, and in recruiting advertisements and video games.

A twofold explanation for the expansion of military visual/virtual culture since the institution of the all-volunteer force (AVF) in 1973 includes heightened needs to appeal to the target age group and a concomitant change in the modes that reach those young people (Mead 70).[18] First, the AVF denaturalized the notion of a citizen-soldier and its logic that (male) citizens are obliged to serve their country militarily. Second, the birth of the internet, the ubiquity of cable television, and the proliferation of digital gaming have meant that most of what young people learn about the military is by way of visual/virtual culture. The combination of a decreased disposition to serve, a decline in the number of eligible enlistees (as discussed in the previous chapter), and a simultaneously narrowed and broadened lens by which to convince them to serve means that the military has to fight inventively—using visual/virtual culture—to attract the few suitable recruits. The meanings of visual/virtual culture's images, however, are not fixed or stable, nor can they be dismissed as "just entertainment" and thereby escape critical analysis. Instead, images require constant replay and interpretation as they "instruct us how to see and how to think . . . as important agents in shaping how military events are understood, judged, and remembered" (Miller 279). Furthermore, because images proliferate in the current American visual/virtual culture, it is the rhetorical frame—such as the logics that discriminate between what is a "legitimate" versus a "gimmick" tribute or what is an authentic or inauthentic demonstration of patriotism—that apportions meaning to an image.[19] Even that framing containment is impermanent, however, and so has to be reinforced repeatedly. "In this internet age," Bonnie Miller concludes in her brief history of American war's visual culture, "the tendencies toward democratizing image production and distribution via global pathways is too strong a force for any policy of containment to succeed" (304). Hence, the repeated DoD-sponsored displays at athletic events and Donald Trump's persistent harangue of NFL players are attempts to frame patriotism as "warrior patriotism."

Because of "democratizing image production," visual texts abound that tell the story of warrior patriotism. What follows are analyses of two of those storytelling visual modes. The first story is told through U.S. Army recruiting tactics and demonstrates the military's intent to ally with sporting events and the notion of "team." The second story is told via video games and demonstrates the military's intent to ally with digital games and the internet. Both stories indicate the dominance of warrior patriotism's tale.

Recruiting Advertisements and Joining "the Greatest Team You Will Ever Be a Part Of"

Chapter 4, "Military Judgment," indicates that, given the neoliberal imperatives of the AVF, recruiting is critical to populating the armed services, especially the at-once largest and least attractive branch, the U.S. Army. Recruiting pressures have required substantial financial and personnel resources in addition to visual inventiveness at all levels of the military. The Congressional Budget Office reports that between 2000 and 2014, the U.S. Defense budget increased from $384 billion to $502 billion, "mainly because of higher costs for military personnel and operation and maintenance" (Congressional Budget Office). According to Geoff Martin and Erin Steuter, the entire Defense Department's recruitment budget ballooned from $590 million in 2003 to $20.5 billion requested for FY2009 (147). Meghann Myers reports in the November 7, 2018, Army Times the amounts spent since 2013 on recruitment by the U.S. Army alone: from $121 million (2013), to $290 million (2017), to estimates of $600 million in 2018 and $700 million in 2019.[20] Just as McCain and Flake found there were no effectiveness measures of the "paid patriotism," Myers also found that audits of Army recruiting expenditures could not identify their effectiveness. Nonetheless, from 2005 through 2017, the U.S. Army met recruitment goals and did not meet them in 2018 (Long). These monies are spent in many ways, not least of which are recruiting advertisements aired through assorted visual media.

For instance, a series of six 2014–2018 "Tunnel" Army recruiting advertisements indicate the branch's association with athletics and advocacy of "warrior patriotism." The ads signal this advocacy by arguing for team membership that is both exclusive and also makes a difference. Each ad is thirty seconds long, begins uniformly, and concludes slightly differently. Echoing the "Soldier's Creed" above, the upshot of the "Tunnel" ads is that one joins a team when one enlists in the Army, each team requiring either jumping out of airplanes ("Tunnel: HALO"; 2015), allying with Middle Eastern forces ("Tunnel: Special Forces"; 2015), providing medical assistance ("Tunnel: AMEDD"; 2015), repairing power grids ("Tunnel: Power Grid"; 2016), launching drones ("Tunnel: Microdrone"; 2017), or conducting amphibious assaults ("Tunnel: Amphibious Assault"; 2018).[21] With more than 15,000 airings, "Tunnel: Amphibious Assault" has been shown the most frequently; at 2,653 airings, "Tunnel: AMEDD" has been shown the least often. According to iSpot.tv, the ads appeared on YouTube, on the GoArmy website, and most recently on networks such as NBC during high school football games, and on BET, Univision, and TNT.

The first ten seconds of the "Tunnel" ads depict in unfocused black-and-white silhouette what appears to be a group of players walking in slow motion through a dark tunnel toward a bright light. The dominant sound is of feet tromping, as though cleated, while the outline of the players' rounded helmets is unmistakable. The camera's perspective is from the head level of one of those walking through the tunnel toward the light but from the rear of the group. It looks as if this is a helmeted football team walking through the tunnel that leads to the field, and the bright light ensures that no one person is distinct in this image. Except for the close-up on two faces in the AMEDD ad and one in the Special Forces and HALO ads, among the six advertisements only the voiceover during these ten seconds differs. As the group reaches the light at the end of the tunnel, at once the same brassy, triumphal music begins, and images come into focus and at normal speed.

Though the voiceovers differ, they all imply that to join this football-team-like group is to enact a very specific form of warrior patriotism, one that includes action, decisiveness, teamwork, daring, and conquest. Take, for instance, the voiceovers of two of the most frequently and recently aired ads (on NBC during high school football games), "Tunnel: Amphibious Assault" and "Tunnel: HALO," and note the emphasis on "team." "Every *team* trains hard. Every *team* prepares to win," says the baritone male voice in "Amphibious Assault" while the group walks through the tunnel. When they emerge from the dark tunnel and leap, as though from the rear of a cargo airplane, into the bright light of the water and race across it in inflatable landing craft, the triumphal music sounds and the voiceover resumes. "But when U.S. Army soldiers *take the field*," the voiceover gloats, "it's best if the other guys don't bother showing up." The screen then reads, "Join the *team* that makes a difference," followed by the voiceover urging, "See if you have what it takes at goarmy.com/team" (emphasis added). "Tunnel: HALO," meanwhile, features two voices. (In this version, the original emphasis is underlined and the added is italicized.) The first voice, speaking as the group walks through the tunnel, says, "Alright, listen up. Out on *that field* today, you <u>will</u> be ready for anything. And I want you to always remember, <u>this</u> is the greatest *team* you will ever be a part of." As the team members emerge into the light to parachute from the rear of a cargo airplane, a second voice says, "When they're asked what did you do to make a difference in the world . . . they can say, 'I became a soldier.'" "Can you make the cut?" then appears in script on the screen. Clearly, in an era when opting to enlist is itself regarded as heroic, these two advertisements synonymize being on an athletic team with being a patriot who makes the cut, has what it takes, and thereby makes a difference in the world.

Spotlighting the appeal to a patriotic athletic ethos in "Amphibious Assault" and "HALO" is the "Tunnel" ad least aired, according to iSpot.tv, "Tunnel: AMEDD." It begins just as the others do in the tunnel and features the same coachlike voiceover exhorting the team that "HALO" does before the team emerges into the light. Like "HALO" and "Special Forces," "AMEDD" also features individual faces of members in the tunnel, consequently suggesting that these units require of their members special abilities and verve. Once the AMEDD members reach the end of the tunnel, they walk toward what appears to be a newly built military field hospital in, like "Special Forces," an arid climate. Unlike "HALO" and "Special Forces," however, the appeal to being exceptional is mitigated by the voiceover urging, "Join the team that makes a difference." Meanwhile, "HALO" and "Special Forces" conclude with "Can you make the cut?" subtly suggesting that it is the individualistic and athletic skydivers, amphibious assaulters, and Special Forces, not those collectivists with medical know-how, who are the most venerable of warrior patriots.

Perhaps the "Tunnel" ads were too subtle a call for warrior patriots, though, given the Army's missing its 2018 recruitment quotas. An explicit call for warrior patriots is not at all subtle in a May 2019 Army recruiting advertisement aired, according to iSpot. tv, on NBC Sports' website *Pro Football Talk*. Entitled "We Stand Ready," it features a small artillery unit on the edge of a green, leafy forest near mountains, so not the stereotypically arid Middle East. As a rapid-fire montage of artillery images scroll—fire direction orders, adjusting barrels, heaving rounds to the guns and then firing them simultaneously—and of what sounds like a digital metronome ticking to suggest urgently that time is passing, a baritone voice intones, "There are those who stand forever ready. Ready to defend the nation. Ready to fight for what matters. No matter what." Those spoken words are followed by six howitzers firing simultaneously and then unspoken script on the screen: "Warriors

Wanted." The voiceover resumes with a question similar to those asked at the conclusion of the three "Tunnel" ads more overtly promoting warrior patriotism: "Do you have what it takes?" The implication is that if you do, you are a warrior, and you are ready not only to defend the nation but also to know what matters and to battle for it.

One might ask why team sports are represented as the best medium for the enactment of patriotism, or why militarism and patriotism are constructed as synonymous. William Astore asks a related question: "If we're so strong . . . why do we need so much steroidal piety, so many in-your-face patriotic props, and so much parade-ground conformity?" ("Whatever Happened"). One might conclude that these ads, conflating as they do sports teams (only of a certain ilk), patriotism, and militarism, not only are protesting too much (as Astore implies) but also are naturalizing militarism and thereby making it benign.

Call of Duty and *America's Army*: Freedom of Choice

Like recent U.S. Army recruiting ads, war-themed video games also tell stories appealing to warrior patriotism, both through the exclusivity of "having what it takes" or "making the cut," and also joining a team to make a difference. While the alliance between Hollywood and the Pentagon formed early in the film industry, the coalition between visual/virtual and martial cultures was foreseen late in the twentieth century and has accelerated since.[22] Although the typical concern about many video games is their desensitization of players to violence and the lures of authoritarianism, scholars recently discern more nuanced effects related to the warrior patriotism that games promote. For instance, John Wills points out in his cultural history *Gamer Nation* (2019) that in twenty-first-century America, the "real national pastime involves joypads and keyboards, not shoulder pads and footballs" (3), and he argues that the stories told in this pastime have a role in informing and perpetuating the national ethos. Echoing Tom Engelhardt's *The End of Victory Culture* assertion that there were attempts post-9/11 to revive the conventional story of America as a persecuted and righteous underdog, Wills explicates how post-9/11 gamic stories "reflect the resurgence of traditional values" and a "neo-conservative payback ideology" (151), thereby relying on a backward-looking appeal to traditional American myths of individual heroism and sacrifice to convince players that in playing as combatants they are warrior patriots. "Games depicted a nation under attack," Wills asserts, "but thanks to the player's skill, the nation was capable of overcoming all odds and emerging victorious." "As virtual soldiers," Wills continues, "gamers fought for good old American values, protecting their brethren in violent conflicts and dangerous war zones" (149). Reverberating the tension in American culture between the core values of individualism and collectivism discussed in chapters 2 and 3, the games' fetishization of "an individual player's success at killing, rather than the hard work, democratic values, or migratory forces that shaped real nations" (221) worries Wills, however.

In *War Play*, Corey Mead also worries about the stories told by video games, especially because in his estimation the military tends to use video games as the solution to most training challenges without knowing whether the games are effective (164). Mead outlines the technological links between education and the U.S. military, focusing chiefly on military training's use of video games. This use "helps to plug the holes, to address the issues that previous military instruction wasn't set up to address," (4) and is economical when a downsizing, neoliberalizing DoD can task corporations to develop its virtual war worlds at cut-rate costs (22, 68). The video games featuring these worlds are intended to teach service members how to contend with combat's information overload, explains Mead, a responsibility in the past assigned largely to officers and noncommissioned officers. Mead applauds the responsibility conferred on recruit-players as they become "agents of knowledge, as opposed to 'passive recipients'" (67). Mead has reservations, however, about the story told through this education, as he alleges its overvaluation of STEM (science, technology, engineering, mathematics) and devaluation of grappling with the ethical and moral quandaries endemic to warfare may, in the end, lead to more war.

In *Virtuous War*, James Der Derian presages Wills and Mead's unease. Riffing on Dwight D. Eisenhower's "military-industrial complex," Der Derian christens the expanded alliance the "military-industrial-media-entertainment network" (MIME-NET), one that produces "virtuous war," or the projection of "a technological and ethical superiority in which computer simulation, media dissimulation, global surveillance, and networked warfare combine to deter, discipline, and if need be, destroy the enemy" (xx). While this alliance enables the economic, human, and technological efficiencies of the neoliberal AVF, virtuous war is hazardous, as it promotes "bloodless, humanitarian, hygienic wars" in which "one learns how to kill but not to take responsibility for it" (xxxii). Video games, Der Derian says, as a "maelstrom of simulation, patriotism, and profit" (89) are complicit in this "virtuous" risk to peace (96). "From Bosnia to Kosovo, from Afghanistan to Iraq, virtuous war had taken on the properties of a game of high production values, mythic narratives, easy victories, and few bodies," concludes Der Derian, a visual parallel he extends in "War in the Twenty-First Century." "Images of violence," he contends in the 2017 essay, "no matter how degraded, night-scoped, or pixelated, grab more eyeballs and engender more controversial interpretations than even the most well-crafted print story" (260). Plainly, these images exceed the containment or meaning-making framing that Bonnie Miller cautions.

Roger Stahl's conception of the "weaponized gaze" in his 2018 monograph *Through the Crosshairs* is instrumental to understanding how video games "grab more eyeballs" and thereby cultivate warrior patriotism.[23] Stahl asserts that "habits of vision" have been fostered through visual war stories since the camera's invention, shaping American citizenship and conceptions of war by training American audiences to view combat through weapons' lenses. "The war machine," Stahl declaims, "has learned to steer the civic gaze through its stockpiles in order to 'rationalize its own operation.'" The core of the weaponized gaze, he continues, "is an authoritarian discourse that trains citizens to see like weapons," to be interpellated, while at the same time gaslighting citizens into thinking there is nothing unusual to be seen. This weaponized gaze, he contends, is a "perfect combination of 'Hey, look!' and 'Nothing to see here!'" (16–17). Stahl outlines five modes of vision by which Americans have been tutored to see: smart bomb, satellite, drone, sniper, and helmet cam. Together, the ubiquity and subsequent normalization of these ways of seeing have the effect of rationalizing warfare, so much that, in a prime example of Foucault's panoptic discipline, citizens cannot and may not see otherwise. Through this "seduction of the eye," these ways of seeing, citizens are shaped as warrior patriots.

Not only does warrior patriotism conclude that militarism is the answer to all national challenges, but it also subsequently commands that Americans unquestioningly support and emulate the ultimate warrior patriots, "troops," and their activities. Wills, Mead, Der Derian, and Stahl illustrate how that support is constructed in video games: players are encouraged to imagine themselves as warrior patriots; empirical STEM skills are privileged over moral and ethical skills; games make the case for war being a virtuous amalgam of technology, patriotism, and efficiency; and before American citizens ever become players, they are educated to visualize themselves as righteously deadly weapons—aka warrior patriots. These constructions are useful to analyzing various first-person-shooter (FPS) and multiplayer video games, especially the long-running *Call of Duty* franchise and *America's Army*, the U.S Army's "most cost-effective recruitment tool ever" (Mead 72). Additionally, game theorists argue for at least two approaches to understanding the storytelling of digital games: the content-concerned "narratological," about the somewhat real-world stories told by games; and the form-concerned "ludological," about the aesthetic and experiential effects of playing.[24] Tom Bissell provides a way to differentiate these approaches:

> Games with any kind of narrative structure usually employ two kinds of story-telling. One is the framed narrative of the game

itself, set in the fictional "present," and traditionally doled out in what are called cut scenes or cinematics, which in most cases take control away from the gamer, who is forced to watch the scene unfold. The other, which some game designers and theoreticians refer to as the "ludonarrative," is unscripted and gamer-determined—the "fun" portions of the "played" game—and usually amounts to some frenetic reconception of getting from point A to point B. The differences between the framed narrative and the ludonarrative are what make story in games so unmanageable: One is fixed, the other is fluid, and yet they are intended, however notionally, to work together. Their historical inability to do so may be best described as congressional. (36–37)

It is this storytelling clash endemic to video games that complicates how some visual stories are told, sometimes leading to a papering-over of the fixed/fluid clash in order to meet rhetorical ends. Such is the case with *Call of Duty* and *America's Army.*

The first of the fifteen renditions of *Call of Duty* was released in October 2003, the same year the Army's "Soldier's Creed" was instituted and only months after the U.S. invasion of Iraq.[25] Set in a "good war" era, World War II, the first three versions (2003, 2005, 2006) were accepted as fun and, given the setting, benignly patriotic and militaristic.[26] In this sense, then, the game was ludological: the effect of the playing experience itself was paramount, and stories of the past served secondarily as the neutral medium for that experience. Once the series moved out of the "good war" era and into the present day with the "Modern Warfare" level in 2007, however, this acceptance was more grudging as the game's patent advocacy of warrior patriotism—or militarism above all—became evident. In this sense, then, the game became more narratological as it represented the known world. Wills reports that the violence depicted in the "Modern Warfare" version was so offensive, so threatening to the world as it is now, especially with 2009's *Call of Duty: Modern Warfare II* having players visualize themselves as terrorists, that the *Salt Lake Tribune* named it "the most controversial game of the year" and the British Parliament debated the game's violence (149). According to the gaming review website *Kotaku*, "In Japan and Germany, the game was altered to trigger a mission failed screen if players [as terrorists] decided to shoot the civilians. In Russia, it was straight up *removed*" (Klepek). Roger Stahl contends in "Digital War and the Public Mind" that since 2007 the entire franchise has aimed to legitimize the Global War on Terrorism by representing war as a naturally foregone conclusion, imbuing players with feelings of superiority in "making the cut" (as urged in the U.S. Army's "Tunnel" ads), and perhaps more importantly, absolving citizens of responsibility for authorizing this state-sponsored violence. In effect, Stahl concludes, playing the game is not an exercise of agency, as the ludic interactivity of video games insinuates and players want to believe, but one of following orders. As Bissell's "congressional" characterization suggests, this difference between agent and order-follower muddies the sharp distinction between video games as either ludic or narrativistic, as either play or lesson. That *Call of Duty* players imagine they are willfully, delightedly, and righteously exercising their own will to wreak havoc in a world closely approximating the present one is disturbing enough.[27] That they may do this imagining they are agents without recognizing they are command-driven is perhaps more disturbing, because they cannot discriminate between what is choice and what is obligation. The inability to distinguish between the two while imagining oneself as exercising uninhibited choice demonstrates how some video games promote warrior patriotism.

The *America's Army* video game franchise also faces this dilemma of agency, obligation, and warrior patriotism but with heightened stakes as an overt military recruiting instrument. How does one employ a genre grounded in interactivity and choice— agency—to deliver institutional lessons in following orders or surrendering agency? How does one at once deliver pleasure in free play and also ensure that proper lessons are learned? To what extent do those lessons need to be mitigated in order to entice recruits? As Mead points out, the military has to be assured that its trainees have learned their lessons (67). After all, the game's stated objective since its July 4, 2002, release is didactic/narratological: "to *tell* the public the true life of a Soldier by exploring Army values, careers and technology" and "to kind of *get across* to the community that there is more to being a Soldier than just guns" (Smith; emphasis added). This "telling" and "getting across" implies that the gamic representations are nonideological and objective lesson-delivery systems. The Army values purportedly promoted by the *America's Army* franchise—loyalty, duty, respect, selfless service, honor, integrity, personal courage—are represented by the U.S. Army in this way, as universal, irrefutable human and humane qualities.[28] But most importantly, the "telling" implies fixed meanings, an implication at odds with Miller's "democratizing image production" and the definition of "video game" as interactive. In video games, a player's illusion of uninhibited choice is fundamental.[29]

Obviously, however, as visual constructs, video games are rhetorical and therefore limit choice based on elements such as designer biases, technological capabilities, aesthetic preferences and trends, affective objectives, economic bottom lines, willingness of players and audiences to suspend disbelief, references to stories of the national past, and cultural norms promoted and challenged by the games. Instruction, too, is rhetorical in its attention to audience and how best to persuade that audience through visual storytelling. As Mead argues, this rhetoric hinges on the values and assumptions of the game designer, qualities that players agree to implicitly but unknowingly when they play the games (160–161). Says one of *America's Army*'s designers about this instructive element: "We focus on rewarding the player for sticking together as a team, for being mission focused, and taking objectives. We try to structure the mechanics such that one guy can never be the best. You always have your battle buddy. You always have your team, your unit, and you're always going to stick together to achieve victory" (Smith). Thus, games are didactic narratives controlled by their ideological underpinnings, as Stahl's discussion of *Call of Duty* indicates, but appeal to players with the promise of ludic autonomy. Individual autonomy and the possibility of disobedience, however, as outlined in chapter 3, contradicts the uniformity, collectivity, and obedience demanded by the armed forces. Thus, the genre or form of "video game" paradoxically contradicts the essence of military service.[30]

Mead details tensions in the early development of *America's Army* between the game's teaching lessons vital to the Army's recruitment objectives and the pleasure of autonomous action (90–94). A meaningful share of this tension is in the intended audience of the recruitment tool, twelve-to-thirteen-year-old boys inexperienced enough not to know yet what they want to do with their lives and yet also enamored by a free-of-charge video game that promises fun and excitement.[31] Controlling the narrative for this youthful group was imperative since, as one of the game's originators remarks, "the first information you get is the most important" (Mead 83).[32] Not only did potential recruits need to be attracted at an age when they could not yet imagine their own mortality or morality, but they also needed to be protected from stories—like war films and the tales of veterans—that might inhibit their desire to join the Army at eighteen (Mead 83–84). This need to control the effects of the game by minimizing the interactive, ludic qualities and maximizing the linear, narrative qualities for impressionable boys might help to explain the 2009 introduction of the *America's Army* digital graphic novel. In an official press release, the Army said this about the graphic novel: "This exclusive online novel allows readers to explore the storyline behind the [newly released] AA3 game through stories that showcase Army operations, Military Occupational Specialties, and high tech equipment while following the lives of U.S. Army Soldiers at home station and while deployed. Readers will discover stories of bravery and teamwork by Soldiers whose jobs include Intelligence Analyst, Medic, UAV Operator, Infantryman, and Apache Helicopter Pilot" (CBR Staff). Tellingly, in this same release, the novel's executive producer encouraged game players to read the novel, saying they "may find useful game tips that may give them an edge when playing AA3 this summer." These so-called "tips" seem not to have been aimed at enhancing the mechanics of players' gaming abilities but instead at deepening their understanding of the game's storylines. Thus, they may operate as prescriptions for how to play the game and learn the desired-by-the-Army lessons. The novel depicts the missions and characters in visual but text-heavy ways, leading to mixed reviews such as this in *Wired*: "In short, *America's Army* [the graphic novel] shoots for ultrarealism for all the things that don't really matter, and glosses over the stuff that counts. Like, you know, believable emotions, real countries and conflicts, enemies with actual personalities and any admission at all that the good guys aren't perfect and even the U.S. Army fights bad wars. The failure of *America's Army* [the graphic novel] reflects its creators' ambivalence" (Axe). The reviewer ascribes this "ambivalence" to the uncertain objectives of the novel. Is it entertainment? Propaganda? Or by way of "tips," is it a way to stress the narrative over the ludic qualities of the game, thereby mitigating the generic, interactive, free-choice qualities of "video game" that pressure the conformity of warrior patriotism?

In 2009's "Whatever Happened to Gary Cooper?," William Astore argues for a turn away from a protesting-too-much "comic-book-style militarism" and toward "a quieter, less muscular patriotism." "If we're so strong," Astore asks, "why do we need so much steroidal piety, so many in-your-face patriotic props, and so much parade-ground conformity?" These three venues—the stadium, the moving picture advertisement, and the video game—illustrate Astore's protesting-too-much and how stories of patriotism can be told in ways neither overtly storytelling nor concerned with patriotism. Moreover, the imbrication of post-9/11 militarism and twenty-first-century professional athleticism to produce "warrior patriotism" suggests that the traditionally nationalist recruiting appeals to heroism and to sacrificial duty, to citizen-soldier, are no longer effective, so much so that a warrior patriot may as likely be an employee of a private military contractor as of the Department of Defense. The "Soldier's Creed" makes this evident, as it pledges more explicitly and repeatedly to uphold the aggressive warrior ethos than the defensive "Army values" it purports to uphold.

These recruiting and video game stories indicate the dominance of the warrior version of patriotism, and their ubiquity suggests it is the most valued version. A recent 2019 analysis by the online financial app *WalletHub* confirms this valuing (McCann). The result, "2019's Most Patriotic States in America," uses a variety of military and civic indicators to determine which state in the United States is most patriotic. In weighting most heavily current or past employment in the warrior-themed armed forces, it equates "warrior" to "patriot" and consequently deems as "most patriotic" the states with a disproportionate share of military volunteers. At the same time, the analysis underweights "civic engagement," especially volunteering locally, serving in the Peace Corps or AmeriCorps, participating as a juror, and receiving some form of civics education. Finally, this weighting tells a story whose plot is that *all* engagement with the federal or state armed forces is motivated by patriotism, whereas some civic engagement—like serving in the Peace Corps, AmeriCorps, and volunteering generally—is regarded as far less so. This indicates the effects of proliferating warrior patriotism stories: the most authentic patriotism is enacted in the warrior mode, a mode demanding adherence to the dictates of authority in all its many forms.

Coda

Prices Paid for the War Stories We Tell

The traditionally narrow notion of "war story" that makes it shelvable may make war seem inconsequential and unrelated to everyday American life—in short, as compartmentalized—which may explain why it is that so many Americans, especially students like mine, have fixed ideas about war generally and American war in particular. The narrow boundaries of what constitutes a "war story" and the willingness to dismiss the didactic effects of war-related stories through an "It's just entertainment" refrain apparently can lead students like mine—and, I would wager, Americans generally—to suppositions unsupported by historical records. Broadening the genre of "war story," as this study urges, enables seeing more plainly some of the stories recited about the nation's armed conflicts, the means by which they are communicated, and the lessons imparted by them.

"State of Crisis" (chapter 1), for instance, illustrates two lessons: knowledge of the past always is incomplete and in the process of being revised as more is studied and discovered; and regarding knowledge of the past as static leads Americans to see the nation as an exception to the forces of history. "Staging War" (chapter 2) demonstrates how exhortations of collective solidarity in war commemoration may be foiled or confounded by equally vocal exhortations to honor the individual. The lesson is that memorials and monuments subsequently can function as literal and figurative stages for war, not against it. "Lone Wolf Family Man" (chapter 3) builds on the tension between American individualism and collectivism discussed in the previous chapter, exhibiting how blockbuster films may construct American combatants as the individualist/collectivist heroes American audiences apparently prefer and will pay to see. "Military Judgment in a Neoliberal Age" (chapter 4) suggests that the neoliberal all-volunteer force has enabled a semantic alteration—"military judgment"—to who is permitted to be employed in the armed forces and under what conditions. Despite a long and ongoing record of discriminatory practices, this deployment of military judgment has enabled the story of a democratic, egalitarian armed forces to flourish. Finally, "The Soldier's Creed" (chapter 5) demonstrates how patriotism and militarism have been conjoined in stories during the AVF era, teaching Americans that the best way to perform patriotism is to accept if not enact militarism. Learning the origins of these lessons can reveal some of the prices paid for them: unending wars, civilians pacified with shame at not enlisting, the militarization of civilian life, confusion about whether individualism and collectivism can coexist in a democracy, a willingness to ignore the offensiveness of some war monuments, versions of "hero" that would in other contexts be threatening. But there are yet even more obvious stories told and prices paid, often fiduciary ones—prices that oddly but largely go uninspected.

For instance, in *Taxing Wars*, Sarah Kreps details how the United States has paid for its wars since World War II. She submits that the country's leaders, desiring maximum flexibility in whether and how to wage wars, deliberately aim to quell the dissent among the populace that may depress the national will to fight well before the potential for armed conflict. In the past seven decades, United States leaders have achieved this in two major ways, according to Kreps: first, by ending the draft, thereby curtailing who pays the blood sacrifice required of the public in a democracy; second, by borrowing money to fund wars as opposed to real-time taxation, thereby delaying and obscuring the public's fiscal sacrifice. Kreps alleges that these two practices result in a story that says the American public has little at stake and leaders are not answerable when the United States goes to war. The consequences, or prices paid, of this story are longer and costlier American wars and the erosion of democratic principles. "Bearing the burden in both blood and treasure is part and parcel of democratic accountability in war," Kreps concludes. "The absence of those visible costs is the reason we end up with the limitless, unaccountable war scenarios" experienced since World War II's end (222).

Throughout her study, Kreps emphasizes that the components of war's conduct need to be "shielded" from the public, that the costs of war, as dire and far-reaching as they are, must not be _felt_. Escalating fiscal and physical prices still are incurred; the American public is just made less aware of and attentive to them. Feelings of outrage or indignation and scrutiny of leaders' motivations and methods of war are appeased when so little appears to be at stake, as so few Americans volunteer the blood sacrifice needed to conduct war and as the fiscal sacrifice is deferred to later generations.

Just as volunteering and borrowing deflect critiques of American war conduct by creating the illusion of costless war, the war stories examined in this study also contribute to that proscription and prescription of feeling. Stories that are not patently concerned with combat but invoke core American values such as exceptionalism, individualism, collectivism, egalitarianism, and patriotism animate some feelings and dampen others. With these invocations, the stories mitigate Kreps's illusion of stakelessness as they tether Americans to war's cause, coaxing Americans into imagining that although they do not contribute their lives or their monies, they still somehow have a stake in the conflicts. Tautologically, Americans' uncritical acceptance of the received notions these stories disseminate because of the core values they invoke fortify those core values, authorizing even more the leaders' decisions to take the country into armed conflict. Problems arise, however. Unwavering acceptance of American exceptionalism in the face of the historical record may facilitate the United States imagining it can succeed at war in places where other countries have failed, for instance. Unqualified faith in the power of individualism can undermine the collectivism required of military ventures, and utter faith in collectivism can undermine the heroism Americans have come to expect of their armed protectors. Moreover, the stories' wide dispersion among genres and media in American culture naturalizes the values they invoke and the feelings they evoke. They are dispersed among differences between popular history and the historical record, between the historical record and commemorative practices, between memoirs and blockbuster films, between expectations for equality and its practices, and between dominant and subordinated versions of patriotism. This Foucauldian dispersion empowers the stories, the storytellers, and the lessons they deliver.

These war stories exact additional and often high prices, furthermore. Certainly they gird the volunteering and borrowing that Kreps claims is undermining participatory democracy. But they also bolster the increasing sanctification of the U.S. armed forces and the subsequent public willingness to fund them at whatever cost, even at the expense of and in debt to other national interests, foreign and domestic.[1] This expensive condition is what Rosa Brooks cites as the "vicious circle" that leads to the military being expected to do "everything." Jessica T. Mathews, a longstanding national security expert, exemplifies this high price in her June 2019 *New York Review of Books* essay with what she terms an "indefensible defense budget," asserting that the American tendency to conflate spending on the military with patriotism (another form of warrior patriotism) has produced a defense fund that, adjusted for inflation, is the highest since World War II. Though defense funding represents a smaller portion of the GDP that has grown in the intervening years, as makes sense, Mathews contends, like Brooks, that the current armed forces' nearly 60 percent share of the discretionary funds appropriated by Congress is a better gauge of the nonsensically disproportionately large share of national treasure allocated to the armed forces and the subsequent disproportionately small share allocated to everyone else. This out-sized share has produced an "extravagant, wasteful, and less agile, innovative, and forward-looking" defense establishment. Concomitantly, the small share has produced, for instance, a "withered" diplomatic arm, so that the national security expertise needed for U.S. engagement with the world has been disrespected and under-funded. "Unqualified campaign contributors are appointed to important diplomatic posts," rues Mathews. More gravely, "the lack of resources [allocated to expert diplomacy] often means that the military is called on to carry out humanitarian and governance tasks for which it is not well suited, because that's where the money and manpower are." As Abraham Maslow's law of the instrument says, if you only have a hammer, everything looks like a nail. In this case, employing an armed force trained to exert lethal power to perform the delicate work of diplomacy risks unintended and enduring conflict.

Another 2019 example of the price paid for these war stories is journalist Andrew Cockburn's. His caution echoes those of Kreps, Brooks, and Mathews: that the overfunding of American defense forces is perilous, the outcome of a military-industrial complex organically organized—like a "virus"—to protect its own viability above all. Thus, rather than defense budget increases prudently cal-culated to respond to or anticipate known threats, the reverse pre-vails: "Wars are a consequence of the quest for bigger budgets" ("Military-Industrial Virus" 65). According to Cockburn, in an echo of Eisenhower's cautions issued nearly six decades earlier, the Department of Defense and the defense industry are more or less one and the same, with both spread across the United States and the world. Not only are these two institutions intertwined, but the federal legislature is also implicated in this knottiness.[2] Cockburn asserts that the defense industry intentionally aims to gain the "fealty" of senators and representatives as it extends its work across congressional districts, thereby pressuring members of Congress regardless of political party to rubber-stamp Pentagon budget requests that potentially bring jobs to their constituents (66). The military-industrial complex that Eisenhower warned against in

1961, says Cockburn, "is embedded in our society to such a degree that it cannot be dislodged, and . . . could be said to be concerned, exclusively, with self-preservation and expansion, like a giant malignant virus" (63).

Using monster imagery similar to Cockburn's, former Pentagon analyst Franklin Spinney cautioned in 2011 that the "voracious appetite" of the military-industrial-congressional-complex (MICC) is what drives strategy, not vice versa.[3] Spinney asserted in the 1980s that the Pentagon's agenda to acquire increasingly expensive and complex weapons systems—an agenda pushed by defense contractors, who need the prospect of war and hugely expensive weapons systems to keep their corporations not just profitable but sustainable—was reckless and would lead to national ruin. The 1991 end of the Cold War and its anticipated "peace dividend" threatened the defense industry and its "powerful political dependents," according to Spinney, so a campaign was begun to "foment an enduring voter-terrifying threat and unending small wars to justify the money flow" (57). That campaign has continued through the intervening decades, a campaign whose methods and effects could be seen to include this study's war stories. "Continuous small wars," Spinney continues, "are essential for the corporate component of the MICC; these companies have no alternative means to survive" (58).

Taken together, the arguments of Kreps, Mathews, Cockburn, and Spinney suggest that the pecuniary motives of the defense establishment are formidable and resilient. They have endured over the course of many decades due in large part to a compliant and trusting public (excepting the anomalous Vietnam War era), a public conditioned by war stories like those outlined in the previous five chapters. Some of the effects of these stories include the willingness—delineated by Kreps, Mathews, Cockburn, and Spinney—to send others to protect American national interests and to burden subsequent generations with the financial costs of war; to fund the armed forces at the expense of other national interests; to permit the economic welfare of the defense establishment to govern when and how the nation engages in conflict; and to accept that "perpetual war" is normal.

Perhaps most indicative of this compliance is the American public's readiness to pay, year after year, decade after decade, astronomical sums to fund an organization that has proven incapable of accounting for how it spends those monies.[4] In 1990, all government agencies not already accounting for their spending of taxpayer monies appropriated by Congress were required by the Chief Financial Officers Act to submit annually audited financial statements.[5] "The government has a responsibility," reads the GAO's comptroller general's preface to the act, "to use timely, reliable, and comprehensive financial information when making decisions which have an impact on citizens' lives and livelihood. Despite good intentions and past efforts to improve financial management systems, this is still not done." Twenty-three years later, in 2013, the Department of Defense was the only federal agency not complying with the mandate, and it was not until 2018 and upwards of a billion dollars paid to audit corporations that the first audit was completed. The Department of Defense, with annual budgets made available to it of more than seven hundred billion dollars, failed its first audit, twenty-eight years after it first was required.[6] The *New York Times* offered a tempered assessment of the failure: "The Pentagon has long prided itself on being a 'can do' organization, firmly committed to protecting the nation. But when it comes to husbanding the billions of taxpayer dollars that pay for the vast military establishment, defense leaders have had less exacting standards" (New York Times Editorial Board). More deprecatingly, Mathews comments, "the $400 million audit released last year revealed a nonfunctional accounting system, systemic weaknesses in cybersecurity, and such pervasive deficiencies that nearly every Pentagon agency can neither track nor accurately account for its spending."

Journalist Matt Taibbi of *Rolling Stone* offers an even more scathing assessment of the failure, suggesting that the military's inability to keep track of its expenditures, its inventory, and the bills it pays to contractors enables the potential not just for rampant waste but also fraud. Taibbi writes that Congress is stymied when it comes to making a difference, neither stick nor carrot effecting change (73), and defense contractors now have been joined by auditors in desiring the system's persistence, broken and wasteful but financially advantageous to them as it is. Taibbi quotes Republican Senator Chuck Grassley of Iowa, one of the primary drivers for audits since the beginning: it's not only that the Pentagon is unable to develop an accounting system, "it seems like they don't want to fix it" (92).[7] Taibbi concludes that, in effect, the Department of Defense is too big to be permitted to fail: "The military has become an unstoppable mechanism for hoovering up taxpayer dollars and deploying them in the most inefficient manner possible." Moreover, Taibbi echoes Brooks's and Mathews's worries that the U.S. military increasingly devours resources that are needed by other U.S. agencies and institutions: "Schools crumble, hospitals and obstetric centers close all over the country, but the armed services are filling up warehouses for some programs with '1,000 years' worth of [what will become obsolete] inventory,' as one Navy logistics officer recently put it'" (93).

How is it possible that American citizens are not objecting to the U.S. armed forces requesting and receiving a massive share of taxpayer money? To the dubious fairness of expecting others to defend what are national interests? To burdening the next generations with the debt of wars fought now? How is it possible that trillions of dollars can be spent without account and taxpayers are not in revolt? This study contends that revising what war stories are and do permits a series of answers to these questions, fundamentally reduced to this: these stories, as contrary as they may be, condition Americans to accept these injustices. The popular war stories told of American history bend toward easy triumph and away from complicated defeat or truce or forever wars. They explicitly encourage a united collective while implicitly expecting individual heroism. These potentially contradictory stories of collectivity and individuality are embedded in the war commemorations erected, and arguments persist about whether the monuments should represent the historical record, how that representation should look, and whether ideological aspirations can possibly be omitted from the monument. Meanwhile, the prevalence of neoliberal thinking encourages Americans to accept that military judgment is best, and that judgment urges regarding the armed forces as the locus for all things egalitarian. This attitude prevails despite a long history of inequality and prejudicial arbitration and extends into the valorization of warrior patriotism as the nation's most authentic version.

Yet broadening the concept of war story affords seeing the costs of the militarism increasingly pervading American culture since World War II, as is demonstrated by each of this study's chapters. This method of seeing is also proposed by Christopher J. Gilbert and Jon Louis Lucaites in "Returning Soldiers and the In/Visibility of Combat Trauma." Gilbert and Lucaites observe how the American public is tutored to regard itself as not responsible for the trauma of the men and women it sends to combat. As one of our "neoliberal failings," they warn, Americans are advised to turn "a blind eye on our own collusion" in the trauma, and they call for a new way of looking, a "civic gaze" that acknowledges our liability for this outcome (64–65). A similar charge to gaze differently is leveled by a 2016 episode, "Men against Fire," in the dystopian Netflix *Black Mirror* series. The series explores the potential and unanticipated costs of new technologies. This particular episode examines how combatants are made to kill other beings, its title identical to S. L. A. Marshall's post–World War II book-length study of how few men in combat actually fire their weapons and how they need to be conditioned psychologically to kill other humans. Patriotism, comradery, and the promised rewards of heroism are not enough to motivate them. In *Black Mirror*'s not-so-futuristic version, the combatants are not only conditioned to kill with repetitive training. Instead, on seeking employment in a quasi-U.S. military/corporate force, they also agree to have devices implanted in their brains. These facilitate the military/corporation's controlling all of their senses, sleeping or waking, but chiefly to make them actually see the enemy as terrifying, aggressive, exterminable monsters, or "roaches."[8] The implant also makes them forget that they agreed to the implantation, so as long as the implant is functioning as designed, the combatants are unable to imagine the roaches as anything but monstrous and their primary life's work as eradicating the vermin. This storyline is distressing enough, that humans can and must be systematically programmed to see the enemy as monstrous, diseased, and a threat to the welfare of the human species. But perhaps more disconcerting is that those humans—"civs"—who are not in the armed forces do not have implants and, first, choose to regard as "roaches" people they can see are humans and, second, out of self-interest actively support the military/corporation's exterminations.

An exchange between the episode's protagonist, Stripe, and a "roach" clarifies this horror. In his very first roach hunt, Stripe's implant begins malfunctioning when he accidentally activates a small device he has found near the body of a roach he had killed. Within days, and despite his being told by officials that the implant was operating properly, Stripe's senses awaken. His vision is unsteady and glitchy, calling his attention to its artifice. He can smell the grass and see it as green, and he can hear birds. Stripe's faltering implant means that during his second hunt, he sees a woman and child as humans, "civs," what his partner, Rai, still only sees as roaches. In the struggle to keep Rai from killing the humans, Stripe is shot by Rai, knocks her unconscious, and escapes with the woman and child. Stripe drives them into the forest, where the woman, Catarina, takes them into her underground home. She explains to Stripe that his implant made him see her and others as monsters, and when he asks why the "civs" also see them that way, she replies, "Everybody hates us," even though they always have seen her and the others as Stripe sees her now: human. "They hate all the same," she adds, "because it's what they've been told." Just as the combatants' implants tell them stories that make them eager to kill, the "civs" are conditioned by stories to hate the people known as roaches and to seek their deaths. This systematic conditioning, or storytelling, Catarina explains, began a decade earlier. "First, the screening program, the DNA checks, then the register, the emergency measures. And soon everyone calls us creatures. Filthy creatures. Every voice—the TV, the computer. Say we have, we have sickness in us. We have weakness. It's in our blood. They say that our blood cannot go on. That we cannot go on."

This "Men against Fire" episode illustrates how such rhetoric does not emerge overnight, in one comprehensive plan or among one group of people. Instead, it evolves over time and in bits and pieces, in stories of various genres from various locations aimed at various audiences. Despite knowing otherwise, the "civs" accept the stories that engender in them fear for themselves, their safety dependent on regarding other humans as exterminable monsters. Their lack of what Gilbert and Lucaites call a "civic gaze" results in a moral compromise mirrored by Stripe's. Rai tracks him to Catarina's home, kills the woman and child whom she sees as roaches, and turns Stripe in as a traitor. He is offered two options by the authorities: either spend the rest of his life in prison with the loop of his viciously murdering other humans being made to run continuously in his head, or agree to have his implant reactivated, his memory erased, his senses redulled, his rejoining the roach-hunters, and the illusion of a beautiful, colorful, happy home life. Neither option offers Stripe a moral choice: he is either tortured with the murderous loop for the rest of his life, or he is the instrument of torture for the officials who want to exterminate the roaches.

In both cases, the "civs" and Stripe suffer what is in this world called moral injury. This concept emerged from the recent American wars in Afghanistan and Iraq, when post-traumatic stress disorder (PTSD) seemed inadequate to explain the effects of these wars on American combatants. During the world wars and the American wars in Korea and Vietnam, whether termed "shell shock" or "combat fatigue," the underlying premise was a Freudian one: that combatants experiencing these effects of war were inherently weak, that there was something inherently wrong in their character before going to war that *created* this response. This meant that the combatants were individually answerable for their abnormal response to war; it was their own weakness that led to what was understood as their "abnormal" psychological and often physical responses to combat.

This notion of blaming the sufferer for his suffering changed following the American war in Vietnam; by 1980 the psychiatric establishment agreed that the conditions of war itself, not combat alone, was traumatizing. That is, the deleterious mental responses of people who had experienced war were not the result of a weakness intrinsic to themselves but the expected, normal reaction to the violence of war. What started as "post-traumatic stress syndrome" and became "post-traumatic stress disorder" was a dramatic change in how to conceive of war's effects on human beings. The condition of war itself was seen as the primary problem, not its participants.

The wars in Afghanistan and Iraq have spurred more thinking about how to understand the impacts of war on military people. PTSD has seemed inadequate to describe what many veterans and active-duty service people have been feeling after having been at war in those two locales: not a psychological wounding so much as a spiritual one. Some veterans of the most recent wars report what has been termed "moral injury," or the sense that what they did or were asked to do as participants in these wars wounded their moral sense of what is right and wrong. This way of categorizing the prices paid of war's violence is in its early stages but seems to be a useful tool for articulating what in the past has been unspeakable.

On the U.S. Department of Veterans Affairs website, authors Shira Maguen and Brett Litz describe this condition (and quote from their own publication) in relation to combatants: "Events are considered morally injurious if they 'transgress deeply held moral beliefs and expectations.' Thus, the key precondition for moral injury is an act of transgression, which shatters moral and ethical expectations that are rooted in religious or spiritual beliefs, or culture-based, organizational, and group-based rules about fairness, the value of life, and so forth." Stripe's objection to killing "civs" is evidence that his expectations are rooted in "group-based rules about fairness" emerging from the implant. It is proper to kill "roaches"; it is improper to kill "civs." The humans who are implant-free, however, the noncombatants, collude in this propriety and so are also morally injured, regardless of whether or not they acknowledge such injury. As Syracuse University's "Moral Injury Project," describes it, "Moral injury is the damage done to one's conscience or moral compass when that person perpetrates, witnesses, or fails to prevent acts that transgress one's own moral beliefs, values, or ethical codes of conduct" (*Moral Injury Project*). The damage is done once the transgression occurs, once the "civs" internalize that it is in their interest to regard other humans as killable.

This injury is not limited to combatants but can be done to and incurred by the nation too. Three previously obscured war stories concerning the Global War on Terrorism (GWOT) came to light at the end of 2019 and can be seen to injure the moral standing of the United States. First, the report sponsored by Seton Hall University's Law School detailing the torture practiced at Guantanamo Bay by Americans and referred to in this book's introduction is morally injurious to the United States because torture—excused by the U.S. government as "enhanced interrogation techniques"—violates all domestic and international codes of human rights and decency (Denbeaux). Second, Brown University's Watson Institute of International and Public Affairs issued a multipart "Costs of War" report calculating the many costs paid around the world for GWOT. The 6.4 trillion dollars budgeted for 2001 to 2020 by the United States for GWOT (also known as "Operation Enduring Freedom") can be regarded as moral injury, as it makes painfully clear that American armed violence supersedes the welfare of the country's own citizens when it denies better schools, infrastructure, peace initiatives, and informed diplomacy, let alone adequate housing, healthcare, and nourishment.[9] But that monetary moral injury to the United States according to the report is compounded if not itself superseded by the hundreds of thousands of deaths and millions of displacements directly attributable to the war violence underwritten by "Operation Enduring Freedom." Certainly the death toll includes the approximately 2,400 deaths of American service people.[10] But it includes also the 801,000 deaths "due to direct war violence, and several times as many indirectly," the over 335,000 civilians "killed as a result of the fighting," and the 21 million "war refugees and displaced persons." These numbers cannot begin to account for the environmental and human rights degradations outlined in the report ("Costs of War").

The moral injury to the nation is profound when the wars are found to have been predicated on false pretenses. The predication for the 1965 whole-force invasion of Vietnam was the alleged 1964 attack in the Gulf of Tonkin, an allegation later found to be at least dubious if not false. The 2003 American invasion of Iraq was Saddam Hussein's government having illicit weapons of mass destruction, an assertion disproven soon after the war's beginnings. The predication for the invasion of Afghanistan was its being a haven for Osama bin Laden, the perpetrator of the 9/11 attacks. Unlike the war in Iraq, it was understood as a legitimate and righteous use of armed violence, "ambushed" by evildoers as the United States had been. Though the war dragged on, the American populace was assured the price being paid was worth it, that progress was being made. Eighteen years after its beginnings, however, the third previously obscured war story was released. Documents acquired only as the result of years of Freedom of Information Act court battles by the *Washington Post* suggest that senior U.S. officials knew from the outset the war in Afghanistan was unwinnable: "With most [of the hundreds of interviewees] speaking on the assumption that their remarks would not become public, U.S. officials acknowledged that their warfighting strategies were fatally flawed and that Washington wasted enormous sums of money trying to remake Afghanistan into a modern nation" (Whitlock). One U.S. Army general responsible for White House policy on Afghanistan during the Bush and Obama administrations is reported to have said bluntly, "We were devoid of a fundamental understanding of Afghanistan—we didn't know what we were doing." Other officials recounted "explicit and sustained efforts by the U.S. government to deliberately mislead the public. They said it was common at military headquarters in Kabul—and at the

White House—to distort statistics to make it appear the United States was winning the war when that was not the case" (Whitlock). The nation and its democracy were damaged by this potential prevarication on the international stage, as it suggests federal officials cannot be trusted to tell their citizens the truth.[11]

American civilians, the nation itself, and American democracy can be morally injured by the American war stories examined, perhaps the most damaging price paid. At the same time the stories invoke American values, they also normalize the high prices and questionable behaviors exacted by the war industry. They assure Americans that as long as troops are supported and honored for their heroic sacrifice done on the nation's behalf, the nation's conduct and their own can be seen as morally just. And yet the moral injury occurs nonetheless. This is the conclusion we might draw from "Men against Fire," where both combatants and civilians are ensnared in a system that requires they make impossible choices, ones that mandate they seek what appears to be least injurious to themselves.

But just as Foucault offers a way to understand the power of story proliferation, he also offers a way out of the inevitability of this trap when he distinguishes between the commonly held belief of power as solely repressive. Regarding power as primarily repressive leads to the trap of impossible choices. Instead, Foucault exhorts, we need to understand that power also produces pleasure and that our objective is to determine how that production happens: "What makes power hold good, what makes it accepted, is simply the fact that it doesn't only weigh on us as a force that says no; it also traverses and produces things, it induces pleasure, forms knowledge, produces discourse. It needs to be considered as a productive network that runs through the whole social body, much more than as a negative instance whose function is repression" ("Truth and Power" 307). It is in comprehending the many ways that war stories appear and instruct in American culture that this production becomes apparent and that Americans can practice the democratic citizenry expected of them.

Acknowledgments

This book was facilitated by the generosity of Denison University, especially in awarding me an R. C. Good Fellowship that gave me time and funding to conduct research at the U.S. National Archives in College Park, Maryland. There I encountered librarians who were eminently helpful and patient with my questions. They are an expert and impressive group; I am so thankful for the work they do and for the archives themselves.

I also appreciate John Wills, the editor of the *European Journal of American Culture*, for giving me permission to include chapter 3, "Lone Wolf Family Man: Stories of Individualism and Collectivism in *American Sniper*(s) and *Lone Survivor*(s)." It previously appeared in a slightly different version in volume 38, no. 2 (2019) of the journal. Many thanks.

I wrote this book at the same time I developed what I hope will be lifelong friendships with the ten scholars of Denison Chicago Posse 15. Their keen interest in all things intellectual, their fierce commitment to making the world a better place, and their resilience in the face of many obstacles convinced me of the book's worth. Thanks to Amirah, Andrea, Armando, Brandon, Daweed, Ja'lia, Jenna, Jesse, Luis, and Mallory—you're the best of what America is.

At the risk of claiming the authority from experience that I trouble in the book, I would be remiss if I did not acknowledge this book's debt to my lifetime relationship to the U.S. Army. I grew up as an "Army brat," during which time my father spent two tours in Vietnam as a combat aviator. I earned a four-year Army

ROTC scholarship in 1975 for college (before the academies were opened to women) and was commissioned as a military intelligence second lieutenant in 1979. I served in what was then West Germany with the Third Armored Division until late 1983, when I left active duty. My relationship continued, though, since many of my eight siblings, their spouses, and their children continued to serve in the U.S. Army. Eight nieces and nephews have been affiliated with the U.S. Army and five remain on active duty in 2020. My relationship changed course when I began scholarly study, first in an international relations master's program while on active duty, then with another master's and a PhD in literature a few decades later. I am grateful for all of these experiences and, especially because I think most of them could not understand why I did this cultural work, for the forbearance of my sibling family members. Thanks for putting up with what you always called my "too deep" thinking.

Finally, I want to acknowledge the unending support of Kirk, Clayton, Liv, and Hannah, and relative newcomers to my support network, Kelsey, Iain, and Carter. With hope, my work will make a difference for Carter's generation.

Notes

Introduction

1. Lutz is a project director of the Costs of War Project at the Watson Institute of Brown University.
2. See Turse (*The Complex*) for more about the pervasiveness of the military-industrial complex.
3. The exception to this claim is Tim O'Brien's *The Things They Carried*, which most of my students tell me they read in high school, especially in AP English classes.
4. Many stories that reflect poorly on Americans and their armed forces remain untold or are suppressed: those about torture (see Turse [*Kill Anything*]); atrocity (see Kendrick Oliver, Jones); chemical warfare (see Martini); suicide, drug and alcohol abuse, and homelessness among returned combatants (see Glantz); moral injury (see Sherman); and white supremacy within the forces (see Belew). Other stories rarely include those concerning the families of armed forces members and the effect of that service on them, the effect of the armed forces billeted in civilian communities, and U.S. policy and material support for autocratic leaders and the blowback effect when the United States ends up in armed conflict with those same nations.
5. "By means of such surveillance, disciplinary power became an 'integrated' system, linked from the inside to the economy and the aims of the mechanism in which it practiced. It was also organized as a multiple, automatic and anonymous power; for although surveillance rests on individuals, its functioning is that of a network of relations from top to bottom, but also to a certain extent from bottom to top and

laterally; this network 'holds' the whole together and traverses it in its entirety with effects of power that derive from one another: supervisors, perpetually supervised" (*Discipline and Punish* 176–177).

6. "A real subjection is born mechanistically from a fictitious relation. So it is not necessary to use force to constrain the convict to good behavior, the madman to calm, the worker to work, the schoolboy to application, the patient to the observation of the regulations" (*Discipline and Punish* 202).

7. Rosa Brooks calls this "the vicious circle" dominant since the beginning of the millennium: "Asking the military to take on more and more nontraditional tasks requires exhausting our all-volunteer military force and necessitates higher military budgets. Higher military budgets force us to look for savings elsewhere, so we freeze or cut spending on civilian diplomacy and development and domestic social programs. As budget cuts cripple civilian agencies and programs, they lose their ability to perform as they once did, so we look to the military to pick up the slack, further expanding its role in both foreign and domestic activities and further straining the volunteer forces. This requires still higher military budgets, which continues the devastating cycle" (20–21). Nonetheless, it would be "political suicide" for any national politician to suggest cutting the defense budget (19).

8. In 2000, Enloe presaged what the 2018 RAND study later concluded, that a populace needs to be readied to fight well before armed conflict is more than potential: "Militarizers seem to believe that if women cannot be controlled effectively, men's participation in the militarizing enterprise cannot be guaranteed. Thus women and the very ideas about feminine respectability, feminine duty, feminine sexuality, and feminine skills will have to be, they decide, the objects of policy and persuasion. Decisions about women will have to be made not just in the midst of that conflict, but in the years preceding any anticipated conflict and in the years following that conflict" (294). This assertion that the control of women's gender roles is central to effective national security is echoed in Faludi's *The Terror Dream*: according to denouncers of feminism following 9/11, "women's liberation had 'feminized' our men and, in so doing, left the nation vulnerable to attack" (23).

9. There are many stories not discussed in these chapters: the motivations and conduct of the wars in Korea, Vietnam, Iraq, and Afghanistan, or of the many "small" and/or covert wars since 1945; the growing reliance on the use of Special Forces since their beginnings in 1952; the growing reliance on the use of private military companies since the turn of the millennium; the use of drones, cyberwarfare, and surveillance devices; or the impact on American militarism of the National Rifle Association. Those constituting the chapters and those listed here are only a sample of the various stories that have multiplied in the national discourse.

1. State of Crisis

1. Ken Burns and Lynn Novick's recently released miniseries, *The Vietnam War* (2017), has been lauded for its inclusion of stories of the French and by Vietnamese people. Nonetheless, of the ten episodes, only the first deals with the century of French colonization of and war in Vietnam. This eighty-three-minute episode represents less than 8 percent of the eighteen-hour series, indicating the perceived relevance of the story of the French war to the story of the American war.

2. See these for histories of the era: Bradley (*Imagining*), Cain, Dalloz, Devillers, Gardner, Lawrence (*Assuming the Burden*), Lawrence and Logevall, Logevall (*Choosing and Embers*), Marr, Patti, Scheer, Statler, and Tønnesson.

3. James Der Derian adds that enumerating past wars provides continuity to these conflicts, but the ex post facto assignment provides a dangerous logic as it justifies war ("War" 254–255).

4. A similar absolving story is told about the war's end in April 1975, though all U.S. combat forces and POWs had been withdrawn from Vietnam by mid-1973.

5. See Walt. For more about American exceptionalism, see Pease.

6. In 1967, the *Pentagon Papers* dismissed the conclusion that American policy during and immediately after World War II was clear in its intents. Instead, the *Papers* asserted, policy was contradictory, simultaneously supporting French colonial possession and also national

self-determination (I.A.A-1). See also Lawrence, *Assuming* and "Forging."

7. Bradley reiterated this charge to tell other stories about the Vietnam wars at the 2018 American History Association meeting. On a panel about the 2017 Ken Burns and Lynn Novick documentary, *The Vietnam War*, Bradley argued that the documentary glosses over "previous U.S. military involvement in Asia and overall framing of the war as a 'tragedy' rather than a series of 'immeasurable and irredeemable' mistakes" (Flaherty).

8. This claim is repeated in many histories but is outlined specifically in Bradley ("Slouching" 19–21, and *Imagining* 59–64).

9. Another often-cited quote reveals Johnson's homophobia: "If I don't go in [to Vietnam] now, and they show later that I should have, they'll push . . . Vietnam up my ass every time" (Herring 439).

10. Archimedes Patti blames French recalcitrance for American involvement with the Viet Minh at the end of World War II: "Had they worked honestly toward the defeat of the Japanese within the Allied framework, it is most doubtful that there would have been any need to resort to a joint military action with the Viet Minh" (188).

11. See Hofstadter for American anti-intellectualism.

12. See also chapter 6 of Tumblety.

13. See chapters 1 through 4 of Cain for a detailed discussion of this period.

14. See Lawrence, "Forging," for postwar British involvement in Indochina. See also chapter 1 of Tønnesson.

15. For "indecisive," see *The Pentagon Papers*, I.A.A-1-5.

16. In *Facing the Abyss: American Literature and Culture in the 1940s*, George Hutchinson says, "The 1940s is not only the vortex of the past century but a period in which literature—especially contemporary American literature—mattered to more people than ever before or since" (7).

17. See also "Secret Blacklist: Untold Story of the USIA" by Scrutineer, which reports that both Hemingway and Thoreau were blacklisted by the USIA.

18. Sussman says the USIA became more conservative in 1970, and its book selection reveals that conservatism: Eugene Burdick and William Lederer's 1958 novel, *The Ugly American* was not accepted for distribution in its libraries (10).

19. See Butterworth and Wallner.

20. See chapter 3 of Belkin, *Bring Me Men*, for more about "penetration."

21. See Reed's October 23, 1946, letter to Moffat and Wallner: "In no other country except Yugoslavia has the program had to be curtailed because of local official opposition."

22. See chapter 2 of Page for a discussion of the distinction during the American war in Vietnam. See also Stephens for a post–World War II discussion of propaganda's uses.

23. For intemperate measures, see Martini on the uses of Agent Orange, Turse (*Kill Anything*) on the uses of "kill anything that moves" operations, and Sheehan and Valentine about the Phoenix Program.

24. The "Afghanistan Papers," troves of documents acquired by the *Washington Post* through a Freedom of Information Act request, indicates so (Whitlock).

25. See Susan Faludi's *Terror Dream* for discussions of gender since 9/11.

2. Staging War

1. In his 2005 recollection about this photograph, Van Es says the building housed senior CIA employees and that the rooftop had been reinforced weeks earlier to support the weight of a helicopter.

2. See also Hass (*Sacrificing*). For more on commemoration, memory, and/or the Vietnam War, see Bodnar, Danto, Doss, Espiritu, Foote, Gillis, Hixson, Nguyen, Senie, Tatum, and Winter and Sivan.

3. The Vietnam Veterans Memorial Fund announced in September 2018 that because it had not been able to raise the funds needed since the center was approved in 2001, it would no longer pursue building the education center but would focus instead on virtual/digital dissemination for its educational mission. See "Vietnam Veterans Memorial Fund."

4. An example of telling the discomfiting stories of the United States' past is the National Memorial for Peace and Justice, dedicated at Montgomery, Alabama, in April 2018 to memorialize stories of lynching in the United States. Its website declares that its founding organization, Equal Justice Initiative, "believes that publicly

confronting the truth about our history is the first step towards recovery and reconciliation." It continues: "A history of racial injustice must be acknowledged, and mass atrocities and abuse must be recognized and remembered, before a society can recover from mass violence. Public commemoration plays a significant role in prompting community-wide reconciliation" (https://eji.org/national-lynching -memorial). Patrick Hagopian echoes this thought in relation to the VVM's discourse of healing and its forwarding by the nation's leaders: "Before forgiveness can be sought, even from oneself, there must be some honest acknowledgement of wrongdoing; otherwise, self-forgiveness is simply a euphemism for absent-minded responsibility. 'Healing' gave a new and superficially attractive cast to the consistent policy of America's postwar leaders, which was to refuse to consider anything to do with U.S. culpability" (*Vietnam* 402). Christian Appy offers a similar evaluation: "If the legacy of the Vietnam War is to offer any guidance, we need to complete the moral and political reckoning it awakened. And if our nation's future is to be less militarized, our empire of foreign military bases scaled back, and our pattern of endless military interventions ended, a necessary first step is to reject—full and finally—the stubborn insistence that our nation has been a unique and unrivaled force for good in the world. Only an honest accounting of our history will allow us to chart a new path in the world" (*Reckoning* xix).

5. Meredith Lair asserts that arguments made for the education center indicate that atonement to Vietnam veterans continues well into the twenty-first century. Given the many stories of the sins against them in a "support the troops" milieu, she cannot foresee a point when there will have been enough atonement (40). David Kieran similarly argues there is "a long-standing revisionist narrative that obscures the imperialist origins of the Vietnam conflict and America's devastation of Vietnam through claims that it was waged for peace and that American soldiers made the primary sacrifices . . . [a narrative] that remains tenuous and must be constantly reasserted" (3).

6. This "new" story became the familiar "band of brothers" myth, a trope Megan Mackenzie unpacks in *Beyond the Band of Brothers* (10).

7. For Reagan's saying the conflict was a noble cause, see his 1980 address to the Veterans of Foreign Wars and his 1988 Veterans Day remarks at the VVM.

8. Lair reports that the educational program initiated by the VVM's founders since 2002 has distributed a free kit of teaching materials to more than 40,000 public and private high schools and middle schools (40). See the VVM Fund's website for its education program: http://www.vvmf.org/teaching-the-vietnam-era. See Hagopian (*Vietnam*) for the widespread discourse that reshaped the narrative about the war since the VVM's beginnings, especially chapters 7 and 11.

9. In a May 2016 personal email from the National Park Service Museum Resource Center, Favorite is told that the archives of objects left at the VVM record "74 objects categorized as Iraq, 12 categorized as Afghanistan, and 22 categorized as both" (201, note 26).

10. See "Items left at the Wall, Catalog number Vive 14944" (http://www.vvmf.org/items/1217/VIVE14944). For more about these objects in the National Park Service's archive, see "Vietnam Veterans Memorial: Collections" (https://www.nps.gov/vive/learn/collections.htm).

11. Documented noncitizens are further assured that their chances of becoming citizens will be enhanced by serving in the U.S. military. See https://www.usa.gov/join-military for details about joining the military as a noncitizen, and https://www.uscis.gov/military/naturalization-through-military-service for information about noncitizen veterans becoming naturalized citizens. For other incentives to joining the U.S. military since the end of the draft in 1973 and the creation of the all-volunteer force, see Mittelstadt (*The Rise*).

12. In today's parlance, these stories might be termed "viral."

13. See Dudziak, who argues that "a confusion about *time* obscures our understanding of contemporary war" (4). Using "wartime" loosely, without clear definition, leads to the indiscriminate imposition and expansion of government power. See also Belew, who in her study of the white power movement as an outgrowth of the Vietnam War, says, "War is not neatly contained in the space and time legitimated by the state. It reverberates in other terrains and lasts long past armistice. It comes home in ways bloody and unexpected" (16).

14. Richard B. Fitzgibbon Jr.'s 1956 death was added to the Wall after its 1982 celebratory opening, or "Salute." See http://thewall-usa.com /names.asp.

15. For Reagan's error, see Hagopian (*Vietnam* 47). For Reagan's first recorded "noble cause" speech, see Reagan, Candidate.

16. Christian Appy makes a similar point: "South Vietnam would not have existed without American intervention. Had the United States committed to self-determination in the mid-1950s it would have honored the Geneva Accords, allowing nationwide elections to reunite Vietnam peacefully" (*Reckoning* 224). See also both of Logevall's books. For American immunity to international law, see Hagopian (*American Immunity*).

17. See Hagopian's discussion of how Americans are depicted in Vietnam War memorials. "In these depictions," Hagopian explains, "Americans are not the agents of violence but its victims. The war is rendered in passive voice" (*Vietnam* 268). The rhetoric of selfless aid also is used in a 1962 booklet designed for American servicemen being sent as "military advisors" to Vietnam, a country distinct from the apparently illegitimate "Communists": "The Vietnamese have paid a heavy price in suffering for their long fight against the Communists. We military men are in Vietnam now because their government has asked us to help its soldiers and people in winning their struggle" (Department of Defense, *Pocket Guide* iii).

18. See chapter 3 of Boyle (*Masculinity*).

19. See Glantz, Kieran and Martini, Sherman, and Simons and Lucaites. See also "Critical Issues Facing Veterans and Military Families" (https://www.samhsa.gov/veterans-military-families/critical-issues).

20. Hagopian comments that by 1979, most veterans thought the U.S. government had prevented them from winning the war. According to a 1980 Harris poll that Hagopian cites, "At least some of the veteran respondents must have believed two mutually exclusive ideas: that politicians prevented them from winning the war, and that the war could never have been won. Both exonerate veterans from responsibility for the outcome of the war" (*Vietnam* 31). Sturken also comments on exoneration ("Wall" 130).

21. In *Dispatches*, Michael Herr remarks that as a correspondent he was permitted to go to wherever he could hitch a ride. For more about media in wartime, see Belknap.

22. See "Reagan, Candidate" for the United States on not being permitted to win. See Kalb 197–198 for a list of reasons for why the war was lost.

23. See Espiritu and Nguyen for analyses of this focus on American victimhood and neglect of Vietnamese and Vietnamese American suffering. See Schwenkel and Tatum for analyses of commemoration in Vietnam.

24. This erroneous idea that the Vietnam War was the United States' most tragic is repeatedly objected to by professors of American history, who recount often that if their students think anything about the war, it concerns this tragedy. See Lair and Savage ("Education Center"). Hagopian repeats this accounting: "Only two-thirds of a March 1990 national poll sample recalled that the United States was fighting on the side of South Vietnam. Irrespective of the shakiness of the public's knowledge of this basic fact, the Vietnam syndrome appeared to be alive and well in the public's inflated sense of the costs of Vietnam compared with other American wars: a plurality believed that more Americans lost their lives in Vietnam than in any other war" (*Vietnam* 262).

25. See Doubek generally for the evolution of "recognition" into "healing." As one of the VVMF's founders, Doubek explains: "While some Vietnam veterans truly needed more benefits, most didn't. What all did need, however, was some recognition and acknowledgement of their service in war" (7).

26. See Daddis for more about the American experience in Vietnam.

27. See Hess (121), Hagopian (*Vietnam* 79–83), and the 1988 made-for-TV-movie about Scruggs, *To Heal a Nation*. Throughout his memoir, VVMF cofounder Robert Doubek refers to Scruggs in derogatory terms: a "lone wolf" (5); having a "cocky attitude" (11); being naive about fundraising (13) and public announcements (29); being inept and disorganized (32); of being "often reckless . . . and would have to be protected from himself" (45); of Scruggs's indiscretion (38, 71, 132, 196); and being "dumb" (111). At the same time, Doubek says Scruggs had a "magic touch" in getting the buy-in of "major player[s]" (25) and made

good public relations copy (96). Although it could be said that Doubek's own class, ethnic, racial, and gender-based insecurities lead him to these interpretations, his conclusion that the press "lionized" Scruggs is not disputable (242).

28. Another problem is that the memorial permits its viewers to forget (or never to know) that the United States was only one of many allies of the southern part of Vietnam during what is known as the Vietnam War, a group that included South Korea, Australia, New Zealand, the Philippines, Taiwan, and Thailand. Many of the Vietnamese from the south became refugees to the United States after 1975, and though they want to be included in commemoration, have most often been prevented. See Nguyen (194–198), Espiritu, and Tran for accounts of these efforts.

29. See Hagopian's discussion of the contradictions in Carter's speech (*Vietnam* 90–92).

30. See Hagopian (*Vietnam*), Doubek, and Scruggs and Swerdlow.

31. Once the National Park Service assumed control of the VVM following its 1982 celebratory opening, it and the VVMF agreed that "it should not be used for political demonstrations or for commercial activities" (Hagopian, *Vietnam* 193). "Political" never has been fully defined, however, and so some voices have been permitted and others have not.

32. As a structure that commemorates the Vietnam War's dead and its surviving veterans, the VVM may be trying to be both memorial and monument.

33. On silencing, see Appy, "Muffling"; Berlant, introduction and chapter 1; and Pease, chapter 1.

34. See Hass (*Carried*) for a full analysis of objects left at the Wall. See the National Park Service regulations on objects (https://www.nps.gov /vive/learn/collections.htm). Notably, the regulations prohibit the leaving or spreading of human remains.

35. See Savage ("Education Center"): "Official speakers at the wall have used it as a platform to defend the war and the military more generally."

36. In an odd echo of Obama's "Presidential Proclamation: Commemoration of the Fiftieth Anniversary of the Vietnam War," on Veterans Day 2017, President Trump issued a "Presidential Proclamation

Commemorating the Fiftieth Anniversary of the Vietnam War." In this proclamation, Trump announced that hereafter March 29 will be National Vietnam Veterans Day. As did Bush and Obama, Trump recited the truisms initiated by Reagan. See "Presidential Proclamation."

37. Obama's proclamation clarifies two points: First, the 2012–2025 program of events primarily is to "pay tribute to the more than 3 million servicemen and women who left their families to serve bravely . . . fighting heroically to protect the ideals we hold dear as Americans." Even clearer is the program's intent to remember these valiant heroes in relation to 1975, the starting point of "the fiftieth anniversary," when in April the North Vietnamese army completed its push south into Saigon and drew to a close the Second Indochina War. See "The United States of America Vietnam War Commemoration (http://www.vietnamwar50th.com) for the program events.

38. See "Vietnam Veterans Memorial Fund Changes Direction" (https://www.vvmf.org/News/Vietnam-Veterans-Memorial-Fund-changes-direction-of-Education-Center-campaign/)for the amount of money that was raised and the center's revised aims. See Senie (37–39) and Favorite (198, note 3) for details about legislative attempts to authorize the center.

39. See Hass (*Sacrificing*) for more about memory on the National Mall: "In fact, on the Mall in the recent past it is almost as if once we *gesture* toward memory, we divest ourselves of the obligation to remember what actually happened" (9).

40. See Favorite (202, note 44) for a list of Content Advisory Committee members as of 2016.

41. Senie refers to these moves as tactics of "diversion and denial" (171).

3. Lone Wolf Family Man

1. The U.S. government also perpetuates this autobardolatry through the Library of Congress's "Veterans History Project," specifically its "memoir toolkit" at http://www.loc.gov/vets/memoirkit.html. Additional sites encouraging veterans' storytelling include the *Journal of Veterans Studies* (https://journals.colostate.edu/jvs); the Veterans

Writing Project (https://veteranswriting.org); the Wrath-Bearing Tree podcast (https://soundcloud.com/user-449758953); the Military Writers Society of America (http://www.mwsadispatches.com); the Veterans Writing Workshop (http://veteranswritingworkshop.org/index.html); Warrior Writers (http://www.warriorwriters.org); and a 2018 competition, "Untold Stories," hosted by *Flyaway: Journal of Writing and Environment* that was only for veterans and their families (https://flyway.submittable.com/submit/107333/untold-stories-contest-2018). Publishing houses also promote stories of and by veterans. See, for instance, the new University of Massachusetts Press series "Veterans," whose monographs "explore the lived experiences of military veterans."

2. See also Cowen, who asserts that the basis for the all-volunteer force, neoliberalism, rejects collectivism (169–170).

3. In *Bring Me Men*, Aaron Belkin outlines how contradictions in military culture confuse the troops, thereby sustaining compliance (4). For the militarization of U.S. culture, see Brooks, Bacevich (*New American*), and Dudziak. For gender, see Boyle (*Masculinity*), Brittan, Butler (*Gender*), Combe and Boyle, Connell and Messerschmidt, Faludi, Goldstein, Halberstam, Kimmel, and Phillips (*War!*).

4. The intersection of individualism, collectivism, national character, and gender is explored most in the field of cultural psychology. For examples of research studies, see Fischer et al.; Forbes et al.; Hamamura; Kashima et al.; Omi; Twenge, Campbell, and Gentile; and Vargas and Kemmelmeier.

5. See Chapman, Dwyer, Eberwein, Huebner, Hynes, McLoughlin, Peebles, Ray, and Vernon for discussions of the war story genre.

6. See Bederman and Mann for more on the difference between "manhood" and "masculinity."

7. In "The Red and the Blue," Brian Van Reet characterizes these two memoirs as "red" books. He distinguishes between "red" and "blue" in this way: "Red war books do better in the marketplace because they offer the type of war story that most appeals to red demographic groups that tend to outnumber the blue readers who are specifically and highly interested in war. Will your average military history buff pick up a book of somewhat oblique literary fiction about veterans

failing to re-acclimate to civilian life, or will he be more interested in a straightforward book offering incredible real-life heroics during World War II? I'd say for that type of reader, it'll be the book of heroes, most times. Additionally, there is some evidence that the red/blue political divide in America correlates to levels of empathy, which is relevant to the selection of war literature. Red war readers generally don't want to feel your pain: they want to feel the pain as it is doled out on the battlefield to terrorist enemies who, by the end of the story, will be found twitching on the floor. Meanwhile, for sensitive blue readers, ongoing real wars may be too painful a subject to want to sit with for the length of a book, fictional or not. They may feel like the nightly news is enough, and they can barely stand to watch that anymore."

8. The "lone wolf family man" can be seen as a composite of Robert Ray's "outlaw" and "official" heroes, outlined in *A Certain Tendency*.

9. As Philip Dwyer says about war memoirists, "All put pen to paper in the knowledge that they have lived through, and survived, something extraordinary, that they have been part of a larger historical moment. The memoirist does not, however, set out to write history, but to give a privileged point of view, a personal perspective of what has been witnessed, experienced, and suffered" (4).

10. See Boyle ("Rescuing Masculinity").

11. See chapter 5 of Stahl (*Through the Crosshairs*) for a discussion of the "sniper vision" in the film *American Sniper*.

12. See Butler (*Frames of War*) for a discussion of whose lives deserve to be "grievable."

13. In his analysis of *American Sniper*, Lennart Soberon rebuts the screenwriter's claim that the story is about an individual, not war or politics (para. 2).

14. See Combe and Boyle for analyses of masculinity and monstrosity in Hollywood films.

15. Michael Boughn outlines how both films (and another, *Fury*) adhere to or defy the war film genre: "As much as these three films are alike, or at least close, in their treatment of war, and in the conventions they mobilise, they are infinitely different in their attention to and disposition of those conventions" (70).

4. Military Judgment in a Neoliberal Age

1. In his history of the U.S. military draft, George Flynn refers to "the myth of egalitarianism" that says "the draft should offer no class or group deferments, and no substitutes or bounties should be allowed" (6). For more about recruiting, see Segal.

2. The institutions and 2017 levels of "great deal/quite a lot" of confidence include (1) church or organized religion (41 percent); (2) Supreme Court (40 percent); (3) Congress (12 percent); (4) organized labor (28 percent); (5) big business (21 percent); (6) public schools (36 percent); (7) newspapers (27 percent); (8) military (72 percent); (9) presidency (32 percent); (10) medical system (37 percent); (11) banks (32 percent); (12) television news (24 percent); (13) police (57 percent); (14) criminal justice system (27 percent); (15) small business (70 percent); (16) news on the internet (16 percent); (17) health maintenance organizations (19 percent).

3. See Woodruff and Kelty about sacrifice. See also Hass (*Sacrificing Soldiers*).

4. The Pew Research Center report "Six Facts" says that 0.4 percent of the U.S. population serves in the active-duty military (see Parker et al.). Two items in the December 2018 *Harper's Magazine* "*Harper's* Index" indicate this American peculiarity: "Chance that an American believes that all members of the armed services should be described as heroes: 1 in 2; That a German does: 1 in 7." See "*Harper's* Index."

5. See Stachowitsch, who, for instance, explains that even in the last several decades, the media representation of women in the armed forces has varied widely, depending on the political makeup of Congress, whether or not the military is downsizing or upsizing, and whether there is a military intervention. "Military women," she concludes, "predominantly become an issue in the media when it serves the positive portrayal of the nation, the military, and the current war effort" (132). Furthermore, this vacillation between accepting and rejecting women has been mitigated by private military companies, "a new male-dominated military labor market . . . which is largely uncontrolled by the state" (133).

6. See Wendt (*Warring over Valor*).

7. According to Parker et al., in 2017, the U.S. Army constituted 36 percent of the active-duty armed forces.

8. Still, according to 2015 data, approximately 20 percent of active duty personnel qualify as obese and over 50 percent as overweight. See Copp.

9. For information about disqualifying factors for enlistment, see Bailey (*America's Army* 253), Haltiwanger, and "Too Fat to Fight: Military Threatened by Childhood Obesity." For the numbers of potentially eligible Americans as of July 2017, see United States Census Bureau and Frey. For research on who enlists and who goes to college, see Kleykamp.

10. As Beth Bailey argues in the introduction to Bristol and Stur's *Integrating the US Military*, though U.S. courts have judged that military mission takes precedence over some individual rights, "military policies are fundamentally important to broader struggles for civil rights" (4).

11. For Army leaders in 2018, enlistment and re-enlistment bonuses were a primary means of populating the service. See Myers.

12. For instance, see Bacevich (*Breach of Trust*).

13. Military statistics complicate this conclusion. According to "Population Representation," the majority of enlisted personnel come from the middle three of five income quintiles of the American population: "In FY16, for example, virtually all [enlisted recruits] were high school diploma graduates, and high school dropout rates are higher in low-income neighborhoods. . . . The military actually gets the largest proportion of its recruits from the middle three quintiles" (20–21). Interestingly, 44 percent of recruits come from the Census Bureau–defined southern region, which includes the South Atlantic, East South Central, and West South Central division states. See also Savell and McMahon, "Numbers and per capita distribution of troops serving in the U.S. post-9/11 wars in 2019, by state," which concludes that South Carolina, Hawaii, Florida, and Georgia send the most troops, per capita, to war.

14. See Wendt ("Instrument of Subjugation").

15. See Kimberley Phillips 278: "A recession became the recruiters' best marketing tool." This rise is especially notable because Bailey reports a

precipitous drop in the enlistments of "black youth" consequent to the 2001 and 2003 wars in Afghanistan and Iraq (229).

16. This percentage was the Army quota established in the 1930s (Kimberley Phillips 22).

17. See Yockelson, and Nalty and MacGregor 73–102.

18. See also Maxwell, who draws a line between integration of African Americans in the military during the war in Korea and discrimination against them: "Segregation might have been dealt its final blow through the experience of combat in Korea, but that did not mean discrimination did not persist within the military" (155).

19. See also Skaine (*Women*).

20. These steps in the Army include longer maternity leaves, more women trained as recruiters, and an increase in the number of female corps members at West Point.

21. According to Stachowitsch, the military and civilian labor markets have become much more technologically oriented. Thus, "changing patterns of gender-specific division of labor in civilian and military sectors . . . [have] changed recruitment conditions and led to competition between civilian and military employers for qualified personnel. Selective integration of women became necessary in the face of recruitment shortages. . . . Because of discrimination against women in the civilian sector, female personnel are cheaper and on average better qualified" (3–4).

22. Webb was a graduate of the Naval Academy, served in the Vietnam War, and has occupied many governmental positions, including secretary of the Navy. He was also vocally opposed to Maya Lin's design for the Vietnam Veterans Memorial (Hagopian, *Vietnam War* 106–108). In 2015, Webb sought the Democratic nomination for president.

23. Despite this attitude, Webb subsequently was given positions of authority over and responsibility for these women in the federal government, most notably as the secretary of the Navy in the Reagan administration.

24. This series of comments by Trump are particularly insensitive, following as they do the release of 2012's documentary about sexual assault in the military: *The Invisible War*. The comments suggest at the very least ambivalence about women in the military. As Kelly Oliver

asserts in *Women as Weapons of War*, "Even as the presence of women in the military seems to signal their 'liberation' from patriarchal traditions, the rhetoric surrounding their involvement betrays the lingering association between women, sexuality, and death" (19).

25. Charles Moskos, noted military sociologist, is quoted in Frank (*Unfriendly Fire*) as arguing that the natural compassion of women would be "a hindrance in combat, where the worst instincts in soldiers must be aroused" (125).

26. See Ables, who argues in response to MacDonald's inflammatory essay in the *Wall Street Journal*, "Changing a culture is never without headache or heartache. Racial integration of the Army was not easy, either—it had more than its fair share of stutters and missteps, from social isolation to all-black units to segregated facilities. But flawed standards and imperfect implementation are not good reasons to scrap worthy policies. We should not penalize a capable and competent minority of women because the majority may not be qualified to serve in combat arms units; instead, let's fix the real problem so that *all* of our combat forces adhere to a higher standard."

27. Mackenzie also contends that the band-of-brothers myth has been used to exclude from the military African Americans and people who identify as gay: "The band of brothers, then, is not simply a myth about an all-male unit; it is a myth about a white, heterosexual man and his nonsexual bonds with his comrades" (15).

28. For more on "cohesion," especially at the Naval Academy, see Burke. See also Frank 128–134.

29. Frank cites the first discharge for sodomy as 1778 (1–3).

30. See Frank, chapter 1, "The Long History of the Military Closet." See also Haggerty 12–14.

31. See Lehring, chapter 1, "What Is an Official Gay Identity?" (9–33).

32. Aaron Belkin says that the military's judgment on this point is about morality, not its usual invocation of "unit cohesion" ("Politics of Paranoia" 77).

33. Haggerty describes the Cold War fears underlying this supposition as the "'commie-pinko-queer' syndrome," whose tenets were that "homosexuals were secretive and pervasive and had infiltrated key positions in the government and civilian life" (19).

34. See Hall.

35. Frank says that in the 1980s, women made up 25 percent of force-wide discharges for homosexuality (when 10 percent of the forces) and one-third of those discharged from the Marines (11). Linda Bird Francke reports a similar targeting (176–181). For histories of gays and lesbians in U.S. culture, see Abelove, Barale and Halperin; Bérubé; D'Emilio and Freedman; Estes; Lehring; Parco and Levy; Scott and Stanley; and Shilts.

36. For sources addressing DADT, see especially Belkin and Bateman; Parco and Levy; and "Report of the Department of Defense Working Group."

37. See Lee, "Comprehensive Review Working Group" for a description of the process leading to repeal.

38. The report informing the repeal of DADT notes that in regard to the integration of African Americans and women into the armed forces, the Department of Defense was forced despite resisting such change. See Lee 175–176.

39. Wells-Petry concludes: "The profession of arms is unlike any other. It is not a profession of individual aspiration, nor is it a profession of social pro-action. In evaluating military personnel policies or decisions about the composition of the armed forces, the touchstone cannot be how the policy or decision furthers the interest of the individual or the enlightenment of society at large" (187).

40. See Belkin et al. 587 and that document's note 3.

41. See Goldich for more on this gap and its echo of Bailey's caution about the civilian-military gap: "The U.S. military has become the shield behind which civilian society can hold fast to its pacifist views about the absolute supremacy of kindness and compassion. The entire military, in turn, not just the career force, has become a refuge for those who question the basic orientation of civilian society and do not wish to live within many of its central boundaries. There appears to be a gap—if not a chasm—between an increasingly sensate, amiable, and emotionally narrow civilian world and a flinty, harshly results-oriented, and emotionally extreme military, for career and non-career personnel alike" (Bailey, *America's Army* 68).

42. See Parco et al. 238. See also Harrison-Quintana and Herman, who point out that until July 2015, transgender people had been medically disqualified from employment in the U.S. military (2).

43. For research supporting the open service of transgender people, see Elders et al.; Parco, Levy, and Spears; Quam; and Schaefer et al. For documents not supporting this open service, see "Department of Defense Report and Recommendations" and Center for Military Readiness, "Trump Transgender Policy."

5. The Soldier's Creed

1. These four lines in the creed—"I will always place the mission first. I will never accept defeat. I will never quit. I will never leave a fallen comrade"—constitute the "Warrior Ethos."

2. This and several other creeds can be found at "Army Values." (https://www.army.mil/values/soldiers.html): NCO, Ranger, and Army Civilian Corp. The 2003 "Soldier's Creed" replaced this post–Vietnam War creed (Bailey 248–249):

   I am an American Soldier. I am a member of the United States Army—a protector of the greatest nation on earth. Because I am proud of the uniform I wear, I will always act in ways creditable to the military service and the nation it is sworn to guard. I am proud of my own organization. I will do all I can to make it the finest unit in the Army. I will be loyal to those under whom I serve. I will do my full part to carry out orders and instructions given to me or my unit. As a soldier, I realize that I am a member of a time-honored profession—that I am doing my share to keep alive the principles of freedom for which my country stands. No matter what the situation I am in, I will never do anything, for pleasure, profit, or personal safety, which will disgrace my uniform, my unit, or my country. I will use every means I have, even beyond the line of duty, to restrain my Army comrades from actions disgraceful to themselves and to the uniform. I am proud of my country and its flag. I will try to make the people of this nation proud of the service I represent, for I am an American Soldier.

Note at least two differences: "warrior" does not appear in the pre-2003 version, suggesting a post–Iraq War rhetorical adjustment; and the insinuation that a service member could behave disgracefully is erased. In *America's Army*, Bailey suggests that the 2003 creed makes clear the Army's departure from "an army that defined its purpose as the provision of social good" (249).

3. See Haerens for a timeline of the NFL protests.

4. See Curran. Snopes says about this practice that "what actually changed in 2009, according to NFL spokesman Brian McCarthy, was that (due to network timing issues) players had previously remained in their locker rooms during the playing of the national anthem for *primetime* games. After 2009, players appeared in the sidelines for the anthem during primetime games, just as they had been doing all along for Sunday afternoon games." See Garcia. See also an interview (McNicoll and Schreiber) with sports journalist and professor Kevin Blackistone, who says, "The [Colin] Kaepernick thing wouldn't be an issue had the NFL not—in 2009—decided to make the anthem a part of the 'theater,' and demanded that players be on the sideline for the anthem and flying of the flag. That was a conscious political decision by the NFL."

5. This can explain the adulation of Pat Tillman, an Arizona Cardinals NFL player who left his team in 2002 to volunteer for service in the U.S. Army Rangers and who was killed by friendly fire while deployed to Afghanistan in 2004. See Boyle, "The Tillman Story."

6. See Kilgore for an outline of the relationship between the NFL, the American military, and American patriotism. Also, it is clear that there is no single form of patriotism; it may be more a process than a condition. See Liu and Hanauer, and McCann.

7. Such a financial turn risks transforming the teams and the players into mercenaries, anathema to Americans who want to see their warrior patriots as self-sacrificing (see Hass, *Sacrificing*). Yet modern mercenaries constitute a "multibillion-dollar industry" that likely will grow in the "security vacuum left by US forces" (McFate xiii).

8. William Astore implicates professional sports for the development of warrior patriotism through the reverence for service people: "In conjunction with the military and marketed by corporations,

[professional sports] have reshaped the very practice of patriotism in America" ("Why Can't We").

9. Indeed, Trump's outrage at a professional athlete's not behaving as he expects when the national anthem is played was not directed at soccer player Megan Rapinoe. While Trump called her behavior inappropriate, he did not demand that she be punished for it. The degree of his outrage seems to be connected to "the economics of it," or the financial value of a player's activity. That is, a player's duty to play the role of warrior patriot is relative to that player's financial compensation and the income he or she generates for the team's owners. One might ask if Trump's conception of appropriate player behavior is a form of "paid patriotism." See Russell.

10. Since at least 2008, to call military service members "warriors" is contentious. See Kosuta for an outline of the debate.

11. In "Warmaking as the American Way of Life," Catherine Lutz says the military "has helped to define true manhood and true womanhood and has suggested that certain values that are championed in the military—discipline, loyalty, courage, respect for authority among them—are ultimately American values and superior to other kinds" (53).

12. See Lucaites and Simons, "Introduction," where they claim, "By seeing struggle and victory on the athletic 'battlefield,' publics are invited to *not* see what cannot be seen because it is not there: victory on the battlefield of war" (6). "Kinetic" warfare is a euphemism for combat first used in 2002. See Noah.

13. The gendering of these names is evident when "Lady" is appended for girls' and women's teams, e.g. "Lady Wildcats," "Lady Warriors," "Lady Patriots."

14. See "Patriot" for more about the missile system.

15. Andrew Bacevich ("Playing Ball") names "support the troops" a central tenet of "America's civic religion," and William Astore ("Whatever Happened") calls it "the cult of the soldier." For "warrior ethos," see Bailey (*America's Army* 226–260). See also *Spy Culture* for a discussion of dying in combat as a religious sacrifice.

16. In 2015, the Obama administration limited the distribution of military materiel to local police forces. In August 2017, the Trump administration lifted those limits, calling the concerns about distribution of

war-making equipment "superficial." See Goldman. See also Asken and Grossman's *Warrior Mindset*, a tome that teaches police forces to embrace acting and thinking as warriors. (Grossman's distinction between sheep, sheepdogs, and wolves is also featured in this book's chapter 3, "Lone Wolf Family Man.")

17. In 2003, Norman Mailer cautioned that the ubiquity of the military in American life may lead to democracy's demise: "Democracy is the special condition—a condition we will be called upon to defend in the coming years. That will be enormously difficult because the combination of the corporation, the military, and the complete investiture of the flag with mass spectator sports has set up a pre-fascistic atmosphere in America already." See Mailer.

18. See Deshpande for President Trump's claim that his controversial July 4, 2019, spectacle would produce a "big spike" in recruitment. For sources about the conjoining of visuality and war, see Bousquet, Favret, Kozol, Stahl (*Militainment* and *Through the Crosshairs: Reading the Weaponized Gaze* (book and film), and Simons and Lucaites.

19. For more on framing, see Apel, Butler (*Frames*), Der Derian ("War"), Stahl (*Through the Crosshairs: War*), and Steuter and Wills.

20. Recruitment budgets include not only advertising but also items such as recruiting personnel and reenlistment bonuses. James Long reports that these exponentially increasing budgets are not sustainable, nor do they contribute to enhancing military capabilities.

21. These videos with media information can be found online at iSpot.tv.

22. See Bousquet, Kline et al., Parkin, and Virilio.

23. See also Stahl's film, *Through the Crosshairs: Reading the Weaponized Gaze*.

24. See Stahl, "Digital War" (145–146) for a brief overview of these approaches and the theorists propounding them.

25. See Stewart for a complete list of the *Call of Duty* franchise.

26. In *Extra Lives: Why Video Games Matter*, Tom Bissell titles a chapter "The Grammar of Fun." He explains the title thus: "Bleszinski and the other Epic designers came to this form as children. Growing up playing [video] games, they absorbed the governing logic of the medium, but no institutions existed for them to transfer what they learned into a methodology. Gradually, though, they turned a hobby

into a creative profession that is now as complex as any other. I realized, watching them, that part of what they had done [in developing more games] was help to establish the principles of one grammar of fun" (63).

27. According to Andrew Whalen in "'Call of Duty: Modern Warfare' Rewrites the Highway of Death as a Russian Attack, Rather Than American," an "infamous attack" during the first Gulf War conducted by U.S. forces is rewritten to feature Russian forces. Tom Secker calls this "propaganda," both of the players and about Russians.

28. See "The Army Values" at https://www.army.mil/values/.

29. Bissell problematizes this binaristic thinking: "When I am being entertained [by watching television or a film, or reading a novel], I am also being manipulated. I am *allowing* myself to be manipulated. I am, in other words, surrendering. . . . Playing video games is not quite like this. The surrender is always partial. You get control and are controlled. . . . I *want* to be told a story—albeit one I happen to be part of and can affect, even if in small ways. If I wanted to *tell* a story, I would not be playing video games" (38–40).

30. See a pair of 2019 articles discussing when disobedience in the U.S. military is called for: Milburn; Cohn, Margulies, and Robinson.

31. The Wikipedia entry for *America's Army* says that in 2003, after the Army took control of the game from the Naval Postgraduate School, it contracted with a software developer to "reach a wider and younger audience."

32. In *How to Raise an American*, Blyth and Winston are explicit about the need for parents to develop American patriots when they are young, before the children know otherwise and before they are overly influenced by their formal educations: "After all, it is part of our responsibility as Americans and as parents to teach our kids what this nation stands for. To teach them to be grateful for all our country gives to her own people and to people around the world. To teach them about the heroes and the history that will make our children proud to be Americans once again" (6). The authors cite religion, immigration, and armed service as the primary models of "good Americans" (53), and they encourage parents in the "The Patriot Pledge" to raise their children as "informed and loyal citizens" (126). See also the Grossman,

Rogish, and Karwal children's book, *Sheepdogs: Meet Our Nation's Warriors.*

Coda

1. A December 10, 2019, Reuters report about pending legislation to pass the 2020 National Defense Authorization Act says that the legislation had passed for fifty-eight straight years (Zengerle).
2. For more on this issue, see Cockburn, "Follow the Money."
3. This essay also appears in Wheeler, entitled, "Why Is This Handbook Necessary?"
4. On the Pentagon's inability to pass its first audit, see Ali and Stone.
5. See "The Chief Financial Officers Act" at https://www.gao.gov/special .pubs/af12194.pdf.
6. This budget figure does not include the "Overseas Contingency Operations" fund, first appropriated in 2001 as a supplement. According to the Congressional Budget Office, this "funding peaked at 28 percent of DoD's budget in 2007 and 2008. From 2001 to 2018, it has averaged about $116 billion per year (in 2019 dollars), totaling about 20 percent of DoD's total funding." Furthermore, "more than $50 billion in OCO funding per year (in 2019 dollars), on average, has gone toward the costs of enduring activities rather than the temporary costs of overseas operations." The report states that the Trump administration intends to roll what has heretofore been a supplement into the base budget, thereby increasing the budget rather than reducing it. See the Congressional Budget Office, "Funding for Overseas Contingency Operations and its Impact on Defense Spending" at https://www.cbo .gov/publication/54219.
7. Taibbi also cites Senator Bernie Sanders, independent of Vermont, as a driver for reform.
8. See Steuter and Wills for the use of infestation rhetoric to demonize enemies in war.
9. This report includes post-9/11 conflicts in Iraq, Afghanistan, Pakistan, Syria, Yemen, and "other."
10. See "Congressional Research Service." Note that these numbers do not include private military contractors, whose statistics are not publicly

available. The "Costs of War" report, however, derives an approximate number of "U.S. contractors" fatalities from various sources as of October 2019: 7,950 deaths (note 13). See https://watson.brown.edu /costsofwar/files/cow/imce/papers/2019/Direct%20War%20Deaths%20 COW%20Estimate%20November%2013%202019%20FINAL.pdf.

11. At least one critic of the report claims it is untrue: "The story the *Post* is telling is neither wholly true, nor supported by the documents it published. Instead, the *Post*'s reporting puts sensationalist spin on information that was not classified, has already been described in publicly-available reports, only covers a fraction of the 18 years of the war, and falls far short of convincingly demonstrating a campaign of deliberate lies and deceit" (Schroden).

Works Cited

Abelove, Henry, Michèle Aina Barale, and David M. Halperin. *The Lesbian and Gay Studies Reader*. Routledge, 1993.

Ables, Micah. "Women Aren't the Problem. Standards Are." *Modern War Institute at West Point*, February 5, 2019, https://mwi.usma.edu/women -arent-problem-standards/. Accessed July 28, 2019.

Abramson, Daniel. "Maya Lin and the 1960s: Monuments, Time Lines, and Minimalism." *Critical Inquiry*, vol. 22, no. 4, Summer 1996, pp. 679–709.

Aldrich, Robert. "Colonial Wars." *French Masculinities: History, Culture and Politics*, edited by Christopher E. Forth and Bertrand Taithe, London: Palgrave Macmillan, 2007, pp. 123–140.

Ali, Idrees, and Mike Stone. "Pentagon Fails Its First-Ever Audit, Official Says." *Reuters*, November 15, 2018, https://www.reuters.com/article/us -usa-pentagon-audit/pentagon-fails-its-first-ever-audit-official-says -idUSKCN1NK2MC. Accessed August 17, 2019.

Allen, Frederick Lewis. "Must We Tell the World?" *Harper's Magazine*, December 1945, pp. 553–559.

"America's Army." *Wikipedia*, June 17, 2019, https://en.wikipedia.org/wiki /America%27s_Army#America%27s_Army:_Proving_Grounds. Accessed June 21, 2019.

American Sniper. Directed by Clint Eastwood, performances by Bradley Cooper, Sienna Miller, Luke Grimes. Warner Brothers, 2014.

Anderegg, Michael, ed. *Inventing Vietnam: The War in Film and Television*. Temple UP, 1991.

Anderson, Warwick. "The Trespass Speaks: White Masculinity and Colonial Breakdown." *American Historical Review*, vol. 102, no. 5, December 1997, pp. 1343–1370.

Anderton, Lillian D. "USIS Libraries: A Branch of USIA." *Peabody Journal of Education*, vol. 45, no. 2, September 1967, pp. 114–120.

Apel, Dora. *War Culture and the Contest of Images*. Rutgers University Press, 2012.

Appy, Christian G. *American Reckoning: The Vietnam War and Our National Identity*. Viking, 2015.

———. "The Muffling of Public Memory in Post-Vietnam America." *Chronicle of Higher Education*, February 12, 1999, p. B4.

———, ed. *Cold War Constructions: The Political Culture of United States Imperialism, 1945–1966*. U of Mass P, 2000.

"Army Demographics: FY16 Army Profile." *U.S. Army*, https://m.goarmy .com/content/dam/goarmy/downloaded_assets/pdfs/advocates -demographics.pdf. Accessed July 28, 2019.

Asken, Michael J. and Dave Grossman. *Warrior Mindset: Mental Toughness Skills for a Nation's Peacekeepers*. E-book, Killology Research Group, 2011.

Astore, William. "Whatever Happened to Gary Cooper? A Seven-Step Program to Return America to a Quieter, Less Muscular, Patriotism." *TomDispatch*, September 3, 2009. http://www.tomdispatch.com/blog /175134. Accessed May 21, 2019.

———. "Why Can't We Just Play Ball? The Militarization of Sports and the Redefinition of Patriotism." *TomDispatch*, August 19, 2018, http://www.tomdispatch.com/blog/176459/tomgram%3A_william _astore%2C_make_sports%2C_not_war/. Accessed May 16, 2019.

Axe, David. "*America's Army* Comic: Bad Recruiting Tool, Worse Story." *Wired*, July 14, 2012, https://www.wired.com/2012/07/americas-army -comic-con/. Accessed June 22, 2019.

Bacevich, Andrew J. *Breach of Trust: How Americans Failed Their Soldiers and Their Country*. Henry Holt, 2013.

———. *The New American Militarism: How Americans Are Seduced by War*. 2005. New York: Oxford UP, 2013.

———. "Playing Ball with the Pentagon." *Nation*, July 28, 2011, https:// www.thenation.com/article/playing-ball-pentagon/. Accessed May 17, 2019.

Bailey, Beth. *America's Army: Making the All-Volunteer Force*. Harvard UP, 2009.

———. Introduction to *Integrating the US Military: Race, Gender, and Sexual Orientation since World War II*, edited by Douglas Walter Bristol Jr. and Heather Marie Stur, Johns Hopkins UP, 2017, pp. 1–9.

Barnhisel, Greg, and Catherine C. Turner, eds. *Pressing the Fight: Print, Propaganda, and the Cold War*. U of Mass P, 2010.

Barnhisel, Greg, and Catherine Turner. Introduction to *Pressing the Fight: Print, Propaganda, and the Cold War*, edited by Greg Barnhisel and Catherine C. Turner, U of Mass P, 2010, pp. 1–28.

Basinger, Jeanine. "The World War II Combat Film: Definition." *The War Film*, edited by Robert Eberwein, Rutgers University Press, 2005, pp. 30–52.

Bederman, Gail. *Manliness and Civilization: A Cultural History of Gender and Race in the United States, 1880–1917*. U of Chicago P, 1995.

Belew, Kathleen. *Bring the War Home: The White Power Movement and Paramilitary America*. Harvard UP, 2018.

Belkin, Aaron. *Bring Me Men: Military Masculinity and the Benign Façade of American Empire, 1898–2001*. Columbia UP, 2012.

———. "The Politics of Paranoia." *Evolution of Government Policy towards Homosexuality in the U.S. Military*, edited by James E. Parco and David A. Levy, New York: Routledge, 2014, pp. 73–77.

Belkin, Aaron, and Geoffrey Bateman, eds. *Don't Ask, Don't Tell: Debating the Gay Ban in the Military*. Boulder, CO: Lynne Rienner Publishers, 2003.

Belkin, Aaron, et al. "Readiness and DADT Repeal: Has the Policy of Open Service Undermined the Military?" *Armed Forces and Society*, vol. 39, no. 4, 2012, pp. 587–601.

Belknap, M. H. *The CNN Effect: Strategic Enabler or Operational Risk?* US Army War College Strategy Research Paper, 2001.

Berlant, Lauren. *The Queen of America Goes to Washington City*. Duke UP, 1997.

Berlatsky, Noah. "The Feminist Objection to Women in Combat." *Atlantic*, January 25, 2013, https://www.theatlantic.com/sexes/archive/2013/01/the-feminist-objection-to-women-in-combat/272505/. Accessed August 16, 2019.

Bérubé, Allan. *Coming Out under Fire: Gay Men and Women in World War Two*. New York: Penguin, 1990.

Bissell, Tom. *Extra Lives: Why Video Games Matter*. New York: Pantheon, 2010.

Blyth, Myrna, and Chriss Winston. *How to Raise an American: 1776 Fun and Easy Tools, Tips, and Activities to Help Your Child Love This Country*. New York: Three Rivers P, 2007.

Bodnar, John. *Remaking America: Public Memory, Commemoration, and Patriotism in the Twentieth Century*. Princeton UP, 1992.

Boughn, Michael. "Reconfiguring Conventions in Three Recent War Films." *Cineaction*, vol. 98, 2016, pp. 69–76.

Bousquet, Antoine. *The Eye of War: Military Perception from the Telescope to the Drone*. U of Minn P, 2018.

Box Office MoJo. American Sniper. http://www.boxofficemojo.com/movies /?id=americansniper.htm. Accessed September 19, 2017.

Box Office MoJo. Lone Survivor. http://www.boxofficemojo.com/movies/?id =lonesurvivor.htm. Accessed September 19, 2017.

Boyle, Brenda M. *Masculinity in Vietnam War Narratives: A Critical Study of Fiction, Films, and Nonfiction Writings*. McFarland, 2009.

———. "Rescuing Masculinity: Captivity, Rescue, and Gender in American War Narratives." *Journal of American Culture*, vol. 34, no. 2, 2011, pp. 149–160.

———. "The Tillman Story." *Journal of American History*, vol. 98, 2011, pp. 291–294.

Boyle, Brenda M., and Jeehyun Lim, eds. *Looking Back on the Vietnam War: Twenty-First Century Perspectives*. Rutgers University Press, 2016.

Bradley, Mark. "Slouching toward Bethlehem: Culture, Diplomacy, and the Origins of the Cold War in Vietnam." *Cold War Constructions: The Political Culture of United States Imperialism, 1945–1966*, edited by Christian G. Appy, U of Mass P, 2000, pp. 11–34.

Bradley, Mark Philip. *Imagining Vietnam and America: The Making of Postcolonial Vietnam, 1919–1950*. U of NC P, 2000.

———. "Making Sense of the French War: The Postcolonial Moment and the First Vietnam War, 1945–1954." *The First Vietnam War: Colonial Conflict and Cold War Crisis*, edited by Mark Atwood Lawrence and Fredrik Logevall, Harvard UP, 2007, pp. 16–40.

Bristol, Douglas Walter. "Terror, Anger, and Patriotism: Understanding the Resistance of Black Soldiers during WWII." *Integrating the US*

Military: Race, Gender, and Sexual Orientation since World War II, edited by Douglas Walter Bristol Jr. and Heather Marie Stur, Johns Hopkins UP, 2017, pp. 10–35.

Bristol, Douglas Walter, Jr., and Heather Marie Stur, eds. *Integrating the US Military: Race, Gender, and Sexual Orientation since World War II*. Johns Hopkins UP, 2017.

Brittan, Arthur. *Masculinity and Power*. New York: Basil Blackwell, 1989.

Brooks, Rosa. *How Everything Became War and the Military Became Everything: Tales from the Pentagon*. Simon and Schuster, 2016.

Burdick, Eugene and William Lederer. *The Ugly American*. Norton, 1958.

Burke, Carol. "Pernicious Cohesion." *It's Our Military, Too!*, edited by Judith Hicks Stiehm, Temple UP, 1996, pp. 205–249.

Butler, Judith. *Frames of War: When Is Life Grievable?* New York: Verso, 2010.

———. *Gender Trouble: Feminism and the Subversion of Identity*. New York: Routledge, 1990.

Butterworth and Wallner. "Saigon's Despatch No. 330." October 3, 1947, and October 7, 1947. U.S. National Archives, College Park, MD. RG 59, Box 6315, NND 760050.

Cain, Frank. *America's Vietnam War and Its French Connection*. New York: Routledge, 2017.

CBR Staff. "'America's Army—The Graphic Novel' Released by the U.S. Army," June 5, 2009, https://www.cbr.com/americas-army-the-graphic -novel-released-by-the-u-s-army/. Accessed August 17, 2019.

Center for Military Readiness. "Policy Analysis: Consequences of the Proposed New 'LGBT Law' for the Military," January 2010, https:// www.cmrlink.org/data/Sites/85/CMRDocuments /CMRPolicyAnalysis%28WEB%29-January2010.pdf. Accessed August 2, 2019.

———. "Trump Transgender Policy Promotes Readiness, Not Political Correctness," April 2018, https://cmrlink.org/data/sites/85 /CMRDocuments/CMRSR_TrumpTransgenderPolicyReport-041518A .pdf. Accessed August 3, 2019.

Chapman, James. *War and Film*. London: Reaktion Books, 2008.

Clark, Michael. "Remembering Vietnam." *Cultural Critique*, vol. 3, Spring 1986, pp. 46–78.

Clinton, William Jefferson, President. "Transcript of Clinton Speech at Vietnam War [*sic*] Memorial," June 1, 1993, https://www.nytimes.com /1993/06/01/us/transcript-of-clinton-speech-at-vietnam-war-memorial .html. Accessed August 21, 2019.

Cockburn, Andrew. "Follow the Money." *The Pentagon Labyrinth: 10 Short Essays to Help You through It.* Washington, DC: World Security Institute's Center for Defense Information, 2011.

———. "The Military-Industrial Virus: How Bloated Budgets Gut Our Defenses." *Harper's Magazine*, June 2019, pp. 61–67.

Cohn, Lindsay, Max Margulies, and Michael A. Robinson. "What Discord Follows: The Divisive Debate over Military Disobedience." *War on the Rocks*, August 2, 2019, https://warontherocks.com/2019/08 /what-discord-follows-the-divisive-debate-over-military-disobedience/ ?utm_source=WOTR+Newsletter&utm_campaign=8597cd659c -EMAIL_CAMPAIGN_10_30_2018_11_23_COPY_01&utm _medium=email&utm_term=0_8375be81e9-8597cd659c-83002473. Accessed August 2, 2019.

Collett, Joan. "American Libraries Abroad: United States Information Agency Activities." *Library Trends*, January 1972, pp. 538–547.

Combe, Kirk, and Brenda M. Boyle. *Masculinity and Monstrosity in Contemporary Hollywood Films.* New York: Palgrave Macmillan, 2013.

"Confidence in Institutions." Gallup Historical Trends, June 7–11, 2017, https://news.gallup.com/poll/212843/confidence-institutions-trends .aspx. Accessed August 3, 2019.

Congressional Budget Office. "Growth in DoD's Budget from 2000 to 2014," November 20, 2014, https://www.cbo.gov/publication/49764. Accessed August 17, 2019.

Congressional Research Service. "American War and Military Operations Casualties: Lists and Statistics," September 24, 2019, https://fas.org/sgp /crs/natsec/RL32492.pdf. Accessed December 13, 2019.

Connell, R. W., and J. Messerschmidt. "Hegemonic Masculinity: Rethinking the Concept." *Gender and Society*, vol. 19, no. 6, 2005, pp. 829–859.

Copp, Tara. "More Doctor Visits, More Money: Obese Soldiers May Be Too Obese to Keep, Army Study Suggests," October 11, 2018, https:// www.armytimes.com/news/your-military/2018/10/11/more-doctor

-visits-more-money-obese-soldiers-may-be-too-expensive-to-keep
-army-study-suggests/. Accessed May 22, 2019.

"Costs of War." Watson Institute of International and Public Affairs,
Brown University, 2019, https://watson.brown.edu/costsofwar/.
Accessed December 13, 2019.

Cowen, Deborah E. "'Fighting for Freedom': The End of Conscription in
the United States and the Neoliberal Project of Citizenship." *Citizenship Studies*, vol. 10, no. 2, May 2006, pp. 167–183.

Crowley, Kacy, and Michelle Sandhoff. "Just a Girl in the Army: US Iraq
War Veterans Negotiating Femininity in a Culture of Masculinity."
Women in the Military, edited by Brenda L. Moore, special edition of
Armed Forces & Society, vol. 43, no. 2, 2017, pp. 221–237.

Cuordileone, K. A. *Manhood and American Political Culture in the Cold War*.
New York: Routledge, 2005.

Curran, Tom E. "NFL Teams Being on the Field for the Anthem Is a
Relatively New Practice," August 29, 2016, https://www.nbcsports.com
/boston/new-england-patriots/nfl-teams-being-field-anthem-relatively
-new-practice. Accessed April 9, 2020.

Daddis, Gregory A. *Withdrawal: Reassessing America's Final Years in Vietnam*.
New York: Oxford UP, 2017.

Dalfiume, Richard M. *Desegregation of the U.S. Armed Forces: Fighting on
Two Fronts, 1939–1953*. U of Miss P, 1969.

Dalloz, Jacques. *The War in Indochina, 1945–1954*. Translated by Josephine
Bacon. Dublin: Gill and Macmillan, 1990.

D'Amico, Francine, and Laurie Weinstein, eds. *Gender Camouflage: Women
and the U.S. Military*. NYUP, 1999.

Danto, Arthur C. "The Vietnam Veterans Memorial." *Nation*, August 31,
1985, pp. 152–155.

Davidson, Nicholas, ed. *Gender Sanity*. Lanham, MD: UP of America,
1989.

Defense Advisory Committee on Women in the Services (DACOWITS). n.d.,
https://dacowits.defense.gov. Accessed August 21, 2019.

D'Emilio, John, and Estelle B. Freedman. *Intimate Matters: A History of
Sexuality in America*. 3rd ed., U of Chicago P, 2012.

Denbeaux, Mark P., et al. "How America Tortures." Seton Hall University
School of Law Center for Policy and Research, December 2, 2019,

https://papers.ssrn.com/sol3/papers.cfm?abstract_id=3494533. Accessed December 2, 2019.

Department of Defense, Armed Forces Information and Education. *A Pocket Guide to Vietnam*, DoD PG-21A, 1962.

Department of Defense Report and Recommendations on Military Service by Transgender Persons. February 22, 2018, https://media.defense.gov /2018/Mar/23/2001894037/-1/-1/0/MILITARY-SERVICE-BY -TRANSGENDER-INDIVIDUALS.PDF. Accessed August 3, 2019.

Der Derian, James. *Virtuous War: Mapping the Military-Industrial-Media-Entertainment Network*. 2nd ed., New York: Routledge, 2009.

———. "War in the Twenty-First Century: Visible, Invisible, or Superpositional." *In/Visible War: The Culture of War in Twenty-First Century America,* edited by Jon Simons and John Louis Lucaites, Rutgers University Press, 2017, pp. 249–264.

Deshpande, Pia. "Trump Predicts July 4 Rally Will Cause a 'Big Spike' in Military Recruitment." *Politico*, July 5, 2019, https://www.politico.com /story/2019/07/05/donald-trump-military-july-fourth-1399147. Accessed July 5, 2019.

Devillers, Phillip. *Histoire du Viêt Nam de 1940 à 1952*. New York: AMS Press, 1975.

Doss, Erika. *Memorial Mania: Public Feeling in America*. U of Chicago P, 2010.

Doubek, Robert W. *Creating the Vietnam Veterans Memorial: The Inside Story*. McFarland, 2015.

Dudziak, Mary L. *Wartime: An Idea, Its History, Its Consequences*. New York: Oxford UP, 2012.

Dwyer, Philip. "Making Sense of the Muddle: War Memoirs and the Culture of Remembering." *War Stories: The War Memoir in History and Literature,* edited by Philip Dwyer. New York: Berghahn Books, 2017, pp. 1–24.

Eberwein, Robert, ed. *The War Film*. Rutgers University Press, 2005.

Ehrenhaus, Peter. "Commemorating the Unwon War: On Not Remembering Vietnam." *Journal of Communication*, vol. 39, no. 1, Winter 1989, pp. 96–107.

Eisenhower, Dwight D. "Military Industrial Complex Speech, Dwight D. Eisenhower, 1961." Yale Law School, Lillian Goldman Law Library,

2008, https://avalon.law.yale.edu/20th_century/eisenhower001.asp.
Accessed April 10, 2020.

Elders, M. Joycelyn, et al. "Medical Aspects of Transgender Military
Service." *Armed Forces & Society*, vol. 41, no. 2, 2015, pp. 199–220.

Elliott, Duong Van Mai. *The Sacred Willow: Four Generations in the Life of a
Vietnamese Family*. New York: Oxford UP, 1999.

Engelhardt, Tom. *The End of Victory Culture: Cold War America and the
Disillusioning of a Generation*. Revised ed., U of Mass P, 2007.

Enloe, Cynthia. *Maneuvers: The International Politics of Militarizing
Women's Lives*. U of Cal P, 2000.

Espiritu, Yen Le. *Body Counts: The Vietnam War and Militarized Refugees*.
U of Cal P, 2014.

Estes, Steve. *Ask and Tell: Gay and Lesbian Veterans Speak Out*. U of NC P,
2007.

Faludi, Susan. *The Terror Dream: Fear and Fantasy in Post-9/11 America*.
New York: Metropolitan Books, 2007.

Favorite, Jennifer K. "'We Don't Want Another Vietnam': The Wall, the
Mall, History, and Memory in the Vietnam Veterans Memorial
Education Center." *Public Art Dialogue*, vol. 6, no. 2, 2016, pp. 185–205.

Favret, Mary A. *War at a Distance: Romanticism and the Making of Modern
Wartime*. Princeton UP, 2010.

Fiala, Andrew. "General Patton and Private Ryan: The Conflicting Reality
of War and Films about War." *The Philosophy of War Films*, edited by
D. LaRocca, UP of Kentucky, 2014, pp. 335–353.

Fischer, Ronald, et al. "Individualism-Collectivism as Descriptive Norms:
Development of a Subjective Norm Approach to Culture Measure-
ment." *Journal of Cross-Cultural Psychology*, vol. 40, no. 2, 2009,
pp. 187–213.

Fitzpatrick, Dick. "Telling the World about America." *Public Opinion
Quarterly*, Winter 1946, pp. 582–592.

Flaherty, Colleen. "Professors Debate the Role of the Historian (or Lack
Thereof) in Ken Burns and Lynn Novick's Vietnam Documentary."
Inside Higher Ed, January 9, 2018, https://www.insidehighered.com
/news/2018/01/09/professors-debate-role-historian-or-lack-thereof-ken
-burns-and-lynn-novicks-vietnam. Accessed August 2, 2019.

Flynn, George Q. *The Draft, 1940–1973*. UP of Kansas, 1993.

Foote, Kenneth E. *Shadowed Ground: America's Landscapes of Violence and Tragedy*. UP of Texas, 1997.

Forbes, Gordon B., et al. "Relationships among Individualism-Collectivism, Gender, and Ingroup/Outgroup Status, and Responses to Conflict: A Study in China and the United States." *Aggressive Behavior*, vol. 37, 2011, pp. 302–314.

Forth, Christopher E., and Bertrand Taithe, eds. *French Masculinities: History, Culture, and Politics*. London: Palgrave Macmillan, 2007.

Forth, Christopher E., and Bertrand Taithe, eds. "Introduction." *French Masculinities: History, Culture, and Politics*, edited by Christopher E. Forth and Bertrand Taithe, Palgrave Macmillan, 2007, pp. 1–14.

Foucault, Michel. *Discipline and Punish: The Birth of the Prison*. Translated by Alan Sheridan, 2nd Vintage Books ed., New York: Vintage, 1995.

———. *The History of Sexuality*, vol. 1, *An Introduction*. Translated by Robert Hurley, New York: Vintage, 1990.

———. "Truth and Power." *The Essential Foucault: Selections from the Essential Works of Foucault, 1954–1984*, edited by Paul Rabinow and Nikolas Rose, New York: New P, 2003, pp. 300–318.

Francke, Linda Bird. *Ground Zero: The Gender Wars in the Military*. Simon and Schuster, 1997.

Frank, Nathaniel. *Unfriendly Fire: How the Gay Ban Undermines the Military and Weakens America*. St. Martin's P, 2009.

Frey, William H. "The U.S. Will Become 'Minority White' in 2045, Census Projects." *Brookings*, March 14, 2018, https://www.brookings.edu/blog/the-avenue/2018/03/14/the-us-will-become-minority-white-in-2045-census-projects/. Accessed April 21, 2020.

Friedl, Vicki L. *Women in the United States Military, 1901–1995: A Research Guide and Annotated Bibliography*. Research Guides in Military Studies, no. 9. Westport, CT: Greenwood P, 1996.

Froeba, Kristine. "DC Comics' Frank Miller Reinvents Clark Kent as Man of SEAL." *Military Times*, June 17, 2019, https://www.militarytimes.com/news/your-military/2019/06/17/dc-comics-frank-miller-reinvents-clark-kent-as-man-of-seal/. Accessed June 23, 2019.

Garcia, Arturo. "Why Are NFL Players on the Sidelines for the National Anthem?" October 25, 2016, https://www.snopes.com/fact-check/nfl-sideline-anthem. Accessed April 9, 2020.

Gardner, Lloyd C. *Approaching Vietnam: From World War II through Dienbienphu, 1941–1954*. W. W. Norton & Co., 1988.

Gilbert, Christopher J., and Jon Louis Lucaites. "Returning Soldiers and the In/Visibility of Combat Trauma." *In/Visible War: The Culture of War in Twenty-First Century America*, edited by Jon Simons and John Louis Lucaites, Rutgers University Press, 2017, pp. 48–68.

Gillibrand, Kirsten, Senator. "After All Four Military Service Chiefs Confirm Transgender Troops Have Not Harmed Unit Cohesion, Discipline, or Morale, Gillibrand Leads Bipartisan Group of 50 Senators in Telling Defense Secretary Mattis Transgender Troop Ban Is Harmful to Military," press release, April 26, 2018, https://www .gillibrand.senate.gov/news/press/release/after-all-four-military-service -chiefs-confirm-transgender-troops-have-not-harmed-unit-cohesion -discipline-or-morale-gillibrand-leads-bipartisan-group-of-50-senators -in-telling-defense-secretary-mattis-transgender-troop-ban-is-harmful -to-military-. Accessed August 16, 2019.

Gillis, John R., ed. *Commemorations: The Politics of National Identity*. Princeton UP, 1994.

Glantz, Aaron. *The War Comes Home: Washington's Battle against America's Veterans*. U of Cal P, 2009.

Goldich, Robert L. "American Military Culture from Colony to Empire." *Daedelus*, vol. 140, no. 3, Summer 2011, pp. 58–74.

Goldman, Adam. "Trump Reverses Restrictions on Military Hardware for Police." *New York Times*, August 28, 2017, https://www.nytimes.com /2017/08/28/us/politics/trump-police-military-surplus-equipment.html. Accessed June 6, 2019.

Goldstein, Joshua S. *War and Gender*. New York: Cambridge UP, 2001.

Goscha, Christopher. Series foreword to *Vietnam, 1946: How the War Began*, by Stein Tønnesson, U of Cal P, 2010, pp. xi–xii.

Griswold, Charles L., and Stephen S. Griswold. "The Vietnam Veterans Memorial and the Washington Mall." *Critical Inquiry*, vol. 12, no. 4, Summer 1986, pp. 688–719.

Grossman, Dave, and Loren W. Christenson. *On Combat: The Psychology and Physiology of Deadly Conflict in War and in Peace*, PPCT Research Publications, 2004.

Grossman, Dave, Stephanie Rogish, and Joey Karwal. *Sheepdogs: Meet Our Nation's Warriors*, West Bend, WI: Delta Defense, 2013.

Guillemot, François. "'Be Men!' Fighting and Dying for the State of Vietnam (1951–1954)." *War and Society*, vol. 3, no. 2, August 2012, pp. 184–210.

Haerens, Margaret. *The NFL National Anthem Protests*. Denver, CO: ABC-Clio, 2019.

Haggerty, Timothy. "History Repeating Itself: A Historical Overview of Gay Men and Lesbians in the Military before 'Don't Ask, Don't Tell.'" *Don't Ask, Don't Tell: Debating the Gay Ban in the Military*, edited by Aaron Belkin and Geoffrey Bateman, Boulder, CO: Lynne Rienner Publishers, 2003, pp. 9–49.

Hagopian, Patrick. *American Immunity: War Crimes and the Limits of International Law*. U of Mass P, 2013.

———. *The Vietnam War in American Memory: Veterans, Memorials, and the Politics of Healing*. U of Mass P, 2009.

Halberstam, Judith. *Female Masculinity*. Duke UP, 1998.

Hall, Simon. "Leonard Matlovich: From Military Hero to Gay Rights Poster Boy." *Warring over Valor: How Race and Gender Shaped American Military Heroism in the Twentieth and Twenty-First Centuries*, edited by Simon Wendt, Rutgers University Press, 2019, pp. 113–127.

Haltiwanger, John. "America Is so Out of Shape and Fat, It's putting U.S. Army Soldiers in Danger." *Newsweek*, January 1, 2018, https://www .newsweek.com/america-so-out-shape-and-fat-its-putting-us-army -soldiers-danger-778840. Accessed April 21, 2020.

Hamamura, T. "Are Cultures Becoming Individualistic? A Cross-Temporal Comparison of Individualism-Collectivism in the United States and Japan." *Personality and Social Psychology Review*, vol. 16, no. 1, 2012, pp. 3–24.

"*Harper's* Index." *Harper's Magazine*. December 2018, p. 9.

Harrison, Benjamin T., and Christopher L. Mosher. "The Secret Diary of McNamara's Dove: The Long-Lost Story of John T. McNaughton's Opposition to the Vietnam War." *Diplomatic History*, vol. 35, no. 3, June 2011, pp. 505–534.

Harrison-Quintana, Jack, and Jody L. Herman. "Still Serving in Silence: Transgender Service Members and Veterans in the National

Transgender Discrimination Survey." *LBGTQ Policy Journal at the Harvard Kennedy School*, vol. 3, 2012–2013, pp. 1–13.

Harvey, David. *A Brief History of Neoliberalism*. New York: Oxford UP, 2005.

Hass, Kristin Ann. *Carried to the Wall: American Memory and the Vietnam Veterans Memorial*. U of Cal P, 1998.

———. *Sacrificing Soldiers on the National Mall*. U of Cal P, 2013.

Herbert, Melissa S. *Camouflage Isn't Only for Combat: Gender, Sexuality, and Women in the Military*. NYUP, 1998.

Herr, Michael. *Dispatches*. New York: Alfred A. Knopf, 1977.

Herring, George C. *The American Century and Beyond: U.S. Foreign Relations, 1893–2014*. New York: Oxford UP, 2017.

Hess, Elizabeth. "A Tale of Two Memorials." *Art in America*, April 1983, pp. 121–128.

Hillman, Elizabeth L. "Outing the Costs of Civil Deference to the Military." *Evolution of Government Policy towards Homosexuality in the U.S. Military*, edited by James E. Parco and David A. Levy, New York: Routledge, 2014, pp. 177–191.

Hixson, Walter L., ed. *Historical Memory and Representations of the Vietnam War*. New York: Garland, 2000.

Hofstadter, Richard. *Anti-intellectualism in American Life*. New York: Vintage, 1963.

Hofstede, Geert, ed. *Masculinity and Femininity: The Taboo Dimension of National Culture*. Thousand Oaks, CA: Sage, 1998.

Hoganson, Kristin L. *Fighting for American Manhood: How Gender Politics Provoked the Spanish-American and Philippine-American Wars*. Yale UP, 1998.

Huebner, Andrew J. *The Warrior Image: Soldiers in American Culture from the Second World War to the Vietnam Era*. U of NC P, 2008.

Hutchinson, George. *Facing the Abyss: American Literature and Culture in the 1940s*. Columbia UP, 2018.

Hynes, Samuel. *The Soldier's Tale: Bearing Witness to Modern War*. New York: Penguin, 1997.

Jarvis, Christina S. *The Male Body at War: American Masculinity during World War II*. DeKalb: Northern Illinois UP, 2004.

Jeffords, Susan. "Telling the War Story." *It's Our Military, Too! Women in the U.S. Military*, edited by Judith Hicks Stiehm, Temple UP, 1996, pp. 220–234.

Jones, Howard. *My Lai: Vietnam, 1968, and the Descent into Darkness.* New York: Oxford UP, 2017.

Kalb, Marvin. *The Road to War: Presidential Commitments Honored and Betrayed.* Washington, DC: Brookings Institution Press, 2013.

Karlin, Mara, and Alice Hunt Friend. "Military Worship Hurts US Democracy." *Brookings Institution*, September 24, 2018, https://www .brookings.edu/blog/order-from-chaos/2018/09/24/military-worship -hurts-us-democracy/?utm_campaign=Brookings%20Brief&utm _source=hs_email&utm_medium=email&utm_content=66163363. Accessed August 2, 2019.

Kashima, Yoshihura, et al. "Culture, Gender, and Self: A Perspective from Individualism-Collectivism Research." *Journal of Personality and Social Psychology*, vol. 69, no. 5, 1995, pp. 925–937.

Kerry, John. "Testimony before the Senate Foreign Relations Committee," April 22, 1971. *Legislative Proposals relating to the War in Southeast Asia, Hearings before the Committee on Foreign Relations, United States Senate, Ninety-Second Congress, First Session (April–May 1971).* Washington: Government Printing Office, 1971.

Kieran, David. *Forever Vietnam: How a Divisive War Changed American Public Memory.* U of Mass P, 2014.

Kieran, David, and Edwin A. Martini, eds. *At War: The Military and American Culture in the Twentieth Century and Beyond.* Rutgers University Press, 2018.

Kilgore, Adam. "For Decades, the NFL Wrapped Itself in the Flag. Now, That's Made Business Uneasy." *Washington Post*, September 6, 2018, p. D1.

Kimmel, Michael. *Guyland: The Perilous World Where Boys Become Men.* HarperCollins, 2008.

King, Anthony C. "Women Warriors' Female Accession to Ground Combat." *Armed Forces & Society*, vol. 41, no. 2, 2015, pp. 379–387.

Klepek, Patrick. "That Time *Call of Duty* Let You Shoot Up an Airport." *Kotaku: Gaming Reviews, News, Tips and More*, October 23, 2015,

https://kotaku.com/that-time-call-of-duty-let-you-shoot-up-an
-airport-1738376241. Accessed June 16, 2019.

Kleykamp, Meredith A. "College, Jobs, or the Military? Enlistment during a Time of War." Princeton University Office of Population Research, June 15, 2005.

Kline, Stephen, Nick Dyer-Witheford, and Greig De Peuter. *Digital Play: The Interaction of Technology, Culture, and Marketing.* Montreal: McGill-Queen's University Press, 2003.

Kosuta, Matthew. "Warrior and Soldier, What's the Difference?" *H-Net: Humanities and Social Sciences Online*, July 19, 2018, https://networks.h -net.org/node/12840/discussions/2075887/warrior-and-soldier-what's -difference. Accessed May 28, 2019.

Kozol, Wendy. *Distant Wars Visible: The Ambivalence of Witnessing.* U of Minn P, 2014.

Kreps, Sarah E. *Taxing Wars: The American Way of War Finance and the Decline of Democracy.* New York: Oxford UP, 2018.

Kyle, Chris, with Scott McEwen and Jim DeFelice. *American Sniper: The Autobiography of the Most Lethal Sniper in U.S. Military History.* Harper, 2012.

Laderman, Scott. "Hollywood's Vietnam, 1929–1964: Scripting Intervention, Spotlighting Injustice." *Pacific Historical Review*, vol. 78, no. 4, November 2009, pp. 578–607.

Lair, Meredith. "The Education Center at the Wall and the Rewriting of History." *Public Historian*, vol. 34, no. 1, Winter 2012, pp. 34–60.

Lamothe, Dan. "Under Pressure, Jim Webb Declines to Be Recognized as a Distinguished Naval Academy Graduate." *Washington Post*, March 28, 2017, https://www.washingtonpost.com/news/checkpoint/wp/2017/03/28 /jim-webb-has-been-named-a-distinguished-naval-academy-graduate -and-some-alumni-are-furious/?utm_term=.a6af7f68426e. Accessed August 2, 2019.

Laugeson, Amanda. "Books for the World: American Book Programs in the Developing World, 1948–1968." *Pressing the Fight: Print, Propaganda, and the Cold War*, edited by Gregory Barnhisel and Catherine C. Turner, U of Mass P, 2010, pp. 126–144.

Lawrence, Mark Atwood. *Assuming the Burden: Europe and the American Commitment to War in Vietnam.* U of Cal P, 2005.

———. "Forging the 'Great Combination': Britain and the Indochina Problem, 1945–1950." *The First Vietnam War: Colonial Conflict and Cold War Crisis*, edited by Mark Atwood Lawrence and Fredrik Logevall, Harvard UP, 2007, pp. 105–129.

Lawrence, Mark Atwood, and Fredrik Logevall, eds. *The First Vietnam War: Colonial Conflict and Cold War Crisis*. Harvard UP, 2007.

Lee, Jonathan L. "The Comprehensive Review Working Group and Don't Ask, Don't Tell Repeal at the Department of Defense." *Evolution of Government Policy towards Homosexuality in the U.S. Military*, edited by James E. Parco and David A. Levy, New York: Routledge, 2014, pp. 147–176.

Lehring, Gary L. *Officially Gay: The Political Construction of Sexuality by the U.S. Military*. Temple UP, 2003.

Lembcke, Jerry. *The Spitting Image: Myth, Memory, and the Legacy of Vietnam*. NYUP, 1998.

Linehan, Adam. "Sebastian Junger: Over-Valorizing Vets Does More Harm Than Good." *Task and Purpose*, May 24, 2016, http:// taskandpurpose.com/sebastian-junger-we-need-to-stop-over -valorizing. Accessed September 11, 2017.

Linenthal, Edward Tabor. *Sacred Ground: Americans and Their Battlefields*. U of Il P, 1993.

Liu, Eric, and Nick Hanauer. *The True Patriot*. Seattle: Sasquatch Books, 2007.

Loewen, James W. *The Lies My Teacher Told Me: Everything Your American History Textbook Got Wrong*. 2d edition. New York: New P, 2018.

Logevall, Fredrik. *Choosing War: The Lost Chance for Peace and the Escalation of War*. U of Cal P, 2001.

———. *Embers of War: The Fall of an Empire and the Making of America's Vietnam*. Random House, 2012.

Lone Survivor: Based on True Acts of Courage. Directed by Peter Berg, performances by Mark Wahlberg, Taylor Kitsch, Emile Hirsch, and Ben Foster. Universal, 2013.

Long, James. "It's Not the Economy: Why the Army Missed Its Recruitment Goals and What to Do about It." *Modern War Institute*, February 14, 2019, https://MWI.usma.edu/not-economy-army-missed -recruitment-goals/. Accessed May 19, 2019.

Lucaites, John Louis, and Jon Simons. "Introduction: The Paradox of War's In/Visibility." *In/Visible War: The Culture of War in Twenty-First Century America*, edited by Jon Simons and John Louis Lucaites, Rutgers University Press, 2017, pp. 1–24.

Luttrell, Marcus, and Patrick Robinson. *Lone Survivor: The Eyewitness Account of Operation Redwing and the Lost Heroes of Seal Team 10*. Little, Brown and Co., 2007.

Lutz, Catherine. "Warmaking as the American Way of Life." *The Insecure American: How We Got Here and What We Should Do About It*, edited by Hugh Gusterson and Catherine Besteman, U of Cal P, 2010, pp. 45–62.

MacDonald, Heather. "Women Don't Belong in Combat Units." *Wall Street Journal*, January 4, 2019, A17, https://www.wsj.com/articles /women-dont-belong-in-combat-units-11547411638. Accessed August 2, 2019.

Mackenzie, Megan. *Beyond the Band of Brothers: The US Military and the Myth That Women Can't Fight*. Cambridge: Cambridge UP, 2015.

Maguen, Shira, and Brett Litz. "Moral Injury in the Context of War." U.S. Department of Veterans Affairs, https://www.ptsd.va.gov /professional/treat/cooccurring/moral_injury.asp. Accessed July 10, 2019.

Mailer, Norman. "Gaining an Empire, Losing Democracy?" *International Herald Tribune*, February 25, 2003, https://ratical.org/ratville/CAH /linkscopy/gainEloseD.html. Accessed May 16, 2019.

Makeschin, Sarah. "'From Louboutins to Combat Boots'? The Negotiation of a Twenty-First-Century Female Warrior Image in American Popular Culture and Literature." *Warring over Valor: How Race and Gender Shaped American Military Heroism in the Twentieth and Twenty-First Centuries*, edited by Simon Wendt, Rutgers University Press, 2019, pp. 143–164.

Mann, Bonnie. *Sovereign Masculinity: Gender Lessons from the War on Terror*. New York: Oxford UP, 2014.

Marcus, Ruth. "Jeers, Cheers, Greet Clinton at the Wall." *Washington Post*, June 1, 1993, https://www.washingtonpost.com/archive/politics/1993/06 /01/jeers-cheers-greet-clinton-at-the-wall/c10afb5e-d7f5-4b7b-a308 -200627a47c0c/?utm_term=.9bc1afa797be. Accessed August 2, 2019.

Marr, David. *Vietnam: State, War, Revolution (1945–1946)*. U of Cal P, 2013.

Martin, Geoff, and Erin Steuter. *Pop Culture Goes to War: Enlisting and Resisting Militarism in the War on Terror.* Lanham, MD: Rowman & Littlefield, 2010.

Martini, Edwin A. *Agent Orange: History, Science, and the Politics of Uncertainty.* U of Mass P, 2012.

Marty, Martin E. *The One and the Many: America's Struggle for the Common Good.* Harvard UP, 1997.

Mathews, Jessica T. "America's Indefensible Defense Budget." *New York Review of Books,* July 18, 2019, https://www.nybooks.com/articles/2019/07/18/americas-indefensible-defense-budget/. Accessed July 27, 2019.

Maxwell, Jeremy P. *Brotherhood in Combat: How African Americans Found Equality in Korea and Vietnam.* U of OK P, 2018.

McCain, John, and Jeff Flake. "Tackling Paid Patriotism: A Joint Oversight Report." May 13, 2015, https://archive.org/details/TacklingP aidPatriotismOversightReport/page/n4. Accessed May 13, 2019.

McCann, Adam. "2019's Most Patriotic States in America." *WalletHub,* June 24, 2019, https://wallethub.com/edu/most-patriotic states /13680/?utm_source=Task+%26+Purpose+Daily&utm_campaign =568fafc51b-EMAIL_CAMPAIGN_2019_06_24_07_01&utm _medium=email&utm_term=0_67edd998fe-568fafc51b-76835255&mc _cid=568fafc51b&mc_eid=28a377f211#methodology. Accessed June 25, 2019.

McFate, Sean. *The Modern Mercenary: Private Armies and What They Mean for World Order.* New York: Oxford UP, 2014.

McGurl, Mark. *The Program Era: Postwar Fiction and the Rise of Creative Writing.* Harvard UP, 2009.

McLoughlin, Kate, ed. *The Cambridge Companion to War Writing.* New York: Cambridge UP, 2009.

McNerney, Michael J., et al. *National Will to Fight: Why Some States Keep Fighting and Others Don't.* Santa Monica, CA: RAND Corporation, 2018.

McNicoll, Alex, and Julie Schreiber. "In the Locker Room with Professor and Columnist Kevin Blackistone." *Oberlin Review,* October 16, 2017, https://oberlinreview.org/14538/sports/in-the-locker-room-with -professor-and-columnist-kevin-blackistone/. Accessed May 13, 2019.

Mead, Corey. *War Play: Video Games and the Future of Armed Conflict.* Houghton Mifflin Harcourt, 2013.

"Men against Fire." *Black Mirror*, Season 3, Episode 5. Directed by Jakob Verbrueggen. Netflix, 2016.

Michel, Craig. "Dispelling Myths about Special Operations Forces." *War on the Rocks*, March 17, 2016, http://warontherocks.com/2016/03 /dispelling-myths-about-special-operations-forces/. Accessed March 17, 2016.

Mieszkowski, Jan. *Watching War*. Stanford UP, 2012.

Milburn, Andrew. "When Not to Obey Orders." *War on the Rocks*, July 8, 2019, https://warontherocks.com/2019/07/when-not-to-obey-orders/. Accessed July 8, 2019.

Miller, Bonnie. "War in Visual Culture." *At War: The Military and American Culture in the Twentieth Century and Beyond*, edited by David Kieran and Edwin A. Martini, Rutgers University Press, 2018, pp. 279–307.

Mittelstadt, Jennifer. "Neoliberalism in the American Military and Its Impact on Civilians." *OpenDemocracy*, December 7, 2012, https://www .opendemocracy.net/opensecurity/jennifer-mittelstadt/neoliberalism-in -american-military-and-its-impact-on-civilians. Accessed August 2, 2019.

———. *The Rise of the Military Welfare State*. Harvard UP, 2015.

Monbiot, George. *How Did We Get into This Mess? Politics, Equality, Nature*. London: Verso, 2017.

———. "Neoliberalism—the Ideology at the Root of All Our Problems." *Guardian*, April 15, 2016, https://www.theguardian.com/books/2016 /apr/15/neoliberalism-ideology-problem-george-monbiot. Accessed August 2, 2019.

Moore, Brenda L., ed. *Women in the Military*, special edition of *Armed Forces & Society*, vol. 43, no. 2, 2017.

Moral Injury Project. Syracuse University, http://moralinjuryproject.syr.edu /about-moral-injury/. Accessed July 10, 2019.

Myers, Meghann. "With Retention Up and Recruiting Down, Here's How the Army Plans to Add 7,500 More Soldiers to the Ranks." *Army Times*, May 7, 2018, https://www.armytimes.com/news/your-army/2018 /05/08/with-retention-up-and-recruiting-down-heres-how-the-army -plans-to-add-7500-more-soldiers-to-the-ranks/. Accessed May 7, 2018.

Nalty, Bernard C., and Morris J. MacGregor, eds. *Blacks in the Military: Essential Documents*. Wilmington, DE: Scholarly Resources, 1981.

Nashel, Jonathan. "The Road to Vietnam: Modernization Theory in Fact and Fiction." *Cold War Constructions: The Political Culture of United States Imperialism, 1945–1966*, edited by Christian G. Appy, U of Mass P, 2000, pp. 132–154.

New York Times Editorial Board. "The Pentagon Doesn't Know Where Its Money Goes." *New York Times*, December 1, 2018, https://www.nytimes.com/2018/12/01/opinion/sunday/pentagon-spending-audit-failed.html. Accessed August 17, 2019.

Nguyen, Viet Thanh. *Nothing Ever Dies: Vietnam and the Memory of War*. U of Mass P, 2016.

Nixon, Richard M., President. "President Nixon Announces Agreement on Ending the War in Vietnam and Restoring Peace," January 23, 1973, https://www.youtube.com/watch?v=wiKulZK-ddI. Accessed August 21, 2019.

Noah, Timothy. "Birth of a Washington Word." *Slate*, November 20, 2002, https://slate.com/news-and-politics/2002/11/kinetic-warfare.html. Accessed June 25, 2019.

Obama, Barack Hussein, President. "Presidential Proclamation: Commemoration of the Fiftieth Anniversary of the Vietnam War," May 25, 2012, https://obamawhitehouse.archives.gov/the-press-office/2012/05/25/presidential-proclamation-commemoration-50th-anniversary-vietnam-war. Accessed August 21, 2019.

Oliver, Kelly. *Women as Weapons of War: Iraq, Sex, and the Media*. Columbia UP, 2007.

Oliver, Kendrick. *The My Lai Massacre in American History and Memory*. Manchester, UK: Manchester UP, 2006.

Omi, Yasuhiro. "Collectivistic Individualism: Transcending a Traditional Opposition." *Culture & Psychology*, vol. 18, no. 3, 2012, pp. 403–416.

Page, Caroline. *U.S. Official Propaganda during the Vietnam War, 1965–1973: The Limits of Persuasion*. Leicester, UK: Leicester UP, 1996.

Parco, James E., and David A. Levy, eds. *Evolution of Government Policy towards Homosexuality in the U.S. Military*. New York: Routledge, 2014.

Parco, James E., David A. Levy, and Sarah R. Spears. "Transgender Military Personnel in the Post-DADT Repeal Era: A

Phenomenological Study." *Armed Forces & Society*, vol. 41, no. 2, 2015, pp. 221–242.

Parker, Kim, Anthony Cillufo, and Renee Stepler. "Six Facts about the U.S. Military and Its Changing Demographics." Pew Research Center, April 13, 2017, http://www.pewresearch.org/fact-tank/2017/04/13/6 -facts-about-the-u-s-military-and-its-changing-demographics/. Accessed August 2, 2019.

Parkin, Simon. *Death by Video Game: Danger, Pleasure, and Obsession on the Virtual Frontline*. Brooklyn: Melville House, 2016.

"Patriot." *CSIS Missile Defense Project*. 2019, https://missilethreat.csis.org /system/patriot/. Accessed May 17, 2019.

Patti, Archimedes. *Why Vietnam? Prelude to America's Albatross*. U of Cal P, 1980.

Pease, Donald. *The New American Exceptionalism*. U of Minn P, 2009.

Peebles, Stacey. *Welcome to the Suck: Narrating the American Soldier's Experience in Iraq*. Cornell UP, 2011.

Pentagon Papers, The. "Report of the Office of the Secretary of Defense Vietnam Task Force." Vietnam Task Force, Office of the Secretary of Defense, 1967, United States National Archives, https://www.archives .gov/research/pentagon-papers. Accessed August 3, 2019.

Phillips, Kathy J. *Manipulating Masculinity: War and Gender in Modern British and American Literature*. New York: Palgrave Macmillan, 2006.

Phillips, Kimberley L. *War! What Is It Good For? Black Freedom Struggles and the U.S. Military from World War II to Iraq*. U of NC P, 2012.

Pollard, Miranda. "In the Name of the Father: Male Masculinity in Vichy France." *French Masculinities: History, Culture, and Politics*, edited by Christopher E. Forth and Bertrand Taithe, London: Palgrave Macmillan, 2007, pp. 141–156.

"Population Representation in the Military Services: Fiscal Year 2016 Summary Report." Office of the Under Secretary of Defense, Personnel and Readiness, https://www.cna.org/pop-rep/2016/summary /summary.pdf. Accessed August 3, 2019.

Presidential Commission on the Assignment of Women in the Armed Forces. *Report to the President*, November 15, 1992, https://catalog .hathitrust.org/Record/002635968. Accessed August 3, 2019.

Presidential Memorandum for the Secretary of Defense and the Secretary of Homeland Security. "Military Service by Transgender Individuals," August 25, 2017, https://www.whitehouse.gov/presidential-actions /presidential-memorandum-secretary-defense-secretary-homeland -security/. Accessed August 16, 2019.

Presidential Memorandum for the Secretary of Defense and the Secretary of Homeland Security Regarding Military Service by Transgender Individuals, March 23, 2018, https://www.whitehouse.gov/presidential -actions/presidential-memorandum-secretary-defense-secretary -homeland-security-regarding-military-service-transgender -individuals/. Accessed August 16, 2019.

"Presidential Proclamation Commemorating the 50th Anniversary of the Vietnam War." Donald J. Trump, November 10, 2017, https://www .whitehouse.gov/presidential-actions/presidential-proclamation -commemorating-50th-anniversary-vietnam-war/ . Accessed April 21, 2020.

Priest, Andrew. "The Rhetoric of Revisionism: Presidential Rhetoric about the Vietnam War since 9/11." *Presidential Studies Quarterly*, vol. 43, no. 3, September 2013, pp. 538–561.

Proschan, Frank. "Eunuch Mandarins, Soldats Mamzelles, Effeminate Boys, and Graceless Women: French Colonial Constructions of Vietnamese Genders." *GLQ: A Journal of Lesbian and Gay Studies*, vol. 8, no. 4, 2002, pp. 435–467.

Quam, Kayla. "Unfinished Business of Repealing 'Don't Ask, Don't Tell: The Military's Unconstitutional Ban on Transgender Individuals." *Utah Law Review*, vol. 3, 2015.

Ray, Robert B. *A Certain Tendency of the Hollywood Cinema (1930–1980)*. Princeton UP, 1985.

Reagan, Ronald, Candidate for President. "Peace: Restoring the Margin of Safety." Veterans of Foreign War Convention, August 18, 1980, https://www.reaganlibrary.gov/8-18-80. Accessed August 21, 2019.

Reagan, Ronald, President. "Remarks at Dedication Ceremonies for the Vietnam Veterans Memorial Statue, November 11, 1984, https://www .presidency.ucsb.edu/documents/remarks-dedication-ceremonies-for -the-vietnam-veterans-memorial-statue. Accessed August 21, 2019.

———. "Remarks at the Veterans Day Ceremony at the Vietnam Veterans Memorial," November 11, 1988, https://www.reaganlibrary.gov/research/speeches/111188b. Accessed August 21, 2019.

@realDonaldTrump. "26,000 unreported sexual assaults in the military—only 238 convictions. What did these geniuses expect when they put men & women together?" *Twitter*, May 7, 2013, 7:04 p.m., https://twitter.com/realdonaldtrump/status/331907383771148288?lang=en. Accessed February 28, 2019.

Reed, Charles, U.S. Consul General, Saigon (National Archives, College Park, MD). May 31, 1946, report to secretary of state, "Informational Problems, French Indochina," RG 84, Box 2, NND 765027.

———. August 20, 1946, telegram to secretary of state, RG 84, Box 2, NND 765027.

———. October 23, 1946, letter to Moffat and Wallner, RG 84, Box 2, NND 765027.

———. November 25, 1946, telegram to secretary of state, RG 84, Box 2, NND 765027.

———. December 3, 1946, letter to secretary of state, RG 84, Box 3, NND 765027.

———. December 27, 1946, letter to secretary of state, "Outlook for United States Information Service Program in French Indochina," RG 84, Box 2, NND 765027.

———. February 6, 1947, letter to secretary of state, "Newspaper Attacks on This Consulate General and the United States Information Service; Anti-American Feeling," RG 84, Box 3, NND 765027.

———. June 14, 1947, letter to secretary of state, "Situation in Indochina at Date of High Commissioner's Departure for France," RG 84, Box 4, NND 765027.

———. June 20, 1947, telegram to secretary of state, RG 84, Box 3, NND 765027.

———. September 6, 1947, letter to secretary of state, RG 59, Box 6315, NND 760050.

"Report of the Department of Defense Working Group That Conducted a Comprehensive Review of the Issues Associated with a Repeal of Section 654 of Title 10, U.S.C., 'Policy concerning Homosexuality in

the Armed Forces.'" Washington, DC: U.S. Government Printing
Office, 2011.

"Retired Generals and Admirals Warn of Grave Consequences to
Transgender Military Ban." Palm Center: Blueprint for Sound Public
Policy, February 26, 2019, https://www.palmcenter.org/publication
/retired-generals-and-admirals-warn-of-grave-consequences-to
-transgender-military-ban/. Accessed August 3, 2019.

Reynolds, George M., and Amanda Shendruk. "Demographics of the U.S.
Military." Council on Foreign Relations, April 24, 2018, https://www
.cfr.org/article/demographics-us-military. Accessed August 3, 2019.

Robinson, J. A. USIS Director, Saigon (National Archives, College Park).
May 9, 1946, letter to Chartrand, RG 84, Box 2, NND 765027.

———. July 1, 1946, "Special Survey Report," RG 84, Box 2, NND 765027.

———. September 1946, "USIS-OIC Report for September 1946," RG 84,
Box 2, NND 765027.

———. October 1946, "USIS-OIC Report for October 1946," RG 84, Box
2, NND 765027.

———. November 1946, "USIS-OIC Report for November 1946," RG 84,
Box 2, NND 765027.

Roth, Tanya. "An Attractive Career for Women: Opportunities, Limitations, and Women's Integration in the Cold War Military." *Integrating
the US Military: Race, Gender, and Sexual Orientation since World War II*,
edited by Douglas Walter Bristol Jr. and Heather Marie Stur, Johns
Hopkins UP, 2017, pp. 74–95.

Rotter, Andrew J. "Chronicle of a War Foretold: The United States and
Vietnam, 1945–1954." *The First Vietnam War: Colonial Conflict and Cold
War Crisis*, edited by Mark Atwood Lawrence and Fredrik Logevall,
Harvard UP, 2007, pp. 282–306.

———. "Gender Relations, Foreign Relations: The United States and
South Asia, 1947–1964." *Journal of American History*, vol. 81, no. 2,
September 1994, pp. 518–542.

Russell, Jake. "Trump Says Megan Rapinoe's Silence during National
Anthem at World Cup Inappropriate." *Washington Post*, June 25, 2019,
https://www.washingtonpost.com/sports/2019/06/25/trump-says
-megan-rapinoes-national-anthem-protests-world-cup-are
-inappropriate/?utm_term=.64777e65e645. Accessed June 25, 2019.

Sacks, Sam. "First-Person Shooters: What's Missing in Contemporary War Fiction." *Harper's Magazine*, August 2015, pp. 85–91.

Savage, Kirk. "The 'Education Center' at the Vietnam Veterans Memorial." Blog, May 26, 2012, http://www.kirksavage.pitt.edu. Accessed August 3, 2019.

———. *Monument Wars: Washington, D.C., the National Mall, and the Transformation of the Memorial Landscape.* U of Cal P, 2009.

Savell, Stephanie and Rachel McMahon. "Numbers and Per Capita Distribution of Troops Serving in the U.S. Post-9/11 Wars in 2019, by State." https://watson.brown.edu/costsofwar/files/cow/imce/costs /social/Troop%20Numbers%20By%20State_Costs%20of%20War _FINAL.pdf. Accessed April 9, 2020.

Schaefer, Agnes Gereben, et al. "Assessing the Implications of Allowing Transgender Personnel to Serve Openly," Santa Monica, CA: RAND Corporation, 2016.

Scheer, Robert. *How the United States Got Involved in Vietnam: A Report to the Center for the Study of Democratic Institutions.* Santa Barbara, CA: Fund for the Republic, 1965.

Schoendoerffer, Pierre. *La 317ᵉ Section.* Paris: La Table Ronde, 1963.

Schroden, Jon. "There Was No 'Secret War on the Truth' in Afghanistan." *War on the Rocks*, December 16, 2019, https://warontherocks.com/2019 /12/there-was-no-secret-war-on-the-truth-in-afghanistan/?utm_source =WOTR+Newsletter&utm_campaign=fdf2e6b2e1-EMAIL _CAMPAIGN_10_30_2018_11_23_COPY_01&utm_medium =email&utm_term=0_8375be81e9-fdf2e6b2e1-83002473. Accessed December 17, 2019.

Schwenkel, Christina. *The American War in Contemporary Vietnam: Transnational Remembrance and Representation.* Indiana UP, 2009.

Scott, Wilbur J., and Sandra Carson Stanley, eds. *Gays and Lesbians in the Military: Issues, Concerns, and Contrasts.* New York: Aldine de Gruyter, 1994.

Scruggs, Jan C., and Joel L. Swerdlow. *To Heal a Nation: The Vietnam Veterans Memorial.* Harper & Row, 1985.

Scrutineer. "Secret Blacklist: Untold Story of the USIA." *USIA Bibliography*, vol. 259, October 30, 1959, pp. 376–379.

Secker, Tom. "The Politics and Censorship of Video Games." *Medium*, November 4, 2019, https://medium.com/@tomsecker/how-movies-and

-video-games-help-cover-up-us-war-crimes-9f282d306fca. Accessed December 13, 2019.

Secretary of Defense. "Memorandum for the President: Military Service by Transgender Individuals." February 22, 2019, https://media.defense .gov/2018/Mar/23/2001894037/-1/-1/0/MILITARY-SERVICE-BY -TRANSGENDER-INDIVIDUALS.PDF. Accessed August 16, 2019.

———. "Memorandum for Secretaries of the Military Departments: Directive-Type Memorandum (DTM) 16–005. 'Military Service of Transgender Service Members.'" June 30, 2016, https://www.hsdl.org/ ?abstract&did=794019. Accessed August 3, 2019.

———. "Memorandum for Secretaries of the Military Departments: Implementation Guidance for the Full Integration of Women in the Armed Forces." December 3, 2015, https://dod.defense.gov/Portals/1 /Documents/pubs/OSD014303-15.pdf. Accessed August 16, 2019.

Segal, David R. *Recruiting for Uncle Sam: Citizenship and Military Manpower Policy.* UP of Kansas, 1989.

Senie, Harriet F. *Memorials to Shattered Myths: Vietnam to 9/11.* New York: Oxford UP, 2016.

Sheehan, Neil. *A Bright Shining Lie: John Paul Vann and America in Vietnam.* Random House, 1988.

Sherman, Nancy. *Afterwar: Healing the Moral Wounds of Our Soldiers.* New York: Oxford UP, 2015.

Shilts, Randy. *Conduct Unbecoming: Lesbians and Gays in the U.S. Military, Vietnam to the Persian Gulf.* St. Martin's P, 1993.

Shurkin, Michael. "What a 1963 Novel Tells Us about the French Army, Mission Command, and the Romance of the Indochina War." *War on the Rocks*, September 21, 2017, https://warontherocks.com/2017/09/what -a-1963-novel-tells-us-about-the-french-army-mission-command-and -the-romance-of-the-indochina-war/. Accessed August 3, 2019.

Simons, Jon, and John Louis Lucaites, eds. *In/Visible War: The Culture of War in Twenty-First Century America.* Rutgers University Press, 2017.

Skaine, Rosemarie. *Sexual Assault in the U.S. Military: The Battle within America's Armed Forces.* Santa Barbara, CA: Praeger Security International, 2016.

———. *Women at War: Gender Issues of Americans in Combat.* McFarland, 1999.

Smith, Heather R. "America's Army Comics, Game, App Depict Soldier Lifestyle." *US Army*, April 10, 2013, https://www.army.mil/article/100570/americas_army_comics_game_app_depict_soldier_lifestyle. Accessed June 17, 2019.

Soberon, Lennart. "'The Old Wild West in the New Middle East': *American Sniper* (2014) and the Global Frontiers of the Western Genre." *European Journal of American Studies*, vol. 12, no. 2, Summer 2017, https://ejas.revues.org/12086. Accessed September 18, 2017.

Spinney, Franklin. "The Domestic Roots of Perpetual War." *Challenge*, vol. 54, no. 1, January–February 2011, pp. 54–69.

Spy Culture. "Combat Obscura—Tom on Fortress on a Hill." n.d., https://www.spyculture.com/combat-obscura-tom-on-fortress-on-a-hill. Accessed April 9, 2020.

Stachowitsch, Saskia. *Gender Ideologies and Military Labor Markets in the US*. New York: Routledge, 2012.

Stahl, Roger. "Digital War and the Public Mind: *Call of Duty* Reloaded, Decoded." *In/Visible War: The Culture of War in Twenty-First Century America*, edited by Jon Simons and John Louis Lucaites, Rutgers University Press, 2017, pp. 143–158.

———. *Militainment, Inc.: War, Media, and Popular Culture*. New York: Routledge, 2010.

———. *Through the Crosshairs: War, Visual Culture, and the Weaponized Gaze*. Rutgers University Press, 2018.

State Department, Office of Policy and Plans. "Analysis of Information Centers Programs in the Associated States of Indochina." December 1953. National Archives, College Park, MD, RG 306, Box 8, NND 74622.

Statler, Kathryn C. *Replacing France: The Origins of American Intervention in Vietnam*. UP of Kentucky, 2007.

Stephens, Oren. *Facts to a Candid World: America's Overseas Information Program*. Stanford UP, 1955.

Steuter, Erin, and Deborah Wills. *At War with Metaphor: Media, Propaganda, and Racism in the War on Terror*. Lanham, MD: Lexington Books, 2009.

Stevens, Quentin. "Masterplanning Public Memorials: An Historical Comparison of Washington, Ottawa, and Canberra." *Planning Perspectives*, vol. 30, no. 1, 2015, pp. 39–66.

Stewart, Samuel. "Call of Duty Game Order—The Complete List."
    GamingScan, May 11, 2019, https://www.gamingscan.com/call-of-duty
    -game-order/. Accessed June 15, 2019.

Stiehm, Judith Hicks, ed. *It's Our Military, Too! Women and the U.S.
    Military.* Temple UP, 1996.

Sturken, Marita. *Tangled Memories: The Vietnam War, the AIDS Epidemic,
    and the Politics of Remembering.* U of Cal P, 1997.

———. "The Wall, the Screen, and the Image: The Vietnam Veterans
    Memorial." *Representations*, vol. 35, Summer 1991, pp. 118–142.

Sussman, Jody. "United States Information Service Libraries." University
    of Illinois Graduate School of Library Science, Occasional Papers 111,
    December 1973, pp. 1–23.

Taibbi, Matt. "The Pentagon's Bottomless Money Pit." *Rolling Stone*,
    April 2019, pp. 68–93.

Tatum, James. "Memorials of the America War in Vietnam." *Critical
    Inquiry*, vol. 22, no. 4, Summer 1996, pp. 634–678.

Through the Crosshairs: Reading the Weaponized Gaze. Directed by Roger
    Stahl. Northampton, MA: Media Education Foundation, 2018.

Tierney, Dominic. *The Right Way to Lose a War: America in an Age of
    Unwinnable Conflicts.* Little, Brown and Co., 2015.

To Heal a Nation. Directed by Michael Pressman, performances by Eric
    Roberts, Glynnis O'Connor. Lionel Chetwynd Productions, 1988.

"Too Fat to Fight: Military Threatened by Childhood Obesity." *Military
    .com*, 2017, https://www.military.com/daily-news/2017/10/15/too-fat-to
    -fight-military-threatened-by-childhood-obesity.html. Accessed
    April 21, 2020.

Tønnesson, Stein. *Vietnam, 1946: How the War Began.* U of Cal P, 2010.

Tran, Quan Tue. "Broken but Not Forsaken: Disabled South Vietnamese
    Veterans in Vietnam and the Vietnamese Diaspora." *Looking Back on
    the Vietnam War: Twenty-First Century Perspectives*, edited by
    Brenda M. Boyle and Jeehyun Lim, Rutgers UP, 2016, pp. 34–49.

"Transcript of President Dwight D. Eisenhower's Farewell Address (1961)."
    Ourdocuments.gov, https://www.ourdocuments.gov/doc.php?flash
    =false&doc=90&page=transcript. Accessed August 15, 2019.

Tumblety, Joan. *Remaking the Male Body: Masculinity and the Uses of
    Physical Culture in Interwar and Vichy France.* Oxford: Oxford UP, 2012.

Turse, Nick. *The Complex: How the Military Invades Our Everyday Lives*. Henry Holt, 2008.

———. *Kill Anything That Moves: The Real American War in Vietnam*. Henry Holt, 2013.

Twenge, Jean M., W. Keith Campbell, and Brittany Gentile. "Changes in Pronoun Use in American Books and the Rise of Individualism, 1960–2008." *Journal of Cross-Cultural Psychology*, vol. 44, no. 3, 2012, pp. 406–415.

Tyson, Alec. "Americans Divided in Views of Use of Torture in U.S. Anti-Terror Efforts." Pew Research Center, January 26, 2017, https://www.pewresearch.org/fact-tank/2017/01/26/americans-divided-in-views-of-use-of-torture-in-u-s-anti-terror-efforts/. Accessed December 12, 2019.

United States Census Bureau. "Quick Facts." https://www.census.gov/quickfacts/fact/table/US/PST045217. Accessed April 21, 2020.

Valentine, Douglas. *The Phoenix Program: America's Use of Terror in Vietnam*. William Morrow, 1990.

Van Es, Hubert. "Thirty Years at 300 Millimeters." *New York Times*, April 29, 2005.

Van Reet, Brian. "The Red and the Blue: Writing War in a Divided America." Blog, January 11, 2019, https://brianvanreet.com/author/brianvanreet/. Accessed August 1, 2019.

Vargas, Jose H., and Markus Kemmelmeier. "Ethnicity and Contemporary American Culture: A Meta-Analytic Investigation of Horizontal-Vertical Individualism-Collectivism." *Journal of Cross-Cultural Psychology*, vol. 44, no. 2, 2013, pp. 195–222.

Vavrus, Mary Douglas. *Post-Feminist War: Women in the Media–Military-Industrial Complex*. Rutgers University Press, 2019.

Vernon, Alex, ed. *Arms and the Self: War, the Military, and Autobiographical Writing*. Kent State P, 2005.

"Vietnam Veterans Memorial Fund Changes Direction of Education Center Campaign." September 21, 2018, https://www.vvmf.org/News/Vietnam-Veterans-Memorial-Fund-changes-direction-of-Education-Center-campaign/. Accessed August 1, 2019.

Vietnam War, The. Directed by Ken Burns and Lynn Novick. Florentine Films and WETA, 2017.

Virilio, Paul. *War and Cinema: The Logistics of Perception*. Translated by Patrick Camiller, New York: Verso, 1989.

Walt, Stephen M. "The Myth of American Exceptionalism." *Foreign Policy*, October 11, 2011, https://foreignpolicy.com/2011/10/11/the-myth -of-american-exceptionalism/. Accessed July 24, 2019.

Webb, James. "Women Can't Fight." *Gender Sanity*, edited by Nicholas Davidson, UP of America, 1989, pp. 208–222.

Wells-Petry, Melissa. *Exclusion: Homosexuals and the Right to Serve*. Washington, DC: Regnery Gateway, 1993.

Wendt, Simon. "Instrument of Subjugation or Avenue for Liberation? Black Military Heroism from World War II to the Vietnam War." *Warring over Valor: How Race and Gender Shaped American Military Heroism in the Twentieth and Twenty-First Centuries*, edited by Simon Wendt, Rutgers University Press, 2019, pp. 57–78.

Wendt, Simon, ed. *Warring over Valor: How Race and Gender Shaped American Military Heroism in the 20th and 21st Centuries*. Rutgers University Press, 2019.

Westheider, James E. "African Americans, Civil Rights, and the Armed Forces during the Vietnam War." *Integrating the US Military: Race, Gender, and Sexual Orientation since World War II*, edited by Douglas Walter Bristol Jr. and Heather Marie Stur, Johns Hopkins UP, 2017, pp. 96–121.

Whalen, Andrew. "'Call of Duty: Modern Warfare' Rewrites the Highway of Death as a Russian Attack, Rather Than American." *Newsweek*, October 28, 2019, https://www.newsweek.com/call-duty-modern -warfare-highway-death-russia-gulf-war-1468207. Accessed December 13, 2019.

Wheeler, Winslow, ed. *The Pentagon Labyrinth: 10 Short Essays to Help You through It*. Washington, DC: World Security Institute's Center for Defense Information, 2011.

White, Susan. "Male Bonding, Hollywood Orientalism, and the Repression of the Feminine in Kubrick's *Full Metal Jacket*." *Inventing Vietnam: The War in Film and Television*, edited by Michael Anderegg, Temple UP, 1991, pp. 204–230.

Whitlock, Craig. "At War with the Truth." *Washington Post*, December 9, 2019, https://www.washingtonpost.com/graphics/2019/investigations

/afghanistan-papers/afghanistan-war-confidential-documents/.
Accessed December 9, 2019.

Williams, Tony. "Narrative Patterns and Mythic Trajectories in Mid-1980s
Vietnam Movies." *Inventing Vietnam: The War in Film and Television*,
edited by Michael Anderegg, Temple UP, 1991, pp. 114–139.

Wills, John. *Gamer Nation: Video Games & American Culture*. Johns
Hopkins UP, 2019.

Winter, Jay, and Emmanuel Sivan, eds. *War and Remembrance in the
Twentieth Century*. Cambridge: Cambridge UP, 1999.

"Women in the Military: Where They Stand 2013." Women's Research and
Education Institute, http://www.wrei.org. Accessed August 21, 2019.

"Women's Participation in Peace Processes." Council on Foreign Relations, January 30, 2019, https://www.cfr.org/interactive/womens
-participation-in-peace-processes. Accessed August 3, 2019.

Woodruff, Todd, and Ryan Kelty. "Gender and Deployment Effects of
Pro-Organizational Behavior of U.S. Soldiers." *Women in the Military*,
edited by Brenda L. Moore, special edition of *Armed Forces & Society*,
vol. 43, no. 2, 2017, pp. 280–299.

Yockelson, Mitchell. "They Answered the Call: Military Service in the
U.S. Army during World War I, 1917–1919." *Prologue Magazine*, vol. 30,
no. 3, Fall 1998, https://www.archives.gov/publications/prologue/1998
/fall/military-service-in-world-war-one.html. Accessed April 21, 2020.

Zengerle, Patricia. "U.S. House to Vote on Massive Defense Bill Wednes-
day, Democrats Divided." *Reuters*, December 10, 2019, https://apple
.news/ACPZWzD4wRvadUGzKCOdS4w. Accessed December 10,
2019.

Index

Belknap, M.H., 169n21
Berlant, Lauren, 170n33
Berlatsky, Noah, 113
Bérubé, Allan, 178n35
Bissell, Tom, 136–137, 182n26, 183n29
Blyth, Myrna and Chriss Winston, 183n32
Bodnar, John, 165n2
books, American faith in, 34–38
Boughn, Michael, 173n15
Bousquet, Antoine, 182n18, 182n22
Box Office MoJo, 84
Boyle, Brenda M.: with Combe, 172n3, 173n14; *Masculinity*, 168n18, 172n3; "Rescuing Masculinity," 173n10; "The Tillman Story," 180n5
Bradley, Mark P., 164n7; *Imagining*, 33–34, 36, 37, 46–47, 163n2, 164n8; "Making Sense," 19; "Slouching," 22, 164n8
Bristol, Douglas Walter, 106
Brittan, Arthur, 172n3
Brooks, Rosa, 4, 11, 119, 146, 162n7, 172n3
Burdick, Eugene and William Lederer, 164n18
Burke, Carol, 177n28
Bush, George W., President, 68, 80
Butler, Judith: *Frames of War*, 173n12, 182n19; *Gender Trouble*, 74, 172n3
Butterworth and Wallner, 165n19

Cain, Frank, 23, 30, 46, 163n2, 164n13
Carter, Jimmy, President, 61, 170n29
CBR Staff, 140
Center for Military Readiness: "Policy Analysis," 119; "Trump Transgender Policy," 179n43
Chapman, James, 172n5
Clark, Michael, 63
Clinton, William Jefferson, President, 67–68
Cockburn, Andrew: "Follow the

Money," 184n2; "The Military-Industrial Virus," 147
cohesion, 114, 177n28, 177n32
Cohn, Lindsay, Max Margulies, and Michael A. Robinson, 183n30
Collett, Joan, 36
Combe, Kirk and Brenda M. Boyle, 172n3, 173n14
"Confidence in Institutions," 96
Congressional Budget Office, 129, 184n6
Congressional Research Service, 184n10
Connell, R.W. and J. Messerschmidt, 25, 48, 49–50, 82–83, 172n3
Copp, Tara, 175n8
"Costs of War," 155–156
Cowen, Deborah E., 104, 113, 172n2
Crowley, Kacy and Michelle Sandhoff, 113
Cuordileone, K.A., 28
Curran, Tom E., 180n4

Daddis, Gregory A., 169n26
Dalfiume, Richard M., 106, 108, 109
Dalloz, Jacques., 23, 46, 163n2
Danto, Arthur C., 63, 165n2
defense contractors, 60, 147, 148, 150
D'Emilio, John and Estelle B. Freedman, 178n35
democratic citizenship, 2, 6, 8, 17, 55, 66, 102, 104, 135, 136, 157; from "citizen-soldier" to "consumer soldier," 16, 102, 128; military-civilian divide, 105
Denbeaux, Mark P., et al, 5, 155
Department of Defense: *A Pocket Guide to Vietnam*, 168n17; Report and Recommendations, 179n43
Der Derian, James: *Virtuous War*, 135; "War in the Twenty-First Century," 163n3, 182n19
Deshpande, Pia, 182n18
Devillers, Phillip, 163n2
Doss, Erika, 54, 62, 65, 165n2

White, Susan, 75
white supremacy in the military, 161n4.
   See also Belew, Kathleen
Whitlock, Craig, 156, 165n24
Williams, Tony, 75
Wills, John, 133
Winter, Jay and Emmanuel Sivan, 165n2
women in the military, 98–100, 109–115;
   as "honorary man," 114

"Women's Participation in Peace
   Processes," 115
Woodruff, Todd and Ryan Kelty,
   174n3

Yockelson, Mitchell, 176n17

Zengerle, Patricia, 184n1
Zero Dark Thirty, 5

About the Author

BRENDA M. BOYLE is a professor of English and director of the Writing Center at Denison University in Granville, Ohio. Boyle's relationship with the U.S. Army has been lifelong: she grew up in an Army household, served (with many siblings and in-laws) on active duty during the Cold War, and now has more than a handful of nieces and nephews on active duty during the Global War on Terrorism. She is the author of *Masculinity in Vietnam War Narratives: A Critical Study of Fiction, Films, and Nonfiction Writing* (2009), the coauthor of *Masculinity and Monstrosity in Contemporary Hollywood Films* (2013), the editor of and contributor to *The Vietnam War* (2014), and the coeditor of and contributor to *Looking Back on the Vietnam War: Twenty-First-Century Perspectives* (2016).

Printed in the United States
By Bookmasters